Seth – A Misrepresented God in the Ancient Egyptian Pantheon?

Philip John Turner

BAR International Series 2473
2013

Published in 2019 by
BAR Publishing, Oxford

BAR International Series 2473

Seth – A Misrepresented God in the Ancient Egyptian Pantheon?

© Philip John Turner and the Publisher 2013

The author's moral rights under the 1988 UK Copyright,
Designs and Patents Act are hereby expressly asserted.

All rights reserved. No part of this work may be copied, reproduced, stored,
sold, distributed, scanned, saved in any form of digital format or transmitted
in any form digitally, without the written permission of the Publisher.

ISBN 9781407310848 paperback
ISBN 9781407340555 e-book

DOI https://doi.org/10.30861/9781407310848

A catalogue record for this book is available from the British Library

This book is available at www.barpublishing.com

BAR Publishing is the trading name of British Archaeological Reports (Oxford) Ltd.
British Archaeological Reports was first incorporated in 1974 to publish the BAR
Series, International and British. In 1992 Hadrian Books Ltd became part of the BAR
group. This volume was originally published by Archaeopress in conjunction with
British Archaeological Reports (Oxford) Ltd / Hadrian Books Ltd, the Series principal
publisher, in 2013. This present volume is published by BAR Publishing, 2019.

BAR titles are available from:

        BAR Publishing
        122 Banbury Rd, Oxford, OX2 7BP, UK
EMAIL   info@barpublishing.com
PHONE +44 (0)1865 310431
  FAX   +44 (0)1865 316916
        www.barpublishing.com

CONTENTS

List of Figures 2

Acknowledgements 3

Introduction 5

Seth in Predynastic Egypt 9

The early Dynastic period and the Old Kingdom 14

The First Intermediate Period and the Middle Kingdom 20

Second Intermediate Period 24

The New Kingdom (part 1) 28

The New Kingdom (part 2) 34

The Third Intermediate Period 47

The Late Period 51

The Graeco-Roman Period 55

Seth and Foreign gods 65

Concluding Remarks 68

Appendix 1: The Pyramid Texts 71

Appendix 2: The Coffin Texts 85

Appendix 3: The Book of the Dead 101

References 107

LIST OF FIGURES

1. Map of Ancient Egypt 4
2. Bowl from tomb H29 at el-Mahasna 10
3. Hair-comb from el-Mahasna 10
4. The Scorpion macehead 11
5. Detail of Seth-animal from macehead 12
6. Exterior of Unas pyramid 17
7. Pyramid texts inside Unas pyramid 17
8. Body coffin of Khnum-Nakht 22
9. Lintel from temple of Thuthmosis I at Nubt 29
10. Jamb from temple of Thuthmosis III at Nubt 29
11. Stela of Anhotep 30
12. Sketch of Gebel Adda relief 33
13. Lintel of Seti I from Heliopolis 36
14. Offering table of Seti I 36
15. Stela of Aapehty 41
16. Stela of Taqayna 45
17. Edfu- king spearing hippopotamus 60
18. Edfu – Horus upon back of hippopotamus 60

All figures copyright P. J. Turner except 2, 8, 11 (Manchester Museum), 13 (KIK-IRPA), 14 (Metropolitan Museum), 15 (British Museum), 16 (Rijksmuseum van Oudheden) and 17 (A. E. David).

ACKNOWLEDGEMENTS

Many people have helped in bringing this book to life, in particular the author would like to express his gratitude to Professor Rosalie David of the KNH Centre for Biomedical Egyptology, Faculty of Life Sciences, University of Manchester for her continual support and encouragement, and also to Professor David Langslow, Classics and Ancient History, School of Arts, Histories and Cultures, Faculty of Humanities, University of Manchester who was always prepared to act as 'devil's advocate' and encouraged alternative thought processes.

Thanks are also due to my sister, Mrs Beryl Lang for her help with my translation of relevant French documents and to my good friends, Mrs Pauline Smith and Mr Stuart Cunningham for the same service with respect to Greek and German documents.

Drs Salima Ikram and Marcus Muller kindly answered my queries regarding Seth in the two projects that they are involved with, namely: the Dakhleh Oasis Project and the Totenbuch Project and for that I am grateful.

To my wife whom I am sure did not assume on my retirement from Clinical Microbiology that I would begin a second PhD, resulting in the usual late nights and the covering of the house in books and documents, I record my heartfelt thanks for her continual support.

Finally, the opinions expressed throughout this volume are my own and not all readers may agree with my conclusions, in mitigation I quote Sir Alan Gardiner: "Scholars should not shrink from difficult conclusions. At best they may be lucky enough to hit on the right solution. At the worst they will have given the critics a target to hit at." If my conclusions generate discussion then I have succeeded in my aims.

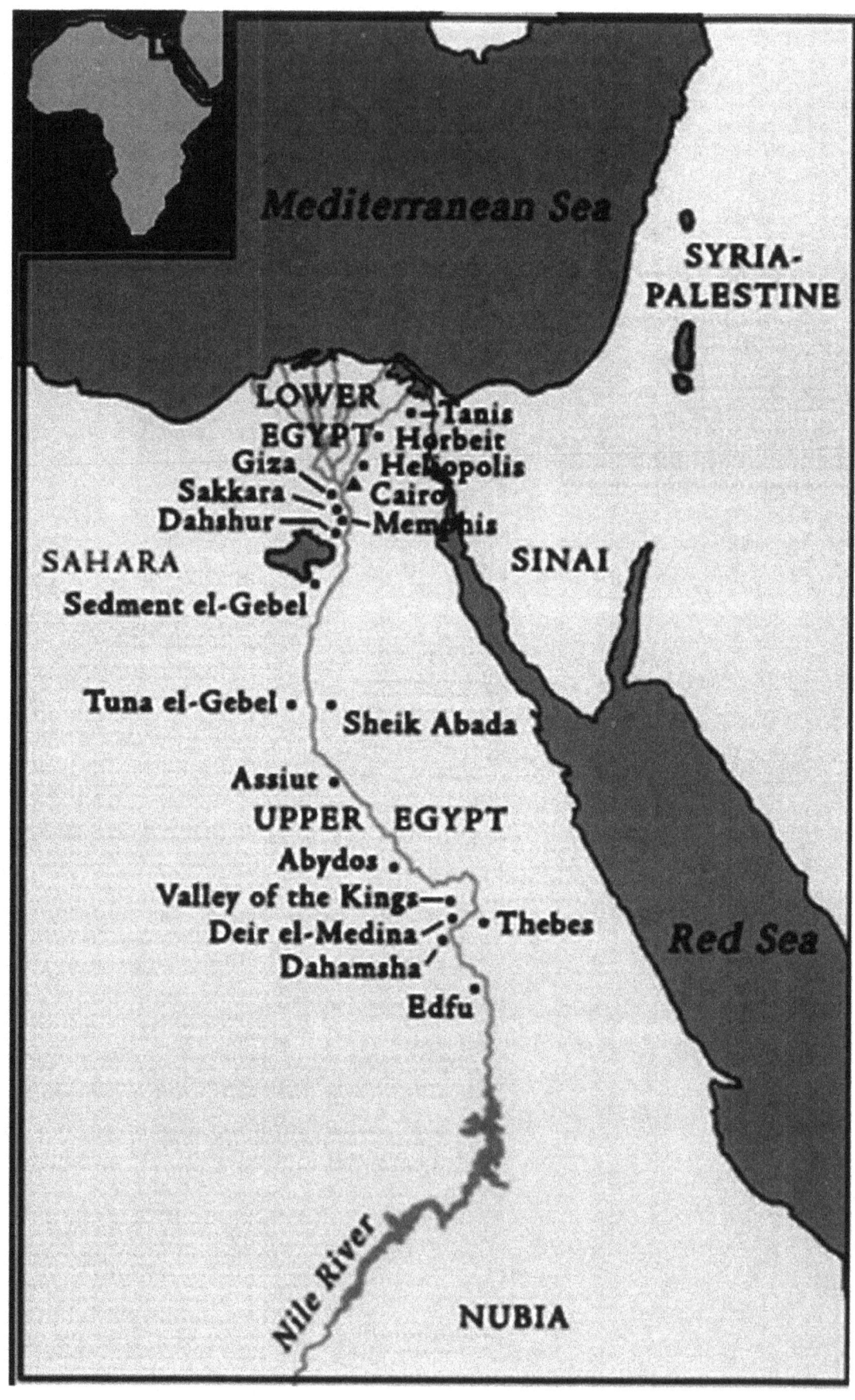

Figure 1: Map of Ancient Egypt

1. INTRODUCTION

Since the study of ancient Egypt first came into fashion, its religion has occupied a major role. Writers have either included chapters on the religion within their books (Gardiner 1961, Mertz 1964, Oakes and Gahlin 2002) or devoted whole books to the subject of the gods and myths of ancient Egypt (Hart 1986, Armour 2001, Pinch 2002, Gros de Beler 2004) or to Egyptian religion (Hornung 1971, Assmann 2001). With several hundred deities mentioned by the ancient Egyptians this is not surprising and some authors have even devoted entire books to one particular deity and their role in the religion (e.g. Witt 1971, Bleeker 1973, Roberts 1995). The overall first impression from this suggests that the ancient Egyptians were a very pious people, but, whilst this may be true, it is probably more accurate to conclude that each god represented a different concept or role or, indeed, could be associated with a particular place. So it was not the case that every deity was worshipped by all the people at any one time, but rather that they worshipped particular deities at particular times depending upon their specific needs (Thomas 1986: 7, Baines 2000).

The state religion occupied a major role which was particularly connected with the pharaoh and his divinity. The state gods were worshipped in major cult centres, e.g. Osiris at Abydos, Amun at Karnak, Re at Heliopolis, Ptah at Memphis, etc. These temples would have been closed to the public with worship at them being conducted mainly by the priests and occasionally by the king in person. At the same time there also developed what is termed a 'people's religion' in which people worshipped in their own homes gods to whom they could relate; these often differed from the state gods (Baines 1987: 83-84, Meeks and Favard-Meeks 1999: 8, Stevens 2009: 10).

Incorporated into the various state gods were different interpretations of the creation of the world so that in the Memphite theology, Ptah brought all things into existence by pronouncing their names (Assmann 1996: 349-351) whereas in the Theban theology, Amun was regarded as the source of the power of all the gods and thus the true, original creator of the universe (Hornung 1971: 149, Strudwick 2006: 103).

In the Heliopolitan creation myth (Assmann 1996: 346-347), the solar deity Atum gave life to Shu and Tefnut, the two gods that represent air and moisture respectively. In turn, this pair then produced Geb and Nut, the earth and sky. These two gods then produced two pairs of gods, the males, Osiris and Seth, and the females, Isis and Nephthys. Osiris is associated with his wife/sister Isis and Seth his wife/sister Nephthys (Strudwick 2006: 103).

As a result of the tale of the murder of Osiris by Seth and his subsequent rebirth as god of the underworld, the pharaohs of the Old Kingdom became identified with Osiris and were believed to experience rebirth upon their deaths in the same way as the god (Hays 2010: 1). Many of the Pyramid Texts are concerned with this (Faulkner 2007). Subsequently, probably because man does not like to believe that his earthly span is all that there is to life and death, the desire to become likened to Osiris and achieve restoration to life and be declared free of wrongdoing became something that all ancient Egyptians aspired to, regardless of their status in life (Smith 2008: 3), and mummification was designed to make the deceased resemble Osiris, thus ensuring an eternal life in the underworld.

Unlike the other deities, Seth always remains something of an enigma to the ancient Egyptians. He exists on the boundary between the transitory and the everlasting, the same boundary that seperates order and chaos (Hornung 1971: 158). Whilst he had originally been worshipped in Ombos where he was seen as chief god of the eastern desert and its rich gold mines, subsequently, following the myths of his murder of Osiris and attempt to usurp the throne from Horus, he appears to represent evil, disorder and everything that was foreign (Pinch 2002: 192).

The vast majority of scholars are content to mention Seth solely in the context of the Osiris/Horus stories and have otherwise largely ignored him. The two notable exceptions are Griffiths (1960) and Te Velde (1967); although both of these mainly concentrate on the usual two stories i.e. the New Kingdom story of the Contendings of Horus and Seth and the Plutarch story: De Osiride et Iside. However these two publications have resulted in some comment, both supportive and critical as we shall see below. Griffiths and Te Velde themselves are unable to agree as to whether these stories are representative of true facts or merely myths.

Griffiths (1960: 134) states, *"I agree with Kees when he upholds the theory that the myth of the fight of Horus and Seth goes back to a time of strife in Upper Egypt. It seems to refer to the conquest of Nubet, the town of Seth,* by the Nakada II people, symbolized by Horus, the special god of their kings, at least at the end of this period." However Te Velde (1967: 75-6) states "None would venture to deny that in Predynastic Egypt, as elsewhere, wars were waged and repeatedly so. Yet we doubt whether actual wars at the time of the uniting of the country were the origin of this religious myth of conflict and reconciliation."

Te Velde followed up his 1967 thesis with an article in 1968 entitled "The Egyptian God Seth as a Trickster" (Te Velde 1968), in this article he states that Seth has the five elements in common with tricksters of other cultures namely that he was disorderly (Te Velde 1968: 37), he was uncivilised (Te Velde 1968: 37-38), he was a murderer (Te Velde 1968: 38), he was a homosexual (Te Velde 1968: 39) and he was a slayer-of-the-monster (Te Velde 1968: 39).

Hornung agreed with this view of Seth, stating that in all of his roles in battles, constant confrontations and confusions and his questioning of the established order that he is engaged as a sort of 'trickster' (Hornung 1971: 213).

Ten years after the publication of 'Seth, God of Confusion,' Te Velde released a second edition. In the preface he points out that during the ten years the book had met with both approval and disapprobation but, rather than now in his turn expressing agreement or disagreement with these pronouncements he merely listed the reviews and requested that the reader judge for themselves (Te Velde 1977: vii-viii).

Amongst these reviews were ones by Zandee (1968), Griffiths (1969) and Hornung (1970). The first of these resembles an article rather than a book review as it runs to six pages and is, somewhat damning in its praise! Zandee had two main criticisms, firstly that Te Velde makes too much of the homosexual nature of Seth and Horus's relationship even suggesting that Te Velde has manipulated some translations to suit his argument and secondly, disagreeing with the statement that Seth was a god of confusion. Zandee arguing that in fact Seth was more a 'god of strength' (Zandee 1968: 184-189). The second reviewer whilst overall praising Te Velde's efforts as a welcome addition to the few monographs that we have that look at an important Egyptian god in some depth also disagrees with the central formulation that Seth is a god of confusion feeling that, like Zandee's comment, that Te Velde has tended to choose texts that support this conclusion and largely ignored the evidence that an early primacy of the Seth-cult in Upper Egypt can be amply demonstrated and that Seth's role in the myths of Horus and Osiris should not blind the reader to the auspicious functions assigned to him. He also takes issue with the prominence given to the homosexual episodes feeling that rather than this being a key to the interpretation of the central myth it should be regarded as a somewhat isolated episode (Griffiths 1969: 226-227). Parkinson (1995: 64-65) has suggested that the homosexual episode in the *Contendings of Horus and Seth* rather than signifying approval of male/male sexual relationships should be regarded as an act of aggression designed to inflict ignominy upon Horus and to emphasise his youth.

Hornung, in his turn, is rather more relaxed with Te Velde's views, agreeing, as outlined above with the view that he was a 'trickster', but in common with the other reviewers feeling that there was more to Seth than being 'a god of confusion' (Hornung 1970: 17-20).

More recent works have examined the varied sides to Seth's character, Borghouts (1973) and Assmann (1995) for example, cite Seth's role in the triumph over Apophis describing how it is Isis with her magic and Seth with his spear that bring about the downfall of the enemy when the sun god's bark is threatened by Apophis (Borghouts 1973: 114-115, Assmann 1995: 51-53).

Assmann in the following year explained how the contrast between Horus and Seth appeared to symbolise the change from the old disorder to new order, Seth as the god of Naqada representing how this period was superseded by the establishment of the state. In the myth order triumphs over chaos, rule over anarchy, and law over force. The legal dispute between Horu and Seth is resolved with a contract and whilst the award of Upper Egypt to Seth is not of any major duration no further conflict is caused when the decision is revoked and Seth is enthroned instead as ruler over the desert and over foreign lands and given the more important role of being entrusted to ward off the serpent, Apophis, who menaces the course of the sun with standstill. Here force which cannot be legalised is being placed in the service of the law (Assmann 1996: 44).

Later in the same book Assmann discusses the demonization of Seth in the age of the Saites and Persians, a subject that I also discuss in Chapter 9 (Assmann 1996: 389-408). Finally in his 2008 book, Assmann, described Seth as 'the iconoclast', citing how on the one hand, upon the cosmic plane Seth acts on the side of Re, the personification of good, and uses his violence to inflict death on the personification of evil, Apophis, but on the other hand, on the plane of life and death represented by Osiris and his mysteries, Seth acts as evil and is himself the object of ritual violence. Thus representing at the same time an evil that is necessary to keep the world going in its "Re" aspect, but that must simultaneously be controlled and contained because it threatens the world in its "Osiris" aspect (Assmann 2008: 33-34).

From all of these sources it can be seen that the character of Seth remains something of an enigma: is he a god of confusion, a trickster, a bisexual god? Or does he represent a change from old to new where his powers of strength and might are still required?

If the references to Seth are examined chronologically we find that Seth and Horus were gods of Upper and Lower Egypt respectively during the Predynastic Period and there was undoubtedly a struggle between the supporters of these two deities from which the followers of Horus emerged victorious although it would be some considerable time before they could be sure of this victory (see Chapter 3). This struggle was probably represented by the Horus/Seth myth. Osiris was drawn into the myth when his cult of eternal life became popular and this probably reflects a religious myth rather than an account of a true event.

In the Pyramid Texts (Faulkner 2007) there are allusions to Seth trampling or rending Osiris and eventually Osiris is seen to stand for everything that is Egyptian and orderly, whilst Seth came to represent disorder and everything foreign. Thus Osiris ruled the 'Black Land' i.e. the Nile valley and Seth the barren red lands of the deserts – maybe this is one of the reasons why he is thought to be red-haired (Wilkinson 1994: 106)? Seth was also the god who caused storms and clouds, and he is in this aspect again the natural opponent of 'Horus the Elder' who represented the solar sky falcon (Pinch 2002: 192).

During the Hyksos Period people from Cannan identified Seth with their god Baal and as such he enjoyed prominence particularly in their capital, Avaris, in the north east of the Delta region, where he had his own temple (Van Seters 1966: 171-180). Conversely in the New Kingdom the story of the *Contendings of Horus and Seth* in which Seth is portrayed in a less than positive manner becomes popular. However, during the Ramesside Period, Seth is seen as a prominent god, once more reflecting his position as a family god of the Ramessides, probably because they originate from Avaris, to the extent that some of this family of rulers, Seti I and II in particular, have his name added to their own.

However, by the Graeco-Roman Period, Seth was confirmed in his role as murderer of Osiris and the god who had attempted to rob Horus of his birthright. This is particularly so in the scenes upon the temple walls at Edfu which depict the *Contendings of Horus and Seth* (Watterson 1998, Kurth 2004).

The conventional position of Seth in ancient Egypt is as a violent and destructive god (Hornung 1971: 103), and this is a position that the majority of authors have been willing to accept. However, whilst he is documented as the murderer of Osiris and the enemy of Horus in the standard accounts, there is reason to doubt whether this is the whole story.

The standard accounts i.e. The Chester Beatty Papyrus I (*The Contendings of Horus and Seth*) and Plutarch (*De Iside et Osiride*) will be extensively examined, the first in Chapter 7 and the second in Chapter 10 in order to ascertain how Seth is depicted in them and how this may have determined how he was perceived at the time of these texts. There is no disagreement over the translation of these texts, their only difference being that Plutarch is not so descriptive of the later events of the *Contendings of Horus and Seth* compared with the Chester Beatty account.

This study will also attempt to examine other aspects of Seth which suggest that throughout Egyptian history he was continually worshipped and indeed, at times, enjoyed some prominence, notably in the Pre- and early-Dynastic periods, during the Hyksos interlude of the Second Intermediate Period and during the Ramesside era of the 19th and 20th Dynasties. Whilst previous authors have devoted some scholarship to these various aspects of Seth I do not believe that anyone has attempted to bring all these together and to demonstrate that rather than being something of an 'outsider' to the Egyptian pantheon, he actually had an important role within it, and as such was continually worshipped throughout ancient Egyptian history. Therefore I propose to examine the role of Seth as he was perceived by the Ancient Egyptians at specific times throughout their history. In order to achieve this aim a chronological approach will be taken beginning with Seth's role in Predynastic Egyptian religion and then progressing through the early Dynastic and Old Kingdom, the First Intermediate period and the Middle Kingdom, the Second Intermediate Period, the New Kingdom, the Third Intermediate Period, the Late Period, and culminating with the Graeco-Roman Period up to the death of Cleopatra. Some of these periods are rich in their evidence concerning Seth and his current worship, others less so, but an attempt will be made to highlight the perception of the god current to the time. A chapter is also included on Seth's relationship with foreign gods.

On a wider issue some thought will be given as to the significance that this study has in the understanding of how to interpret sources dealing with Egyptian religion? Ideally these should be examined carefully and in context, rather than in a general manner which tends to hide the many nuances that occur in Egyptian religion. As an example, can we gain any insight into how the general populace rather than the elite viewed the gods and Seth in particular? Assmann (1984: 9-14) believed that religion completely pervaded early Egyptian civilization, and, it seems as being completely unitary, so that the attested elite forms, which tend to be what we have most information upon, therefore serve as a reliable guide for the whole of Egyptian society. Conversely, Baines (1987: 80) believes that religion need not be a single form that pervades all life from the beginning of history and that diversity is a real possibility. Whilst the 'state religion' was mainly concerned with the relationship between the king and the gods individuals were much more likely to be concerned with the vital points in their own life: birth, puberty, marriage, parenthood and death for example and how their relationship with the gods could influence these.

A map (Figure 1), indicating the major places mentioned in the text is given on page 4.

2. SETH IN PREDYNASTIC EGYPT 5500-3100 B.C.E.

This chapter examines the evidence for the worship of Seth during this early period. The lack of written evidence means that much of the conclusions drawn from this time are speculative. Certainly models of hippotami have been found dating from the Badarian culture, and also occur in the following Amratian culture; given the association of Seth with this animal, the finding of a vase from this period showing a figure harpooning a hippopotamus may be of significance. The development of Ombos as a major site for the worship of Seth is discussed, and the subsequent struggle between the followers of Seth and those of the hawk-headed god Horus, recounted. This struggle resulted in victory for the latter group, and possibly gave rise to the myth of the *Conflict of Horus and Seth*.

Lengthy discussion of the prehistory of ancient Egypt is beyond the scope of this thesis. However, the first element of the Predynastic Period may be said to begin with the 'Badarian culture' (5500-4000 B.C.E.), so called because the culture was first identified in the region of el-Badari in Middle Egypt. The Badarian culture appears to be that of agriculturalists, probably pastoralists, fishers and hunters with a mobile existence influenced by the annual Nile flood cycle and their hunting activities (Midant-Reynes 1992: 160). It was radically different from any cultures that predated it due to the existence of what appears to be a structured and complex society with the presence of what may be described as 'wealthy tombs'. As Midant-Reynes states (1992: 153) *"Each burial was carefully arranged. A mat was placed on the ground to accommodate the contracted body (which was presumably tied up before rigor mortis set in), while the head was sometimes laid on a pillow made from straw or rolled-up animal skin. The whole body was then either covered or completely wrapped up with a mat or a gazelle-skin"*. By the side of the body were placed pottery vessels and these constituted the most distinctive characteristic of the culture; their appearance being of a highly polished, black-topped red-bodied type. Bone tools were also frequently discovered in the tombs and ivory or bone combs with long teeth (Midant-Reynes 1992: 155). Three small figures of women were found in the tombs; two of these, modelled in clay, are now in the British Museum and the third, made from ivory, in the Petrie Museum, London (Midant-Reynes 1992: 157). This would suggest that there was some sort of mother goddess cult prevalent at the time (Baumgartel 1955: 23). The presence of cow burials in the Badarian cemeteries suggest that she was worshipped as a cow and graves of dogs and jackals suggest the existence of a guardian of the dead in canine form. This is not surprising, as presumably the Badarians would have noted the presence of these animals around their cemeteries, no doubt attracted by the existence of meat and bones, and translated this into the presence of a protective deity. What is important is that animal worship in Egypt can be traced back to this period and that it subsequently never dies out throughout the long history of Egyptian religion (Baumgartel 1955: 23).

Apart from the female figurines mentioned above, two ivory amulets representing hippopotamuses and a hippopotamus figurine carved from a hippopotamus tooth were also found (Midant-Reynes 1992: 158). This could, of course, just be an example of a powerful animal being revered for its strength but given the later association of Seth with the hippopotamus (Te Velde 1967: 26, could these objects represent an early occurrence of his worship?

The Amratian culture derives its name from the site of el-Amra which is situated at the beginning of the Naqada meander of the river Nile near to where the Wadi Hammamat, the classic route from the Nile to the Red Sea, begins. It dates from 4000 to 3500 B.C.E., and whilst essentially similar to the Badarian culture, there are differences suggestive of both a local development and an influx of newcomers. Their dead were buried in cemeteries, usually lying upon their left-hand sides, in a contracted position, with the head to the south, looking towards the west (Midant-Reynes 1992: 170). The head looking towards the west (i.e. the setting sun) perhaps suggests that sun-worship was already established. All sexes and ages are buried within the cemeteries with no segregation. The practice of wrapping the bodies in an animal skin appears to have died out and the first wooden or clay coffins make their appearance (Midant-Reynes 1992: 170). The typical black-topped Badarian pottery has been replaced by a red-polished type which is occasionally decorated with white painted designs. These designs represent the fauna: hippopotami and crocodiles dominate, animals which were both associated with Seth (Te Velde 1967: 26), whilst depictions of people were rarer. An important example occurs on a vase from el-Mahasna which depicts a figure confronting a harpooned hippopotamus (Midant-Reynes 1992: Figure 5b; 172). This scene continues throughout Egyptian religious iconography, culminating in the scenes depicted upon the walls in the the Graeco-Roman temple at Edfu which illustrate Horus, in the person of the pharaoh, harpooning the hippopotamus, which represents Seth (Watterson 1998: 115 and Figure 40. This iconography may have influenced the latter portrayal of St George spearing the dragon, a relief popular with early Christians and still in use today (Georganteli 2010: 111-112).

Baumgartel (1955: 30) also recounts the publication of a vase dating to this period, now in the Berlin Museum. Several animals are depicted upon it including one which Scharff (1926: 17) commented looked like a Seth-animal due to the appearance of its head, muzzle and upright pointed ears. Because of the absence of the characteristic raised tail, he later amended this identification to that of an ass. However, as the ass is associated with Seth (Te Velde 1967: 26, Ward 1978: 23-34), I believe that this still could be one of the first depictions of Seth in Predynastic Egypt. Pot marks were also common during this period including one which depicts a hippopotamus (Baumgartel 1955: 33 Figure VI, 8), although whether this again has any association with the god Seth is impossible to prove. Also during this period, a very significant development took place in that the depictions of animals began to protrude from the surface of the vessels rather than being depicted upon the surface (Midant-Reynes 1992: 170). A typical bowl (Ayrton and Loat 1911: 26-27), from the Manchester Museum collection (accession number 5069) with hippotamus figures modelled separately and then attached to the rim, illustrates this and is shown in Figure 2.

Also attributed to this period are a number of ivory combs and hairpins; amongst these is a comb from el-Mahasna (Ayrton and Loat 1911: 27) that is assumed to be the earliest extant depiction of the Seth-animal, although the vase described above may be contemporary with it in date. Once again the typical Seth nose and ears are present but the tail is missing; again, an asinine origin is suggested. Another comb from a grave in the same cemetery was also found which, although its head and tail are missing, probably depicted the same animal (Te Velde 1967: 8). The Manchester Museum collection possesses the example found by Ayrton (accession number 5076); it is shown in Figure 3.

There have been many attempts over the course of the study of Egyptology to identify the so called 'Seth-animal'. These have included a pig, a giraffe, an anteater, a wart-hog and an okapi (Te Velde 1967: 13; Watterson 1984: 112; Manlius 2002: 24-31) amongst others. I would agree with Thomas (2004: 1049) in identifying the animal with the African wild dog, *Lycaon pictus*. Apart from her evidence for this identification- large erect ears, the tail, which is slightly bushy or tufted at the end, and frequently held upright when standing, running or at times of aggression, further proof is possibly provided by the Dakhleh Oasis Project excavations which have revealed many depictions of Seth on an outcrop which the Project has named 'Seth Rock'; this rock also has many caves and holes in its surface which the team believe could have been the lairs of wild dogs (Ikram – personal communication).

Figure 2: A bowl from tomb H29 at el-Mahasna decorated with four hippopotami (copyright Manchester Museum AN 5069).

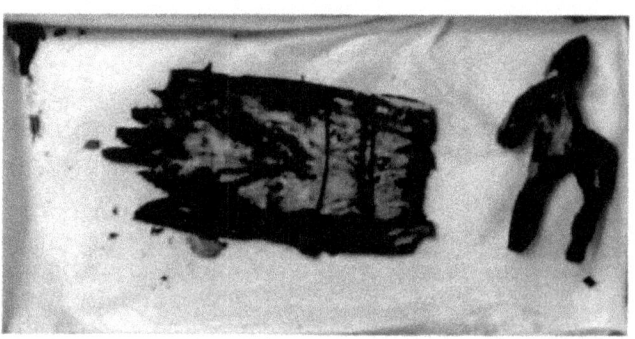

Figure 3: A hair comb from el-Mahasna with the Seth-animal depicted upon it (Manchester Museum AN 5076).

Baumgartel (1955: 34) remarks that the combs *"form the only evidence offered in favour of the opinion that Seth was already worshipped during Naqada I. This may be so but further evidence is needed to make it certain"*. However this may be the only evidence that is ever forthcoming and perhaps an open mind should be kept on the subject. Surprisingly, given her note of caution quoted above, she later states (1955: 36), *"that the religion of Naqada I must have consisted in the cult of animals, trees and an anthropomorphous fertility goddess,"* but then concludes (1955: 50), *"Seth may have been their chief god."*

Figure 4: The Scorpion macehead.

Te Velde (1967: 10) suggests that Baumgartel may have been influenced in this decision by non-archaeological material. In later Egyptian tradition, Seth is often called the *'Lord of Ombos'*, a site which equates to Petrie's 'South Town' at Naqada. However, no representations of the Seth animal have been found in this location or indeed any evidence of a Predynastic Seth shrine or temple. This latter point is perhaps not surprising as any such shrine or temple of that date would not have been constructed in stone but built of perishable materials. Emery (1961: 119-120) makes a much stronger statement: *"In early times, these Seth-worshipping people were a very powerful section of the population of the Nile valley, occupying a large area of Upper Egypt centred round Ombos."*

Compared to the Badarian period there were many more settlements along the Nile valley in the Naqada I period. These settlements demonstrate increasing material wealth, suggesting that the Naqada I people were leading a more settled existence which may have encouraged the development of a more formal religion. If Baumgartel and Emery are correct, this could have resulted in Seth being the first 'state' god, certainly he was closely associated with the kingship in Early Dynastic times (Wilkinson 1999: 37).

The Gerzean culture is named after the type site at el-Gerza which lies 5 kilometres to the northeast of the Meidum pyramid. There has been much conjecture as to whether this period merely illustrates an expansion by the Naqada I people from their sites in the Naqada/Matmar area (Midant-Reynes 1992: 187) or the influx of a people possessing a superior culture from the east (Baumgartel 1955: 38). Certainly the burials of this period differed from those of the Naqada I period in that the precise position of the body seen in the earlier period, was no longer adhered to; also the use of the coffin began to emerge, initially made from basketry, then clay and finally wood. The structure of the tombs became more complex, especially those belonging to the elite (Midant-Reynes 1992: 187).

The wide range of burials encountered within Gerzean cemeteries, ranging from small round pits with hardly any funerary equipment to ones with coffins and separate compartments for grave goods, reflect the growing diversity in the social structure which was becoming more hierarchical (Midant-Reynes 1992: 188). Three principal centres appear to have developed during the Naqada II period: Naqada, Hierakonpolis and Abydos (Midant-Reynes 1992: 198). The first of these was also known as *'Nubt'* (town of gold), indicating its important association with the gold mines of the Eastern Desert, and certainly in the Pyramid Texts, Seth becomes known as *'Seth of Nubt'*. In spite of its long history throughout the Naqada I and II phases, Naqada was eventually eclipsed by Hierakonpolis (*'the city of the hawk'*) as the worship of Horus became more popular, culminating in his rise to become the predominant state god. Excavating at Hierakonpolis, Quibell and Green discovered a damaged large, votive macehead (Figures 4 and 5).

Figure 5: Sketch of one of the Seth animal standards depicted upon the Scorpion macehead.

This macehead, now housed in the Ashmolean Museum, Oxford, depicts a ruler now known as *'Scorpion'* (Whitehouse 2009: 19-25). The macehead is carved with representations shown in three registers, the first depicting dead birds (the hieroglyph denoting "common people") hanging from various *rḫyt* standards surmounted by representations of the local gods with which these standards are associated. Emery (1961: 42) proposed that this represented the standards of the southern tribes from Upper Egypt, with the *rḫyt* birds representing what he termed the 'Confederation of the North' (Lower Egypt). The whole depiction may indicate that the southern tribes led by Scorpion had conquered those of the north. I disagree, and believe that Midant-Reynes (2006: 249) is correct in her interpretation of this register: that it depicts the standards of the tribes that Scorpion had conquered in the south. Importantly, the third and fifth of these standards appear to have a Seth animal atop them, and therefore, I believe that this macehead depicts the first steps towards a united Egypt: Scorpion, as the king of the tribe based at Hierakonpolis (Wilkinson 1999: 39) which worshipped Horus, the hawk god, has subjugated other tribes, including the one that worshipped Seth at Nubt. This victory may also have caused the surviving members of the Seth worshippers to flee to Lower Egypt and relocate to the northeastern area of the Delta where, as will be discussed later, Seth came to have a number of towns associated with him. Further evidence to possibly support this conclusion comes from the '*King Scorpion Tableau*', an eighteen by twenty inch scene carved into a limestone cliff at Gebel Tjauti (Darnell 2002: 9-19). This carved scene has been interpreted by Darnell as showing a triumphal procession of King Scorpion, after he had conquered the rival king and town of Naqada, in which the rival king is being led away to public execution (Wenke 2009: 229-230). Darnell (2002: 19-22) also describes a tableau found at Gebel Tjauti depicting a Horus king and a Seth figure suggesting that this may show either the Horus king, with the assistance of the power represented by the Seth animal, extending his dominion along the Alamat Tal Road or possibly representing the west bank of the Nile, with its mountains, as the home of Seth and the cultivated land as that of Horus. If the first of these is the correct interpretation then this is the first depiction of the idea that the king needed to be an amalgamation of the powers of Horus and Seth. Recent work by the German Archaeological Institute at Abydos has unearthed a large tomb (designated Tomb UJ) which has been attributed to King Scorpion. This tomb contains the oldest extant phonetically readable evidence of hieroglyphic writing on seals, and small inscribed labels which may have been used as wine labels. Amongst these labels are some which appear to have representations of the god Seth upon them (Dreyer 1998: 120-121; Schoer 2004: 37; Wenke 2009: 231). This would suggest that, if these are wine labels, then either the wine came from vineyards that belonged to temples dedicated to the worship of Seth or it was reserved for use in these temples. This is further evidence that the worship of Seth was prevalent at this time, and that his temples were of sufficient importance to possess estates or to be able to purchase the produce of estates.

Although there are few written records from this period the existence of models of hippopotami and ivory combs that possibly depict the Seth-animal appear to indicate that the worship of this god may be traced back to this time. Certainly the Predynastic rulers of Naqada, judging from the size and splendour of the burials, appear to have controlled an area of some size and their local god, Seth, was closely associated with the kingship in Early Dynastic times (Wilkinson 1999: 37). The depiction of the Seth-animal upon the Scorpion macehead would suggest a pictorial depiction of the conquest of the followers of Seth by the followers of Horus, paving the way for the unification of Egypt into one state with Horus as its major god, but with an important role for Seth as we shall see in the next chapter.

2. THE EARLY DYNASTIC PERIOD AND THE OLD KINGDOM 3100 to 2181 B.C.E.

This chapter deals with the period from approximately 3100 B.C.E. to 2181 B.C.E., and examines the continued struggle between the followers of Horus and those of Seth, a situation that appears to have not been settled until the reign of Khasekemwy. Subsequently the importance of Seth was reflected in the title: *'She who sees Horus and Seth'*, borne by the queens of the Old Kingdom. Seth's role in the Pyramid Texts is also examined.

On the Scorpion macehead the king is depicted wearing the White Crown of Upper Egypt (Moorey 1988: 15); this has led scholars to believe that he was only king of this region (Emery 1961: 43) and not of Lower Egypt where he would have been depicted wearing the Red Crown. This may be true; however, he could have been depicted wearing this crown on the missing side of the macehead. The red crown appears to have originated at Naqada and the white crown at Hierakonpolis (Wilkinson 1999: 48-49). If this is correct then the red crown would have symbolised a northern power to the Predynastic rulers of Hierakonpolis allowing for the later association of the two crowns with Lower (red) and Upper (white) Egypt. In 1898 Quibell discovered at Hierakonpolis the famous Narmer palette (Wilkinson 1999: 68), depicting Narmer's triumph in uniting both Upper and Lower Egypt into one country. Narmer, like the rest of the kings of Dynasties 1 and 2, originated from Thinis near Abydos. On one side of this palette Narmer is depicted wearing the White Crown and smiting a captive in the presence of the hawk-god (presumably Horus), and on the obverse he is shown wearing the Red Crown and overseeing the reviewing of decapitated prisoners (Shaw and Nicholson 1995: 196). Whether this palette actually depicts the occasion of Narmer's triumph or was commissioned at a later date to commemorate the ritual re-enactment of the occasion is debatable (Wilkinson 1999: 68) but scholars are agreed that he is the first king of Dynasty 1 and this event is usually dated to around 3100 B.C.E. Unlike the Scorpion macehead there are no depictions of Seth on the Narmer palette. A recent discussion about the iconography of the Narmer Palette is given by O'Connor (2011: 145-152).

It is now agreed (Dodson and Hilton 2004: 44) that the sequence of kings for this Dynasty (c3100 to 3000 B.C.E.) runs:

Narmer, Aha, Djer, Djet, Den, Anedjib, Semerkhet, and Qaa.

All of these rulers built tombs at Abydos which were originally excavated by Amelineau and then by Petrie (Wilkinson 1999: 4-5). These tombs were undecorated so evidence for their owners has mainly come from seal impressions on jars of wine and food (Petrie 1901: 82). All of Narmer's successors had a 'Horus name' which consisted of three elements: a phrase written within a panel that stylistically depicted the palace facade, surmounted by a falcon symbolising Horus (Wilkinson 1999: 201). Many of these rulers of Dynasty 1 had Horus names which expressed an aggressive nature, e.g. Aha ('Horus the fighter'), Djer ('Horus the strong') and Qaa ('arm-raising Horus') (Wilkinson 1999: 202). This suggests that at this time the authority of Horus, and hence the king was reliant upon his military might and that the complete unification of Egypt was still in process.

Aha founded Memphis as a new capital city for the united country. Its position just south of the apex of the Delta illustrates that its site was chosen because it had a geographically good position to exert influence over both Upper and Lower Egypt (Emery 1961: 51). The fact that the kings still chose to be buried at Abydos rather than at the Memphite cemetery at Saqqara would appear to indicate that they all still had allegiance to Thinis and hence to Horus as its local god. Close by Aha's tomb ten donkey burials were discovered (Rossel *et al* 2008: 3617-3717). It has been suggested that these were buried by the king to meet his transportation needs in the afterlife but given the association of donkeys and Seth (Te Velde 1967: 26) could this be evidence of his worship? We will return to this question during the Hyksos period.

The tomb of Aha's mother, Neith-hotep, was discovered by de Morgan in 1897 at Naqada. This town was important during the Predynastic Period and the marriage of Narmer to a princess from this region may well have been political and helped to cement relationships between Naqada and Thinis (Wilkinson 1999: 70). Mereneith, although initially thought by Petrie to be a king, is now acknowledged to be a queen, the mother of Den. It is surmised that Djet died whilst Den was still a child and that Mereneith acted as a regent until the boy was deemed to be of an age to rule independently (Wilkinson 1999: 74). Interestingly, the queens of Dynasty 1 bore the title *'She who sees Horus-and-Seth'* (Sabbahy 1993: 81):

𓅃 𓋴𓏏 𓁹

This may have indicated that, as the wife of the pharaoh, she recognised both gods in her husband or it may have been a title similar to the *Nebty* (i.e. 'Two Ladies') name that linked the pharaoh with the patron goddesses of Upper and Lower Egypt, in this case linking the queen to the two gods associated with Upper and Lower Egypt, i.e. Horus and Seth.

During the reign of Den there are several references to hippopotamus hunting; a sealing attributed to him shows both a figure wearing the Red Crown associated with Lower Egypt and standing in a papyrus skiff harpooning a hippopotamus (Wilkinson 1999: 274 and Figure 8.4) and, unusually, wrestling with a hippopotamus (Wilkinson 1999: 275 and Figure 8.4). Wilkinson (1999: 298) suggests that these figures indicate that the king, as upholder of cosmic order, was controlling an animal that is representing the untamed and aggressive forces of nature, rather than destroying Seth. This may be so but given the earlier representations of hippopotamuses it is possible that, even by this stage, the hippopotamus had come to represent one aspect of Seth. According to Manetho (Waddell 2004: 29), Aha was killed by a hippopotamus, possibly indicating that a ritual hunt and subsequent killing of this creature was expected of the living king.

Den's reign also sees the first attested use of the Golden Horus name (Baker 2008: 512). It has been suggested either that this represents Horus' victory over Seth, as the hieroglyph for gold (*nebu*) symbolises Seth due to his worship at Nebet, or that it indicates a concept of the king being a falcon made of gold (Watterson 1984: 100). However, could it be that like the 'Two Ladies' name it was a way of saying that the king was recognised as being the god of both Lower Egypt (Seth) and Upper Egypt (Horus)? Certainly, as we have seen in the Pyramid Texts, there are numerous mentions of the 'Mounds of Horus' and the 'Mounds of Seth', these being taken as representing the two realms of Egypt and the towns and villages of Lower and Upper Egypt respectively, and indicating that even after the unification the Ancient Egyptians still recognised this division of the realm into two.

The Second Dynasty possibly consisted of nine kings: Hetepsekhemwy, Nebra, Ninetjer, Weneg, Sened, Nubnefer, Peribsen, Sekhemib-perenmaat and Khasekhem(wy). The first five of these are universally accepted and the last is also acknowledged but some of the intervening ones are shadowy figures mentioned in only a few sources, suggesting that this was a time of internal stress within Egypt (Wilkinson 1999: 82-83). Certainly, on the Palermo Stone there is an entry from Ninetjer's reign that reads '*First feast of* dw3-ḥr-pt. *Attacking the towns of* sm-rˁ *and* ḫ3'. On the basis that the name of the second locality may be translated as 'north land', Emery (1961: 93) interpreted this as suppression of a rebellion in Lower Egypt. Certainly, during the time of the Second Dynasty, there was a significant drop in the average height of the Nile's annual inundation compared to that of the First Dynasty and this could well have added to the unrest between the north and the south of the country (Wilkinson 1999: 83). This breakdown in central administration is further attested by the fact that, following Ninetjer's reign, the kingship appears to have been held by a number of shadowy figures, suggesting that at any one time there may have been different rulers in different areas of the country (Wilkinson 1999: 87). For example, Weneg is only attested in the north of Egypt, and Sened and Peribsen only in the south (Wilkinson 1999: 88). Some authors (Shaw and Nicholson 1995: 220) believe that Sekhemib-perenmaat was the name held by Peribsen during the first part of his reign when the cult of Horus was still dominant, indicated by the fact that the *serekh* frame containing this name was surmounted by a Horus falcon. However later in his reign, Seth appears to have been elevated to greater prominence and the king changed his name and the *serekh* containing it is surmounted by a Seth animal (Petrie 1901: 31). Some of the sealings from his tomb at Abydos bear the epithet *inw Stt*, 'tribute (or conqueror) of Setjet'. This has been identified as Sethroe in the north-eastern Delta which was known in later times as a cult centre of Seth (Wilkinson 1999: 89-90). If the term 'tribute' is accepted, could this indicate that the followers of Seth had become sufficiently strong to challenge the rule of the Horus kings and that the only way to keep his throne was for Sekhemib to acknowledge this and to change his name and allegiance? A further sealing from Abydos depicts the god Ash, later to be associated with Seth, holding a *w3s* sceptre (Petrie 1901: pls XXI.176, XXII.178-9; Wilkinson 1999: 189 and Figure 8.1). This sceptre came to be associated with divine power and authority. A late Second Dynasty inscribed stone slab from Helwan belonged to a royal priest called *Nfr-Sts*, 'Seth-is-beautiful', further indicating the popularity of Seth at this time (Saad 1957: 51-53).

The last king of the Dynasty originally appears to have favoured Horus, as the falcon tops his *serekh*, but he only wears the White Crown of Upper Egypt and his name is translated as 'the power has appeared'. His capital appears to have been at Hierakonpolis. However at some time during his reign, as attested by the inscriptions found on a diorite vessel, he defeated the northern enemy (Wilkinson 1999: 91) and was able to reunite the country. To celebrate this fact he changed his name to Khasekhemwy (*'the two powers have appeared'*) and topped his *serekh* not only with the Horus falcon but also the Seth animal (Petrie 1901: 31). Interestingly, in these depictions the Seth animal wears the Red Crown of Lower Egypt whilst the falcon wears the Double Crown (Wilkinson 1999: 92). This may well be the first time that Seth was shown wearing the red crown. In order to cement the reuniting of Upper and Lower Egypt, Khasekhemwy married a northern princess, Nemathap, and a jar-sealing gives her the title, '*The King-bearing Mother*'. Later she would be revered as the ancestral figure of the Third Dynasty.

Khasekhemwy appears to have reunited the land with a stable centralised government and an efficient administrative system. During the next four dynasties the power of Egypt would increase dramatically, the king would be seen increasingly as the reincarnation of Horus and, from the Fifth Dynasty, son of the sun god Re (Emery 1961: 121; Wilkinson 1999: 94).

The first king of the Third Dynasty was Netjerikhet. He was undoubtedly the son of Khasekhemwy as a sealing found at Beit Khallaf (Garstang 1907: Plate X.7) names Nemathap as '*mother of the dual king*'. Why a new Dynasty should begin with him is strange but maybe the final triumph of his father in uniting the two lands was of such importance that his son was deemed to have been the first ruler of a new Dynasty. During his reign the Pyramid Age begins with the construction of his Step Pyramid at Saqqara, breaking with the tradition of the royal tombs being at Abydos. This was perhaps because Netjerikhet wanted to make a statement to the Seth followers of Lower Egypt to show that the South now controlled the North, a fact emphasised with the country's political and economic centre now being fixed in the Memphis area (Kessler 2001: 41). Whatever the reason, his successors also maintained this tradition with the tomb of Sekhemkhet also being located at Saqqara, whilst Khaba built his Layer Pyramid at Zawiyet el-Aryan, just south of Giza (Dodson 2000: 88). A sealing of Khaba was discovered at Elephantine and shows a divine figure, possibly Ash, holding what could well be a *w3s* sceptre flanked by *serekhs* of the king (Wilkinson 1999: 99-100). Huni continued the move away from Abydos, building his pyramid at Meydum.

The Fourth Dynasty (2613-2498 B.C.E.) was initiated with Sneferu's marriage to Huni's daughter, Hetep-heres, whose tomb was discovered in 1925 on the Giza plateau near to her son Khufu's Great Pyramid (Reisner 1927: 14). The Fourth Dynasty represents a peak in the resources devoted to pyramid building and illustrates the rise in the worship of the sun-god Re, the pyramids possibly representing a mythical 'staircase' up which the spirit of the dead pharaoh could ascend to reach and join Re in the heavens. The importance of Re is shown by the incorporation of his name into the names of the pharaohs, e.g. Djedef-re (*'enduring like Re'*), Khaf-re (*'appearing like Re'*), and Men-kau-re (*'eternal like the souls of Re'*). Nevertheless the title '*She who sees Horus and Seth'* was still found associated with queens of this period. It occurs in the tomb, on the Giza plateau, of Meresankh who appears to have been the daughter of Khufu's son, Kaiwab, and his wife Hetepheres; she was married to Khafre (Strudwick 2005: 379-380). It also is found in the mastaba of Khamerernebty II, the daughter of Khafre and wife of Menkaure; she is referred to as "*The mother of the king of Upper and Lower Egypt, daughter of the god who sees Horus and Seth*", (Porter and Moss 1974: III (1):136; Strudwick 2005: 381).

The Fifth Dynasty came about when Userkaf, the grandson of Djedefre, the short-lived successor of Khufu, married Khentkawes, the daughter of Menkaure, thus uniting the two lines of descent from Khufu (Clayton 1994: 61). Once again Khentkawes bears the title "*She who sees Horus and Seth*", (Strudwick 2005: 382). Unlike their Fourth Dynasty predecessors the Fifth Dynasty pharaohs once again built their funerary monuments at Sakkara, although these pyramids were much smaller than previous structures. They also built sun-temples, consisting of a sturdy podium of mudbrick and limestone surmounted by a stubby obelisk (known as the *benben*), further south at Abu-Gurob (Shaw & Nicholson 1995: 10-11). Whilst the architectural achievements of the Fourth and Fifth Dynasty pharaohs is impressive, few documents from this period have survived, so much of our knowledge of this era is incomplete.

This is particularly true with regard to Seth, although the title '*Seer of Horus and Seth*' occurs in the tomb of Nima'ethap on the Giza plateau (Porter and Moss 1974: 136), and one Seth-nubti is shown leading foreign captives in scenes on the causeway of the pyramid-complex of Sahure (Porter and Moss 1974: 326). Further evidence of the importance of the god is shown by the fact that the queens of Unas (Nebet), Teti (Iput I) and Pepy II (Iput II) all bore the title "*She who sees Horus and Seth*" (Strudwick 2005: 383-385). But things were about to change with the appearance of the Pyramid Texts. These funerary texts consisted of some 759 'utterances' written in columns on the interior walls and corridors of ten pyramids of the late Old Kingdom. First encountered in the pyramid of Unas (2375-2345 B.C.E.), (Figure 6), they continue through the pyramids of his Sixth Dynasty successors, Teti, Pepi I, Merenre and Pepi II and their queens, Ankhesenpepi II, Neith, Iput and

Wedjebetni and in the pyramid of Ibi, a king from Dynasty VIII.

Figure 6: The exterior of the pyramid of Unas at Saqqara.

They are conventionally numbered in a sequence progressing from the burial chamber outwards (Allen 2005: 3) although Schott (1950: 149-161) has argued that the opposite arrangement would be more logical. The utterances appear to consist of three major groups of spells: the Offering and Insignia Rituals, the Resurrection Ritual and the Morning Ritual (Allen 2005: 5). The Offering and Insignia Rituals always appear on the north wall of the burial chamber. The Offering Ritual accompanied preparations for and the presentation of a great meal: beginning with a libation it progressed through cleansing with incense and salt-water and culminated in the *'Opening of the Mouth'* ritual in which the deceased's ability to partake of nourishment was restored. The Insigna Ritual consisted of items of royal dress and regalia being offered to the deceased (Allen 2005: 6).

The Resurrection Ritual occupies the south wall of the burial chamber and consists of longer spells designed to release the deceased's spirit from its attachment to its earthly body and to ensure that the dead pharaoh's spirit was united with the sun-god. These rites would have been performed at the actual funeral, where the deceased is addressed as Osiris. There are also accompanying utterances that were designed to be recited personally by the tomb owner (Allen 2005: 6).

The Morning Ritual consisted of spells concerned with awakening the king and dressing and feeding him; these spells always occur upon the east walls of the tombs (Allen 2005: 6).

The remaining spells in the Pyramid Texts comprise ones that are of a personal, rather than a ritual nature (Figure 7).

Figure 7: Pyramid texts upon the west wall of Unas's pyramid at Saqqara.

They are designed to allow the deceased's spirit to find its way safely out of the tomb and to exist in the company of the gods. Composed in the first person they are designed to be spoken by the spirit itself. A subset consists of personal spells directed against such things as snakes and worms that could harm the deceased's body (Allen 2005: 7). Whilst no illustrations accompany the spells, unlike the vignettes associated with the later Book of the Dead, many of the hieroglyphic depictions of humans or animals in these spells are either incomplete or have been deliberately mutilated by knives so that they could not cause any harm to the dead king (Munro 2010: 54).

No single tomb contains all 759 utterances; the maximum number encountered in one place (675), occur in the tomb of Pepi II. It is apparent that out of the 759, Seth is mentioned in 133 (17.5%) and the context can range from his role as the enemy of Osiris and Horus to one where, together with Horus, he is recognised as a dual state-god of Upper and Lower Egypt. Many of the texts use archaic language suggesting origins that perhaps go back to predynastic times; others, with their constant reference to the sun-god, are thought to have been composed by the priests of Re at Heliopolis (Shaw and Nicholson 1995: 236).

Lichtheim (1973: 48) believed that the struggles between Seth and Osiris and Seth and Horus recounted in the Pyramid Texts represented the prototypes of strife within the world.

For convenience I have divided the texts into three categories where Seth is referred to in either a negative, positive or neutral way. Included in the negative texts are descriptions of the struggle between Seth and Horus and the subsequent defeat of the former, his mutilation, subjugation beneath Osiris and the destruction of his followers. The positive texts are concerned with Seth assisting Osiris in his ascent to heaven, either by physically assisting the god or by proclaiming his name and with Seth's role as a protective deity against snakes. The neutral texts are mainly concerned with describing the 'Mounds of Seth and Horus' and certain ritualistic roles that are ascribed to Seth. These selected texts can be found in full in Appendix 1.

As the title of the negative texts suggests all these texts reflect Seth in a 'bad light', many are concerned with the 'Eye of Horus' and either Seth's seizing of it or its recovery by Horus. The 'Eye of Horus' initially represented the left eye that Seth tore out, although Hathor was able to restore the eye, it therefore came to symbolise the general process of 'making whole' and healing (Shaw and Nicholson 1995: 133-134); (see texts 1, 2, 3, 6, 7, 8, 9, 10, 13, 14, 16, 17, 18, 19, 20, 21, 23, 24, 25, 26, 27, 28, 29, 30, 31, 36, 37, 38, 42, 48, 53, 59, 60, 63, 66, 68, and 69). In a similar manner the loss of Seth's foreleg during his battles with Horus is also referred to in text 11. Many of the other texts refer to Osiris's protection and his ultimate triumph over Seth and the fact that Seth was placed under him in a subjugation pose and his followers were destroyed (see texts 12, 15, 22, 32, 39, 40, 43, 44, 45, 46, 49, 51, 52, 54, 55, 56, 57, 58, 62, 64, 65 and 67). Text 51 is of particular interest as it appears to suggest that the followers of Seth should be subjected to cannibalism. This could refer back to some earlier time when perhaps vanquished enemies, or some part of them (e.g., their hearts) were eaten in order to absorb the powers of a rival (Eyre 2002: 155) or more likely it refers to a symbolic cannibalism where the sacrifice of some animal is taken to represent Seth (Eyre 2002: 170-171). This second suggestion is certainly seen in Ptolemaic times in the reliefs upon the walls of the temple at Edfu where Seth is portrayed as a hippopotamus and is depicted being portioned up and fed to the victors (Blackman and Fairman 1943: 2-36. An analogy may be made with the so called Cannibal Hymn (Pyramid Text 273-4) which suggests that the dead king hunts down and eats the gods:

"Their big ones are for his morning meal, their middle-sized ones are for his evening meal, their little ones are for his night meal, their old men and their old women are for his incense-burning."

Eyre (2002: 55) suggests that what is being described here is a ceremony of sacrifice and the meat feast that followed, probably as part of the funeral rite.

Text 33 makes reference to the violent birth of Seth when, *"he broke through his mother's side and leapt forth"* (Te Velde 1967: 27), because of this early indication of the violent aspect of Seth I have included it with these negative texts. Texts 34, 35, 41, 47 and 61 refer to the battles of Horus and Seth and the subsequent judgement in favour of Horus with regard to the throne of Egypt.

In the positive texts Seth's role is more benevolent e.g in texts 7, 9, 10, 11, 12, 16 and 19 he aids in the ascent of the dead Osiris (i.e. the king) to heaven either by physically lifting him up or providing a ladder for the ascent. Seth then proclaims the dead king (texts 4, 56, 15 and 17). The dead king is to be feared (text 2) and has escaped death like Seth (texts 13, 14). Seth also helps protect him against snakes (text 8), helps in removing his fetters (text 18) and in resurrecting him (text 20). He is also invoked in the 'Opening of the Mouth' ceremony where the adze of iron used to complete the ceremony (Taylor 2010b: 88) is attributed to Seth.

In the neutral texts Seth is neither a threat nor a positive influence: many of the texts (7, 8, 10, 11, 18, 23, 24, 25, 26, 28, 36, 37, 38, 42 and 43) refer to the 'Mounds of Seth', a term along with the 'Mounds of Horus' that refers to the two realms of the respective gods represented by the tells (mounds) upon which human settlements were usually sited (Faulkner 2007: 41, note 4), the phrases therefore possibly referring to Lower and Upper Egypt respectively.Other texts are concerned with purification rituals (texts 2, 3, 4, 5, 15 and 22), and with the assumption of kingship (texts 6, 16, 20, 21, 27, 29, 39, 40, 41 and 44).

The dilemma facing the compilers of these utterances as to whether Seth should be shown in a positive, negative or neutral light can clearly be seen in the above examples. Even within individual utterances confusion occurs as can be seen in Utterance 437 (41 in the negative examples) where the deceased is urged to *'arise against Seth'* yet within a line Seth is described as being *'brotherly towards you.'*

The Sixth Dynasty (2345-2181 B.C.E.) came about when Teti married Unas's daughter, Input, thus legitimizing his right to rule. He took the Horus name, Seheteptawy (*'He who pacifies the Two Lands'*); possibly indicating that internal political unrest had once more broken out prior to his rule. By the end of the Dynasty there appears to have been a move away from the central government based at

Memphis, with local governors taking on more responsibility and having only a cursory allegiance to the pharaoh (Dodson and Hilton 2004: 80). This ultimately led to the end of the Old Kingdom and the chaos of the First Intermediate Period (2181-2040 B.C.E.).

Not surprisingly, this period in Egypt's history initially reflected an unsettled time: the land needed time to adjust to being governed by one ruler and to having Horus as the ruler's main deity. This is reflected in the unrest seen during the Second Dynasty culminating in Peribsen acknowledging Seth as his main deity and his successor, Khasekhemwy, acknowledging both Horus and Seth and taking the name *'the two powers are settled.'* The fact that many of the queens of this period used the title *'She who sees Horus and Seth'* would also appear to indicate that either an appeasement with the Seth followers was being sought or that eventually the pharaoh was seen to embody the best characteristics of both gods.

The Pyramid Texts also reflect this quandary; hence Seth's role in them can be either negative, where he is very much seen as the rival of Horus and the plucker out of the 'Eye of Horus'; or positive, where he is seen as a legitimate member of the Ennead who seeks to assist the king in his role as Osiris to ascend to heaven and join the sun god; or in a neutral sense where he is a counter-point to Horus, e.g. the referral to the 'Mounds of Horus and Seth' being used as a term to denote settlements in Upper and Lower Egypt respectively. The occurrence of personal names which include Seth in them e.g. Nfr-Sts and Seth-nubti, may indicate the popularity of Seth in personal, rather than state religion during this period. Birth throughout Egyptian history is associated with gods by parents and this is reflected in the naming of their offspring for gods (Baines 1987: 95), one can therefore imagine that parents who worshipped Seth as a local or personal god could well have named their offspring after him.

4. THE FIRST INTERMEDIATE PERIOD AND MIDDLE KINGDOM 2181-1650 B.C.E.

This chapter initially examines the First Intermediate Period, a time about which, until recently, we had little information. At present, thanks to the work of a number of scholars, we are able to put a little more flesh upon the bones. Central authority broke down and once more there was conflict between south and north, the Herakleopolitan Dynasties (Ninth/Tenth) were only recognised in the north and Thebes was hostile from the outset. Eventually, under Mentuhotep II, the Thebans overcame the blockade at Assiut and also seized the Memphite throne and formed the Eleventh Dynasty, the beginning of the Middle Kingdom. Whilst we have little evidence of Seth's worship during the First Intermediate Period, he features on a number of monuments associated with kings of the Middle Kingdom.

Following the death of Pepy II at the end of the Sixth Dynasty a period of change occurred in Egypt and central control broke down, probably not helped by Pepy's long reign. The conditions in the country at this time are well summarised in the *'Admonitions of a Prophet'* (Lichtheim 1973: 149-163), a literary work dating to the end of the Sixth Dynasty where a wise man named Ipuwer appears at Pepy's court and describes the situation that is prevalent outside the secure palace. Care should be taken however in attributing this as an eye-witness account of the times as more recent research suggests that it was composed during the subsequent Middle Kingdom (Wilkinson 2005: 83). Nevertheless, as can be seen in the following extract, it does paint a picture of the collapse of the Old Kingdom's centralised state.

"Nay, but poor men now possess fine things. He who one made for himself no sandals now possesses riches...

Nay, but many dead men are buried in the river. The stream is a sepulchre, and the Pure Place is become a stream.

Nay, but the high-born are full of lamentations, and the poor are full of joy. Every town says: 'Let us drive out the powerful from our midst.'

Nay, but the gates, columns and walls are consumed with fire; (and yet) the chambers of the king's palace (still) endure and stand fast...

Nay, but gold and lapis lazuli, sliver and turquoise, carnelian and bronze, marble and...are hung about the necks of slave-girls. But noble ladies walk through the land, and mistresses of houses say: 'would that we had something we could eat'...

Nay, but the great and small say: 'I wish I were dead.' Little children say: 'He ought never to have caused me to live.'...

Nay, but the laws of the judgement-hall are placed in the vestibule. Yea, men walk upon them in the streets, and the poor tear them up in the alleys."

(David 1982: 206-207).

Noticeably, unlike texts from the Late Period, Seth here is not blamed for the situation that has arisen, this is possibly because foreigners are not blamed, indeed as Lichtheim states (1973: 162, note 29) the king places the blame for the disorders on the Egyptian people themselves and maintains that Egypt has nothing to fear from foreigners.

However, the situation was not helped by a series of low Nile floods which led to a shortage of food in Egypt, and whereas in the past, a strong central administration had put aside supplies in good harvest years to counteract the yield in poor years, this had not happened on this occasion. Thus the power of individual nomarchs increased, especially those who had kept the irrigation canals in their nomes in good repair and were able to maximise even a poor Nile inundation (Grimal 1992: 139).

Whilst the King Lists preserved in the Turin Papyrus and Manetho's *History* do not testify to this interruption in the line of kings after the Sixth Dynasty, if we look more closely,*"They translate a state of factual disintegration into a form that preserves the outward appearance of continuity."* (Assmann 1996: 81). In fact Manetho, in categorising the Seventh Dynasty, describes it as consisting of seventy kings ruling for seventy days (Manetho 1940: 57). This is probably a ploy to symbolize the breakdown in central control rather than referring to seventy actual rulers.

The kings of the Eighth Dynasty may have been descended from Pepy II as many of their names incorporate his coronation name, Neferkare (Grimal 1992: 140), and have a power base in Memphis. Unfortunately their power appears to be limited to an area around the city (Seidlmayer 2000: 118).

During this period, the Delta was entered by people from the east coming as traders, mercenaries and refugees and the control of Middle Egypt passed to the princes of Herakleopolis. This town occupied an important strategic position lying, as it did, just south of the entrance to the Faiyum region but its influence, especially under Meribre Khety, founder of the Ninth Dynasty, stretched as far south as Aswan (Grimal 1992: 140). Little is known of the remainder of the Eighth and Ninth Dynasty kings.

The Tenth Dynasty was founded by another Neferkare, probably still attempting to show legitimate descent from Pepy II. This Dynasty is marked by an increasing tension with a rival Dynasty (the Eleventh) based in Thebes, culminating in frequent clashes along the border around the area of Abydos (Seidlmayer 2000: 135). These are described in the '*Autobiography of Ankhtifi*', the governor of the third nome of Upper Egypt, Hefat, about 40 kilometres south of Luxor. He also claims to be the nomarch of Hierakonopolis and a follower of the ruler of the Herakleopolitan kingdom (Grimal 1992: 142). Interestingly, it has been suggested by Assmann (1996: 98), that some of the images in Ankhtifi's account - notably '*...but if anyone treads on my tail as on a crocodile*' and '*I tensed my arms like a harpoon in the snout of a fleeing hippopotamus*'- might reflect a Horus/Seth conflict as the crocodile and hippopotamus are animals that symbolise aggressiveness and wildness, traits that are identified with Seth (Te Velde 1967: 26). Certainly in these times of breakdown in central authority, whilst we do not have evidence for it, the original gods of local cults, including Seth and Horus, could well have come to the fore again.

Ankhtifi's main enemy was the founder of the Eleventh (Theban) Dynasty, Prince Inyotef I, who took the Horus name of Seherutawy ('*He who has brought calm to the Two Lands'*). Having achieved victory over Ankhtifi, control over southern Egypt was completed by taking Koptos, Dendera and the three nomes that Hierakonpolis ruled (Grimal 1992: 143). Inyotef II continued the conflict, this time in Middle Egypt, until the country was finally reunified under Mentuhotep I (2060-2010 B.C.E.). The progression of his career can be seen from his successive Horus names: '*He who gives heart to the Two Lands*', followed by '*Lord of the White Crown (Upper Egypt)*' and finally '*Uniter of the Two Lands*' (Clayton 1994: 73). In his temple tomb at Deir el-Bahari, in the hypostyle hall, Naville discovered a block showing Mentuhotep on a throne with Seth and Hathor standing behind him (Porter and Moss II 1972: 391), indicating that the former of these gods was certainly not abhorred during this time. Following the death of Mentuhotep he was succeeded by his son, Mentuhotep II and he, in turn, by Mentuhotep III. After his death in 1991 B.C.E. there appears to have been yet another period of strife which culminated with the vizier Amenemhet claiming the throne and setting up the Twelfth Dynasty.

Amenemhet used literature to legitimatise his position. In the story attributed to Neferti, a Heliopolitan sage, the end of the Eleventh Dynasty is depicted as a dour time only saved by the appearance of Amenemhet (called Ameny in the story):

"*Gone from the earth is the nome of On,*

The birthplace of every god.

Then a king will come from the South,

Ameny, the justified, by name,

Son of a woman of Ta-Seti, *child of Upper Egypt.*

He will take the white crown,

He will wear the red crown;

He will join the Two Mighty Ones,

He will please the Two Lords with what they wish."

(Lichtheim 1973: 143)

The 'Two Mighty Ones' represent the vulture goddess Nekhbet and the cobra goddess Wadjet and the 'Two Lords' mentioned here are undoubtedly Horus and Seth in their roles of gods of Upper and Lower Egypt respectively, the two phrases representing the unified kingdom (Lichtheim 1973: 145, note 16). In the Cairo Museum there is the right half of a lintel from Amenemhet's pyramid temple at Lisht which depicts the king at his *sed*-festival being presented with the symbol for countless years by the god Seth (Hawass 2003: 329). His successor, Senusret I, is depicted on a block found in the court of the 'Temple of Amun' at Karnak showing him before Amun and Seth and upon his throne, with Horus and Seth binding the *sma*-symbol below (Porter and Moss 1972: 135). In a similar manner, the fifth king of the Twelfth Dynasty, Senusret III (1874-1855 B.C.E.), also has a very fine relief of his *heb-sed* festival, in the Cairo Museum, showing the king seated in his special pavilion and wearing, on the left, the Red Crown of Lower Egypt with Horus offering to him and on the right, the White Crown of Upper Egypt with Seth offering to him (Willeitner 2001: 453; Cruz-Uribe 2009: 211). This is unusual as one would have expected Horus to be offering to the White Crown and Seth to the Red given their normal associations with Upper and Lower Egypt, whether this was an error by the sculptor, or, Senusret was making a point we unfortunately do not know. But all of these reliefs suggest that the cult of Seth was functioning well during this period.

There is also evidence to suggest that the story entitled *'The Contendings of Horus and Seth'* was also known at this time. A fragment of papyrus, P. Kahun VI.12, dating to the time of Amenemhat III (c1855-1808 B.C.E.), was published by Griffiths in 1898 (Griffiths 1898: 4 plate 3); it concerns the part of the myth where Seth attempts to seduce Horus but is foiled by Isis:

"...and then the person of Seth said to the person of Horus:"How lovely your backside is! Broad are your thighs and..." And the person of Horus said:"Watch out; I shall tell this!" Then they returned to their palaces. And the person of Horus said to his mother Isis:"Look Seth sought to have carnal knowledge of me." And she said to him:"Beware!Do not approach him about it! When he mentions it to you another time, then you shall say to him:"It is too painful for me entirely, as you are heavier than me. My potency shall not match your potency,"so you shall say to him. Now, when he gives his potency to you, you shall thrust your finger between your buttocks. Look, causing it to [...] for him is like [...].Look, it will be sweet to his heart, more than [...]. You shall then catch the semen which has come from his member, without letting the sun see it."(Parkinson 1991: 120-121).

Te Velde believed that this homosexual side of Seth was important (Te Velde 1967: 38-41) and that Seth was disregarding the normal order of sex because he was the spirit of disorder (Te Velde 1968: 39). I disagree, and believe that Seth here is attempting to demonstrate his superiority over Horus who he regards as weak and he wishes to demonstrate his aggression by inflicting ignomity upon Horus (Parkinson 1995: 65). In fact the opposite happens in that, thanks to Isis's wisdom, Horus is able to turn the tables upon Seth and to highlight his aggressive and boorish traits. We will return to this tendency towards homosexuality being exhibited by Seth in later sections.

The Dynasty finally ended in 1782 B.C.E. with the death of Queen Sobeknefru, who had actually ruled as queen-regnant (Grimal 1992: 171).

In the Old Kingdom only the king could become Osiris upon his death and the Pyramid Texts all deal with the king's resurrection. Osiris is the ruler of the underworld and not therefore concerned with the living which was Re's role. The cult of Osiris had been encouraged during the Old Kingdom, possibly as a constraint upon the Re cult and the power of its priests. The king upon his death was identified with Osiris and his successor with Horus, the son and avenger of Osiris (David 1982: 107). With the new 'democracy' of the First Intermediate Period, first the governors of the nomes and other higher officials and, eventually, all people aspired to become united with Osiris upon their death. As a consequence, the Pyramid Texts were adapted into a series of spells that were inscribed upon the rectangular coffins of this period, hence the name Coffin Texts (Figure 8).

Figure 8: Body coffin of Khnum-Nakht, second of two brothers (copyright Manchester Museum).

Apart from spells based upon the Pyramid Texts, newly composed spells were also added (Munro 2010: 54). These texts incorporated direct statements which negated death and affirmed life and attempted to overcome any adverse situation which the deceased might encounter in his passage from this world to the hereafter (David 1982: 115).

Faulkner has translated 1,185 of these texts (1973, 1977 and 1978); 131 of the texts mention Seth (11.1% of total), either directly by name or indirectly ('the other', 'the outcast', 'the Ombite' etc). Of these 131 texts, 72 refer to Seth in a 'negative' way ie., associate him with the death of Osiris or the fight with Horus, 27 in a 'positive' light and 32 in a 'neutral' way, reflecting once again, as in the Pyramid Texts, the way in which Seth could be identified in both a negative and a positive manner. This is not surprising as many of the texts can be shown to be based upon the Pyramid texts. All of the texts that mention him are listed in Appendix 2. Some generalisations are given here about these texts.

Many of the negative texts (1, 2, 3, 4, 7, 10, 12, 16, 19, 20, 23, 37, 47, 48, 49, 50, 68, 69, and 70) are concerned with the vindication of the dead person, likening him to Osiris or Horus and describing their triumph over Seth.

Other texts are concerned with overthrowing Seth and his followers (5, 6, 11, 13, 17, 21, 24, 25, 30, 32, 33, 34, 35, 36, 38, 40, 41, 42, 43, 44, 45, 55, 59, 60, 61, 62, and 64).

Texts 14, 22, 27, 28, 29, 51, 52, 53, 56, 57, 71 and 72 are concerned with either the 'Eye of Horus' or Seth's testicles, alluding to the injuries that both gods received during their battles. The first of these is of particular interest as it explains the reason why the pig came to be abhorred by the Egyptians: the text likens a black pig to the wound that Horus received to his eye and has Re stating that *'the pig is detestable to Horus.'* While the ultimate reason for not eating pork was a health one, this type of analogy can have only helped to reinforce this potential taboo (Asheri, Lloyd and Corcella 2007: 271). However, there is plenty of evidence to indicate that this was not a universal taboo (Ikram 1995: 31-33) possibly it only applied to the priests (Cauville 2012: 21).

Text 15 relates how Isis severed Horus's hands and fashioned new ones for him.

Texts 8 and 9 describe how Isis and Nephthys prevented the corpse from rotting and caused Osiris to live again.

Many of the positive texts refer to Seth in a protective role, probably referring to his position as the strongest of the gods, so in text 1 he is said to help Horus. Text 2 relates that the heart is afraid of his power. Text 3 has Seth protecting the deceased from an assault by an unnamed being. The power of Seth is referred to in texts 4, 5, 6, 7, 11, 16, 19, 20, 24 and 25: the first of these is concerned with Seth's role as protector of the solar barque (Te Velde 1967: 106) and in text 22 Seth assists Horus in helping the deceased to ascend to heaven by means of a ladder (compare positive text 9 in the Pyramid Texts.

The majority of the neutral texts refer to both Horus and Seth in a neutral manner, often referring to the portions of both of these gods (texts 2, 3, 17, and 30). Texts 10, 21, 24, and 25 refer to the 'Eye of Horus' and the testicles of Seth whilst text 20 mentions the 'Mounds of Horus and Seth' (compare these with the many neutral texts amongst the Pyramid Texts, as discussed earlier, that also refer to these).

Whilst there is little evidence for the worship of Seth during the First Intermediate Period, the fact that he is depicted on reliefs associated with Amenemhet, Senusret I and III from the Middle Kingdom indicates that his cult must have survived through this period. The Coffin Texts, not surprisingly given their development from the Pyramid Texts, continue to depict Seth in negative, positive and neutral terms. Whilst the majority are concerned with Seth's negative aspects, it is interesting to see that his power and strength are recognised in the positive texts including his role as protector of the solar barque. Due to the sparcity of evidence it is difficult to ascertain whether he was being worshipped by the general populace at this time but given the ease, as we will see in the next Chapter, in which the Hyksos rulers took him as their god, one is tempted to believe that certainly in the Delta region and possibly elsewhere he was being worshipped as a local god at this time.

5. SECOND INTERMEDIATE PERIOD 1650-1550 B.C.E.

Once again central authority breaks down and not only is the land divided amongst petty nobles but also a foreign race establishes a kingdom in the Delta region. Ryholt's study (1997) has enabled us to 'put some flesh upon the bones of this time' to the extent that it is now known that a king named Seth ruled for short period of time during the early part of this period.

The Fifteenth and Seventeenth Dynasties are important in the context of this thesis as these so called Hyksos rulers took Seth as their god within Egypt, probably because they saw many resemblances with Baal, the god they had worshipped in their original lands. This relationship of Seth with people in the Delta would have later repercussions. Positively, the Nineteenth Dynasty kings coming from this region worshipped him as their family god (see below, chapter 6), but negatively, it reinforced the relationship between Seth and 'things foreign' to the Egyptians, a relationship that was viewed unfavourably following the Assyrian and Persian conquests (see below, Chapters 8 and 9).

The fall of the Middle Kingdom in 1650 B.C.E. saw the start of the Second Intermediate Period (Booth 2005: 6). Five dynasties occur during this period, some of them concurrently, reflecting the division of Egypt into different regions as a consequence of the breakdown of central government following the death of Queen Sobeknefru, the last ruler of the Twelfth Dynasty (Callender 2000: 170). During the Middle Kingdom, and particularly during the reign of Ammenemes III, there had been a migration of people from the east into the Delta Region (Grimal 1992: 182). Whilst some of these would have been prisoners of war, many had been recruited as mercenaries, sailors and craftsmen (Oren 1997: xxii). A typical group can be seen in a relief on the wall of the tomb of Khnumhotep at Beni Hasan dating from the 6th year of the Twelfth Dynasty pharaoh, Sesostris II (Naville 1891: 18). As time progressed, these people began to unite their communities within this region and to gain control of the surrounding territories, helped, no doubt, by the breakdown in central government.

The Thirteenth and Fourteenth Dynasties appear to have ruled concurrently, the former from *Itj-tawy*, near the Fayum, and the latter from an area in the eastern Delta. There are few written records available to us from these two dynasties, and most information has been gleaned from the Turin King-list (Ryholt 1997: 9) and the royal scarab shaped seals (Ryholt 1997: 34-65). Interestingly, amongst the twenty-seven kings listed in the Turin King-list there is one named Seth, whom Ryholt (1997: 284) suggests may have usurped the throne. Unfortunately only two records of this king are known: a stela from Abydos dated to year 4 of Seth's reign, later usurped by Neferhotep I, which is now in the Cairo Museum (Ryholt 1997: 343), and a lintel inscription, also in the Cairo Museum, that contains his prenomen, Meribre (Ryholt 1997: 343). The fact that an individual of this name did rule, albeit for a short time, strongly suggests that abhorrence of the name was not evident at this time and that worship of the god Seth was still occurring. Further evidence for this claim is found in Simpson's description (1976: 41-44) of a statuette of a devotee of Seth which was found in the vicinity of the temple of Heliopolis and refers to the great chapel of Seth in that city.

The Fourteenth Dynasty appears to be the first Asiatic dynasty within the Delta Region (Ryholt 1997: 94), the argument for this being that no monuments of Nehsy (the founder of the dynasty) have been found outside the north-east Delta, and conversely no monuments of the Thirteenth Dynasty have been found in the same region. Unfortunately, the Turin King-list is somewhat damaged in the parts that would have referred to the Fourteenth Dynasty, so it is difficult to determine how many successors Nehsy had. Ryholt (1997: 97) suggests that there may have been as many as fifty-six kings in this Dynasty. Of the king's names that we do have, the majority appear to be of foreign origin, and the culture of the dynasty appears very similar to that of Canaan (Ryholt 1997: 99-102).

The Fifteenth Dynasty (1650-1550 B.C.E.) is attributed to the Hyksos kings, a name derived from the ancient Egyptian term *ḥḳꜣ ḫꜣswt* or *'rulers of foreign lands'* (Booth 2005: 7). Interestingly, the title *ḥḳꜣ ḫꜣswt* has never been found together with the Egyptian titles of kingship except in one case, a door-jamb discovered in Tell el-Dab'a (Ryholt 1997: 123). On this jamb the following titulary was recorded:

[ḥr ... ...] nbty wꜥf-pḏwt bik-nbw iry-tꜣš-f ḥḳꜣ-ḫꜣswt skr-ḥr, '[Horus who ... ...]. The possessor of the Wadjet and Nekhbet diadems who subdues the bow people. The Golden Falcon who establishes his boundary. The *ḥḳꜣ-ḫꜣswt*, Sakir-Har'.

Here, Sakir-Har has the first three components of the Egyptian titles of kingship, namely the Horus, Nebty and Golden Horus names; he does not have the prenomen or nomen, the parts written in cartouches when present. His successor, Khayan, does use both the ḥḳꜣ-ḫꜣswt title and prenomen and nomen but never together, suggesting that they represent two stages in his life. This is important as it was during the reign of Khayan that the whole of Egypt may have been conquered by the Fifteenth Dynasty (Ryholt 1997: 124). This would have been reflected in Khayan's change from the use of ḥḳꜣ-ḫꜣswt to the full Egyptian titulary. Khayan's successors also dropped the ḥḳꜣ-ḫꜣswt term and only used the traditional Egyptian titles.

The Fifteenth Dynasty kings established their capital at Avaris in the north-eastern Delta (modern Tell el Dab'a). They appear to have been a warrior people judging from the weapons found amongst their grave goods and before their rise to power, they may have been recruited into the Egyptian army. However there is no evidence that their takeover was violent: Avaris, although a fortified city, does not appear to have been involved in any battles, and its reinforced enclosure wall was not built until the end of the period when the struggle with the Seventeenth Dynasty Theban kings was taking place. That said, once they had established themselves within the Delta, it took twenty years for them to conquer Abydos and a further thirty years to gain control of the Theban area, suggesting that they did encounter resistance as they travelled further south (Booth 2005: 10).

There appears to be some controversy over the Sixteenth Dynasty. Initially it was thought to consist only of minor kings who ruled under and by the authority of the Hyksos (Clayton 1994: 95), but Ryholt (1997: 151) suggests that this Dynasty was, in fact, the precursor of the Theban Seventeenth Dynasty, and ruled an area that stretched from Hu in the north to Edfu in the south.

The rulers of the Seventeenth Dynasty appear to have extended the kingdom of the Sixteenth Dynasty by pushing their borders to Abydos in the north and Elephantine in the south (Bourriau 2000: 205). An uneasy truce appears to have originally existed between the Seventeenth Dynasty rulers and their Hyksos counterparts. However, this situation could not last, and, in what appears to have been an attempt to cause hostilities to break out, the Hyksos king Apophis sent a letter to King Seqenenre Tao complaining that the sounds from the latter's hippopotamus pool in Thebes were disturbing his sleep in the Delta (Booth 2005: 47)! The story is outlined in the Sallier I Papyrus, which dates from Ramesside times and may well be written deliberately in such a way as to show the Hyksos in a worse light than they actually deserved (Simpson 1972: 77-80). Whatever the truth, hostilities began and Seqenenre Tao embarked upon a campaign to initially push the Hyksos out of Theban territory. He was probably killed in one of the battles, as his mummy shows evidence of terrible wounds to his head, which appear to have been inflicted by the battle axes favoured by the Hyksos (Bickerstaffe 2009: 87). Following the death of Seqenenre Tao, the campaign was continued by his son, Kamose, who recorded his successes on two stelae originally set up at the Karnak temple (Booth 2005: 47).

On one of the stelae Kamose states: *'One prince in Avaris and another in Kush...each holding his slice of the black land – who share this land with me. I will grapple with him* (Apophis) *that I may cleave open his belly – my desire is to deliver Egypt and to smite the* A'amu (Asiatics).'(Booth 2005: 48).

After Kamose's death, his brother Ahmose continued the fight. He first broke contact between the Hyksos in the Delta and Canaan by taking Sile on the Egypt-Sinai border. Then, secure in the knowledge that no reinforcements could arrive from that region, he besieged Avaris, drove the Hyksos out and pursued them to Sharuhen in Palestine (Booth 2005: 48). An account of the battle for Avaris is given in the autobiography of Ahmose, son of Abana, in his tomb at El Kab (Lichtheim 1976: 12-13). Rohl (2007: 115) believes that the departure of the Hyksos was helped by the eruption of Thera which was heard in the Egyptian Delta and likened to the voice of Seth announcing his disapproval of Hyksos rule. Rohl translates the column of hieratic writing found in the margin of the Rhind Mathematical Papyrus as follows:

"*Year 11, the first month of* Akhet (growing season) *the birthday of Seth: the majesty of this god caused his voice to be heard. The birthday of Isis: the sky rained.*"

These two 'birthdays' belong within the five epagomenal days which precede the New Year and that of Isis follows that of Seth. Rohl likens the term *'the sky rained'* to the ash from the eruption of Thera descending upon the Delta.

Rohl also makes the point that because the walls of Avaris were so strong they could not be breached (Rohl 2007: 113) and so Ahmose concluded a treaty with the Hyksos so that they could leave Egypt unmolested. I propose that the Hyksos may also have suffered an outbreak of plague whilst the siege of Avaris was taking place. Certainly Panagiotakopulu (2004: 271) reports upon the existence of black rats (the carriers of plague) at this time and a description of a disease that could be plague is described in the Hearst Medical

Papyrus and named 'the Canaanite illness' (Goedicke 1984: 94).' The passage reads as follows:

"Who is knowledgeable like Re? Who knows the like of this god? When the body is blackened with black spots – to arrest the god who is above. Just as Seth had banned the Mediterranean Sea, Seth will ban you likewise, O Canaanite illness! You shall not intend to pass through the limbs of X, born of Y."

The disease was probably called the Canaanite illness either because of the place in which it started, or because of the Egyptian practice of blaming everything deleterious on foreigners, in which case, if it was first encountered during the siege of Avaris, this could have also influenced its subsequent name, and indeed, hastened the end of the siege of that city.

With regard to the relationship between the Hyksos and Seth the Sallier I Papyrus states in its second paragraph:

'So King Apophis, life, prosperity, health (l.p.h.) adopted Seth for himself as lord, and he refused to serve any god that was in the entire land except Seth. He built a temple of fine workmanship for eternity next to the House of King Apophis, l.p.h., and he appeared at break of day in order to sacrifice ...daily to Seth, while the officials of the palace, l.p.h., carried garlands, exactly as is practiced in the temple of Pre-Harakhti' (Simpson 1972: 78).

Whilst this is obviously written from the Egyptian point of view, there is no doubt that Seth was the one member of the Egyptian pantheon to whom the Hyksos were able to relate. It seems more than likely that, as the Hyksos began to colonise the Delta region, they came into contact with the indigenous Egyptian population. This population would have included descendants of the original Seth worshippers who had possibly been driven into this region by Scorpion (see above), and so the Hyksos would have encountered this Egyptian god very early in their time in Egypt. Certainly the earliest reference to Seth that we have contemporary with this time is on the obelisk of Nehsy, where the inscription *'Seth, the lord of r-3ḥwt'* occurs (Petrie 1885: 8, pl. III; Te Velde 1967: 118; Ryholt 1997: 376). Nehsy was described as the eldest royal son and could well have been serving as a commander of troops in the Delta region, where he would have come into contact with Seth worship.Subsequently, when he became king, he made Seth *'Lord of Avaris'* (Van Seters 1966: 100-101). Apophis, in turn, often mentions his piety towards Seth so we have an offering table, now in the Cairo Museum, with the secondary dedication to *'Seth, Lord of ḥwt-wʿrt'* (Labib 1936: 160-164 and Ryholt 1997: 386) and several usurped monuments that have had a secondary dedication to Seth added to them, e.g. a sphinx of Amenemhet II in the Louvre, and four more sphinxes in Cairo Museum (Ryholt 1997: 386). Interestingly, excavations of some of the tombs in the vicinity of Avaris have revealed evidence of donkey burials (Bietak 1997: 103; Booth 2005: 33). Bietak suggests that this could indicate the importance of donkey caravaneering and that these tombs might be the resting places of expedition leaders; Booth proposes that these were the animals used to pull the funerary carriage; both believe this to be a Canaanite practice as evidenced by Kenyon's description of similar finds at Jericho (1960: 306; see also Van Seters 1966: 47). Perhaps this was a practice associated with Seth worship (see above). This is given support by the fact that two of the burials at Avaris were not connected with any tombs but were found in oval pits in front of Temple V (Booth 2005: 33). The fact that few burials of this type have been described could be due to the problems encountered in excavating in the Delta region.

In the Sallier I Papyrus paragraph quoted at the beginning of this section, later commentators (Simpson 1972: 78; Booth 2005: 29) have translated the god's name as *'Seth'*, but Gunn and Gardiner (1918: 44) were at pains to point out that it should be translated at *'Setekh'*, believing that this was the correct pronunciation in this part of the Delta and an adaptation of the softer *Setesh* or *Setech* that was the original pronunciation of the god's name, and that the Set or Seth pronunciation came in at the time of the New Kingdom. It is evident that from the Eighteenth Dynasty onwards Set or Seth becomes the Egyptian stock-equivalent of any god associated with an Asiatic enemy. So, for example, Ba'al is written with a Seth determinative. Assmann (1996: 199-200) believes that this arose from the time of the worship of Seth by the Hyksos and his transformation in the minds of the Egyptians from being the killer of Osiris and the rival to Horus, to also becoming an Asiatic god. This meant that, rather than being demonised and ostracised and, as a result, the same feelings being attributed to foreigners, both were seen as examples of 'otherness' which could be regarded as adversaries or partners. The first was dealt with by conquest and subjugation and the second by alliances and political marriages. Certainly, the images of Seth from the Delta attributed to the New Kingdom show him with Asiatic characteristics: a streamer falling from his headdress down his back, a fringed kilt and, in some representations, with an Asiatic beard. All are attributes typical of the Canaanite storm god Ba'al (Te Velde 1967: 125, fig. 15; Booth 2005: 30, fig. 19). He is represented this way on the so-called 400 Years Stela (Montet 1933). This stela was erected by Ramesses II to commemorate his ancestors, in particular his great-grandfather Sethos, who was governor of the town of Sile; it records 400 years of worship of Seth in the Delta region. This period begins before the time of the Hyksos, and suggests that Seth in his foreign manifestation was known before the rule of the Hyksos (Te Velde 1967: 126), possibly because of the trade between Canaan and Egypt and/or the settling of people from Canaan in this region, particularly as Sile was positioned on the Egypt/Sinai border. Further evidence for the identification of Seth with Ba'al comes from the fact that they were both recognised as storm-gods (Allon 2007: S20). Thus both peoples would have identified similar characteristics within the two gods and it would have been a simple step for the Egyptians to use the Seth determinative when they referred to Ba'al in their texts. In time, this resulted in the name Ba'al becoming a foreign name for Seth in Egyptian texts.

The legacy of this period proved to be a two-edged sword for Seth. On the one hand, it firmly cemented his worship within the Delta region which was to have important repercussions in the Nineteenth Dynasty when, as the family-god of the Ramesside kings, he would be elevated to be one of the state-gods. On the other hand, because of Seth's identification with 'things foreign', it would ultimately lead to his abhorrence in the Saite and subsequent Graeco-Roman periods (see below for further discussion on both these topics).

Interactions with people from the Near East had occurred throughout Egyptian history up to this point mainly as a result of trade or military campaigns or because people from these areas settled in Egypt (Zivie-Coche 2011: 2). Of greater significance, both at this time and in the future, were the rule of the Hyksos and their adoption of Seth as their principal deity. Native Egyptians could accept this as an example of Seth's 'otherness'; the fact that they chose to write Ba'al's name with the Seth animal as a determinative reveals the close association that they saw between the two deities (Zivie-Coche 2011: 5). As discussed in the last section of this chapter this was to have significant repercussions with regard to Seth and his worship within Egypt. The ease with which the Hyksos were able to assimilate Seth as their god does strongly suggest that, as alluded to in the last Chapter, the worship of Seth as a local god within the Delta region must have been quite marked.

6. THE NEW KINGDOM (part 1: The Eighteenth Dynasty 1550-1295 B.C.E.)

In the first part of the New Kingdom the Hyksos were driven out and Egypt united once more under one pharaoh; because the dynasty originated in the Theban region the god Amun is once more elevated to one of the supreme gods of Egypt. However, there is plenty of evidence to indicate that Seth was still an important member of the pantheon, especially in his role in the king's heb-sed festival. His name was in general use as witnessed by the discovery of the tomb of the Royal Butler, Seth, dating to the time of Amenophis III, and the existence of a wooden statue base in the Florence Museum, dated to the late Eighteenth Dynasty, belonging to the 'Great Singer and Prophet of Seth of Ombos, Userseth'. Even during the Amarna Period there is evidence to show that Seth was still being worshipped by the general populace and upon the reinstatement of the original religion following this period, Seth was certainly acknowledged by Horemheb.

The Hyksos Period had upset the Egyptian concept of *maat*, a word which is generally translated as order or truth. It signified a state where everything was as the gods had ordained that it should be at the time of creation and which had to be maintained to placate them. An important aspect was that a legitimate pharaoh should be on the throne to act as intermediary between the gods and the Egyptians. If this did not occur then *isfet*, the state of chaos and disruption, took over, and this was exemplified by a line of foreign rulers on the throne of Egypt.

The Theban princes, led initially by Sequenre Tao and then by his sons Kamose and Ahmose, presumably for economic and strategic reasons as well as wishing to ensure a state of *maat* over the whole of the country decided that this situation could not be allowed to continue and as related above they eventually succeeded in driving the Hyksos out and establishing their rule over the entire country.

Whereas the Middle Kingdom had equated the First Intermediate Period with internal chaos, the New Kingdom saw the state of *isfet* as being caused by an 'external menace' and as a consequence, concentrated its main concerns upon foreign policy. The ousting of the Hyksos was interpreted and commemorated in terms of the myth of Horus and Seth, with Seth, now being seen as a god of the Hyksos and hence an Asiatic. However, he was not demonised at this stage but foreign things became part of his 'otherness' (Assmann 1996: 199-200).

An example can be seen in Hatshepsut's inscription at the Speos Artemidos which includes the following passage:

'Hear ye, all persons! Ye people as many as ye are! I have done this according to the designs of my heart. I have restored that which was in ruins, I have raised up that which was unfinished since the Asiatics (the Hyksos) *were in the midst of Avaris of the Northland, and the barbarians were in the midst of them, overthrowing that which was made, while they ruled in ignorance of Re.'* (Breasted 1906: Vol 2: 125-126).

Here, whilst speaking against the Hyksos and their supposed destruction of temples, Hatshepsut does not decry Seth's role in this situation; in fact, she does not even mention him. However he is mentioned in her mortuary temple at Deir-el-Bahari where the story of her conception begins with the god Amun addressing the twelve great gods of Egypt; included amongst their number is Seth, described in the accompanying hieroglyphs as *'the great living god'* (Naville 1896: 13 and Plate XLVI; Tyldesley 1996: 103). Seth is also depicted upon a block now in the Karnak Open Air Museum offering a combination 'was-ankh' to the nose of the God's Wife, King Hatshepsut (Cruz-Uribe 2009: 213). Hatshepsut also records upon her obelisk at Karnak Temple the following:

'as I wear the White Crown, as I appear in the Red Crown, as Horus and Seth have united for me their halves, as I rule this land like the son of Isis (i.e. Horus), *as I have become strong like the son of Nut* (i.e. Seth) (Sethe and Helck 1906: 366, Breasted J.H. 1906: (2)133).

Here Hatshepsut is saying that not only can she rule as Horus, but that if she must use force then she can be Seth; neither of these two aspects of kingship can be dispensed with and hence Seth cannot be ignored. So whilst Seth's role as god of the Hyksos cannot be forgotten, his ancient role in the Egyptian kingship needs to be remembered. Indeed Hatshepsut's father, Thuthmosis I, built a temple dedicated to Seth at Ombos where Petrie and Quibell discovered a magnificent lintel (Figure 9), now sadly destroyed, upon which Seth is depicted presenting an *ankh* (signifying life) to a hawk which is perched upon the *ka* name of the king (Petrie and Quibell 1896: 67 and Plate LXXVII).

Figure 9: Lintel from the temple of Thuthmosis I at Nubt (from Petrie and Quibell 1896:67).

Figure 10: Sandstone jamb from temple of Thuthmosis III at Nubt (from Petrie and Quibell 1896: 68).

Thuthmosis III was also active at this temple as shown by the discovery by Petrie of a sandstone jamb of a doorway on which he is called *'the beloved of Seth, the bull of Nubt, lord of the south'* (Figure 10), and by his foundation deposits, all of which have engraved upon them: *'The good god* Men-Kheper-Re, *beloved of Seth of Nubt.'* (Petrie and Quibell 1896: 68 and Plate LXXIX). Also found was a stela (Figure 11), (Petrie and Quibell 1896: 68 and Plate LXXVIII), now in the Manchester Museum (acquisition no 4528), belonging to an official named Anhotep, which has a fine depiction of Seth standing before an altar accompanied by the following inscriptions:

At top: *'Seth of* Nubt, *lord of provisions, great of strength, powerful of arm'*.

To the right of altar: *'(missing) of Amun,* Anhotep*'*

At bottom: *'made by the* wab-*priest of Amun, the chief of craftsmen,* Nedkem*'*.

Figure 11: Stela of Anhotep (Manchester Museum AN 4528). Copyright: Manchester Museum.

The second consequence of the expulsion of the Hyksos was the elevation of Amun, initially a deity local to Thebes. Worshipped in this capacity by Ahmose, the founder of the Eighteenth Dynasty, Amun became a state god and his temple at Karnak became a huge religious centre receiving tribute from the successful war campaigns of the pharaohs of the New Kingdom, who all added various pylons, courts embellished with obelisks, shrines and altars celebrating their accomplishments. But even here at the centre of Amun's cult, Seth is represented. At the rear of the temple complex Thuthmosis III built a sumptuously decorated Festival Hall to commemorate his Sed Festival, where one of the reliefs depicts the pharaoh being instructed by Seth in the use of the bow (Wilkinson 1994: 184), once again emphasising Seth's strength and military acumen.

However, the dichotomy in Seth's role continued; it can be seen in the Amduat, the story of the sungod's journey through the netherworld, that took place every night when the sun set in the west until its rebirth in the east the following morning. The most complete version of this is seen on the walls of the tomb of Thuthmosis III in the Valley of the Kings. The story is divided into twelve hours and in the introduction to the first one can be read (Schweizer 2010: 33):

This god (i.e. Re) enters through the western gateway of the horizon. Seth stands upon the riverbank.

Here in the darkness, danger lies, Seth is here portrayed as the murderer of Osiris and as a possible threat to the sun-god himself. But in the second hour we see portrayed a figure with the heads of both Seth and Horus. Schweizer (2010: 53) believes that this figure personifies the union of opposites, the two faces of everything that exists, once again implying that everyone has a light and a dark side. Re needs to utilise this dark side of Seth in order to defeat the serpent Apophis, who is intent on annihilating the whole of creation and allowing chaos to hold sway. So, in the seventh hour two figures are depicted in the prow of the solar barque confronting Apophis: one is Isis, well known for her magical skills, but the other is Seth, here becoming one of Re's principal defenders and utilising his powers of strength and energy in order to ward off ultimate chaos and catastrophe (Schweizer 2010: 141). As Spell 108 of the Book of the Dead puts it (Faulkner 1972: 101):

"Get back the sharp knife which is in my hand! I stand before you, navigating aright and seeing afar. Cover your face, for I ferry across; get back because of me, for I am the Male! I am hale and I remain hale, for I am the great magician, the son of Nut (i.e. Seth)*, and power against you has been granted to me."*

Thuthmosis III was a great warrior-pharaoh extending the Egyptian Empire far into Syria by his decisive campaigns against that of the rival empire of Mitanni (Bryan 2000: 243). The subsequent vast empire was maintained by the campaigns of his successors, Amenophis II, Thuthmosis IV and Amenophis III. The long reign of the latter, extending as it did for almost 40 years (1386-1349 B.C.E.), was one of the most prosperous and stable in Egyptian history up to that point. Amenophis III had himself depicted between Seth and Horus, who are crowning him, on the pylon of his temple at Sulb, between the second and third cataracts of the Nile (Lepsius 1849: v; 233; Porter and Moss 1975: 169). This scene was later usurped by Amenophis IV, presumably before he became whole-heartedly involved in the cult of the *Aten*.

During this reign we have the first evidence for an actual cult of the *Aten* (the sun's disk) which was based at Heliopolis with its own priesthood and temple (Fletcher 2000: 61).

With regard to the god's name being in general use at this time, in 1996, whilst excavating at Saqqara, the French Egyptologist, Alain Zivie, discovered a tomb belonging to the Royal Butler, Seth, thus indicating that the name of the god could also be a person's name. The name within the tomb was written in two ways, either as the seated Seth-animal or with phonetic signs followed by a kneeling person (Zivie 1997: 373-382) so:

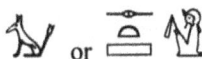

Also dating to the later part of the dynasty is a wooden statue base in the Florence Museum which is inscribed for Userseth,

The owner is described as *'Great Singer and Prophet of Seth at Ombos'* (Pellegrini 1898: 96; Porter and Moss 1964: 787), indicating that this town was still associated with the worship of Seth.

A round-topped limestone stela first described by Moret (1931: 725-750) is dated to this period. Two offering scenes are carved on it: on the left, an official named Amenmose and his wife, Nefertari, are seated before an offering table and, on the right a lady named Baket is depicted with a priest performing rites before her. Below these scenes are twenty-eight lines of hieroglyphs which contain the 'hymn to Osiris.' This hymn gives the fullest account in Egyptian rather than Greek of the conflict of Osiris and Seth. It is unique in this respect, possibly because the slaying of Osiris by Seth was so repugnant to the Egyptians that they could not bring themselves to write it down, presumably as they believed that this would make it real. Even in this example, the actual deed is only alluded to and not fully described (Lichtheim 1976: 81). However, other parts of the story, such as the vindication of both Osiris and his son, Horus, could be described in more detail.

The first part of the text praises Osiris and describes how his father, Geb, recognising his many qualities, gives him the kingship of Egypt. This is followed by a description of how his sister/wife, Isis, was his protector and sought his body after his death, reanimated it and was able to conceive Horus:

'His sister was his guard, she who drove off his foes, who stopped the deeds of the disturber (presumably Seth) *by the power of her utterance. The clever-tongued, whose speech failed not; effective in the word of command; mighty Isis who protected her brother; who sought him without wearying. Who roamed the land lamenting, not resting till she found him, who made a shade with her plumage, created breath with her wings. Who jubilated, joined her brother, raised the weary one's inertness, received the seed, bore the heir, raised the child in solitude, his abode unknown. Who brought him when his arm was strong into the broad hall of Geb.'* (Lichtheim 1976: 83-84).

The text then goes on to describe how pleased the Ennead was to welcome Horus and how they recognised him as the heir to Osiris and the rightful owner of the kingship and how Seth was given to Horus:

'They gave to Isis' son his foe, his attack collapsed, the disturber suffered hurt, his fate overtook the offender.' (Lichtheim 1976: 84).

The final part of the text praises the beneficent rule of Horus, and by association, that of the ruling pharaoh.

In 1352 B.C.E. Amenophis III died, and was succeeded by his son, Amenophis IV. Amenophis III had actively promoted the solar cults, maybe in an attempt to curb the power of the Amun priesthood, who were running a virtual state within a state, based on the vast agricultural estates, gold and slaves that had all been dedicated to the god by the Eighteenth Dynasty pharaohs. He appears to have done this with some skill, managing to keep the priesthood at Karnak happy whilst promoting the sun god in the form of the *Aten*. Amenophis III's successor should have been his eldest son, Tuthmosis, who is known best from his activities around Memphis, where he was the High priest of Ptah (Reeves 2001: 61). Unfortunately, Thuthmosis died before his father, and Amenophis IV was named heir around the time of his father's first Sed-festival in regnal year 30.

By tradition, the pharaoh stood as the intermediary between the gods and men, in life the incarnation of Horus, and in death one with Osiris and the imperishable stars. During the reign of Amenophis III, belief in the divinity of the pharaoh had been deliberately elevated to re-establish kingly authority as against that of the priests of the various cults, particularly of Amun. Amenophis III had been prepared to do this stealthily, but his son wished to see the pharaoh back in the position he had occupied at the start of Egyptian history, i.e. as sole ruler.

Amenophis IV (Akhenaten) was devoted to the *Aten* cult so he initially challenged the cult of Amun in its own centre, the temple at Karnak. Here, Amenophis IV began an extensive building programme of temples dedicated to the worship of the *Aten*. These temples were mainly built using sandstone blocks of two sizes. The first, a series of large blocks carved in traditional style, came from the southern gateway that Amenophis IV constructed at Karnak (Reeves 2001: 91-92); the second, smaller blocks of half-cubit length, are generally referred to as *'talatat'*. These *talatat* were subsequently used, when Amenophis

IV's monuments at Karnak were destroyed by his successors, as in-fill for their monuments. In recent years, computerised study of these blocks has been undertaken by the Akhenaten Temple Project (ATP), a joint American-Canadian-Egyptian venture described by Smith and Redford (1976). From this project it has become apparent that Amenophis IV celebrated a *heb-sed* festival in the second or third year of his reign. This festival was normally celebrated in the thirtieth year of a king's reign (Newby 1980: 85), so why did Amenophis celebrate his so early in his reign? A possible answer is that it may have been thirty years since his father had begun to promote the sun-cult of the *Aten*, a theory given credence by the epithet, *imy-heb-sed*,'he who is in jubilee' which is frequently applied to the *Aten* disc (Smith and Redford 1976: 64). What is interesting from the point of view of this work is that amongst the *talatat* relating to the festival studied by the ATP is one that depicts a couch with the Seth animal above it (Smith and Redford 1976: Plate 85 (1)). Worship by the king of the various gods in the Egyptian pantheon was an important part of a traditional jubilee festival (Frankfort 1948: 82-83) and whilst the *Aten* has been reported as the only god represented at this festival (Reeves 2001: 97), the above finding suggests otherwise, and it may be that in spite of Amenophis IV's misgivings, much of the festival followed the traditional lines. So Amenophis IV would have been crowned with both the White Crown of the south and the Red Crown of the north (Smith and Redford 1976: 65 and plates 85 (7/8) and 67; 75 (2)) and was probably presented with four arrows by priests wearing Horus and Seth masks which he then shot to the four cardinal points in a magic assault on all possible enemies (Newby 1980: 85). Following this jubilee, Amenophis IV decided to abandon both Memphis, the administrative capital, and Thebes, the religious centre, and to change his name to Akhenaten *("He who is effective on the* Aten's *behalf")*. He also moved the capital to a new site, modern Tell-el-Amarna in Middle Egypt, where a new city known as Akhetaten *("the Horizon of the* Aten*")* would be built (Reeves 2001: 103). Then, in Year 10 of his reign, a decree went forth to smash up the divine statues and hack out the names and images of Amun and his consort, Mut, and this was accompanied by a focused attack upon the birth scenes of Hatshepsut at Deir-el-Bahri and Amenophis III at the Luxor temple. Furthermore, the *Aten* was now regarded as the only true deity, so any reference in the hieroglyphs to other 'gods' was also excised. This persecution went as far as small, personal items such as kohl pots and scarabs where the three signs making up Amun's name were removed.

Did the persecution extend to the worship of Seth? If the 400 Year Stela (Breasted 1906: Vol 3, 226-228 and below), is to be believed then this appears unlikely in the Delta region and recent studies at Dakhleh Oasis would also suggest that here the worship of Seth continued uninterrupted (Ikram – personal communication). Furthermore, at Akhetaten itself, recent excavation by Kemp (2008: 41-46) has shown the presence of objects that depict gods, goddesses and symbols that belong to the traditional field of personal belief. So many examples of Bes, the grotesque dwarf figure who warded off evil spirits, have been found, as well as of the goddess-monster, Taweret, part crocodile, part hippopotamus, who was associated with childbirth. Also in the royal workmen's village at Akhetaten, stelae dedicated to Isis and Shed have been discovered (Watterson 1984: 158 and 208). No statues or scarabs depicting Seth have been found up to the present but this does not mean that they did not exist. As Kemp concludes: *"From our perspective Amarna is an accidental experiment in religious belief. Take away a few of the major gods (Amun-Ra and Osiris being the two principal targets) and see what affect this had on the behaviour of the majority of the people. The answer seems to be, not much. The reason is presumably that the combination of household deities and cult of family members brought sufficient satisfaction for it to be viable on its own."*

Inevitably neither Akhenaten nor his chief vizier, Nakht, was able to reorganise the economy of the country to reflect the new power base at Akhetaten. This led to widespread corruption throughout the country with magistrates open to bribery and officials helping themselves. This situation meant that there was a great deal of interest in the naming of Akhenaten's successor. A youth called Smenkhkare was eventually appointed co-regent (David 1980: 172); he constructed his tomb, not at Akhetaten, but at Thebes, suggesting that, as he would have required Akhenaten's permission to do this, some sort of rapprochement was being conducted by the pharaoh with the priests of Amun.

Akhenaten died, after a reign of some 18 years, in 1336 B.C.E. He was possibly pre-deceased by Smenkhkare, as his successor was a boy of nine initially known as Tutankhaten, but who later, as part of the conciliation process with the old religion, changed his name to Tutankhamun (Newby 1980: 132). The court left Akhetaten returning to the ancient capital, Memphis, a move probably engineered by the real power behind the throne, the courtier Ay. Ay managed to survive being chief priest of the *Aten* to succeed Tutankhamun as pharaoh, a move he legitimised by marrying Tutankhamun's widow, Ankhesenamun (Reeves 2001:

189). Ay only reigned for four years and was succeeded by Horemheb who came from Herakleopolis and was a career officer in the army. He had rapidly gained promotion throughout the reigns of various pharaohs of this period. While he was not a young man, on ascending the throne, he set about restoring the status quo, reopening temples and repairing them. His coronation inscription speaks of *'the rejoicing of the gods'* because of his accession and translates as follows: *'Nekhbet, Buto, Neith, Isis, Nephthys, Horus, Seth, all the ennead of gods who preside over the great throne, lifted praises to the heights of heaven, rejoicing in the satisfaction of Amun'* (Breasted 1906: Vol 3: 17). So he certainly regarded Seth as an important deity and had himself depicted between Seth on the left and Horus on the right on the wall of his temple at Gebel Addah (Figures 12).

Although somewhat damaged, the typical ears of the god Seth and his erect forked tail can still be made out in this relief of which Lepsius (1849: iii; 122a) gives an excellent diagrammatic representation (Figure 14). A block at Karnak dating from Horemheb's reign shows Seth, holding a crook, standing before the king (Cruz-Uribe 2009: 214). The death of Horemheb in 1295 B.C.E. brought to a close the Eighteenth Dynasty and heralded what was probably Seth's greatest hour.

Following the re-unification of Upper and Lower Egypt and the expulsion of the Hyksos one could be forgiven for thinking that, as Seth had been so closely associated with the Hyksos, he would subsequently be regarded in an altogether unfavourable light, something that did occur following the Assyrian and Persian invasions (see later). However this appears not to have happened, perhaps because the Egyptians saw Seth's role as that of a 'foreign minister' amongst the gods, i.e. whilst he took foreigners and things foreign under his wing, his main allegiance was still to Egypt. Certainly Thutmosis I and III were active at Seth's temple at Ombos where his worship was probably active, as well as in the Delta and at the oases. Whilst the Great Hymn to Osiris is the best Egyptological written source to describe Seth's role in the death of Osiris, this does not appear to have changed the Egyptians opinion of Seth indeed he continued to be regarded as an important member of the pantheon at this time. As we shall see in the next Chapter he was about to become one of the state gods of Egypt, closely associated with the family from the Delta that was to provide some of Egypt's greatest pharaohs.

Figure 12: Sketch of relief from Gebel Adda – Rock temple; Horemheb depicted between Seth and Horus (from Lepsius 1849: iii; 122a).

7. THE NEW KINGDOM (part 2: The Nineteenth and Twentieth Dynasties 1295-1069 B.C.E.)

This chapter examines the rise to power of a family (the Ramessides) that originated in the Delta and had Seth as their family god. Because of this relationship, when they attained the throne of Egypt Seth also became more prominent than at any time previously. As the early Ramessides began to enlarge the Egyptian empire they were not slow to recognise the war-like attributes of Seth and to liken themselves to him upon the battlefield. The theory that Seti I built a chapel commemorating Seth within the temple at Abydos is discussed below and the many inscriptions referring to Seth during this period are discussed. The presence of a stele dedicated to Seth in the Royal Tomb Workers' village at Deir-el-Medina is significant as it shows acceptance of this god in what was surely a most religious site in Egypt at that time. Finally, Seth's role in the spells that occur in the Books of the Dead is discussed.

During the latter years of Amenophis III and the reign of Akhenaten, a youngster named Seti ('the man of Seth') grew up in the Delta near Avaris. He entered the army and rose to the rank of Commander of Troops, and witnessed the rise of his compatriot, Horemheb, to the position of pharaoh (James 2002: 51). By this time, his son, Pramesse *('Re has fashioned him'),* had followed his father's footsteps and chosen a career in the army. Unlike his father, Pramesse progressed through the ranks, first becoming a *'Commander of Troops'*, a *'Superintendent of Horse'* and *'King's Charioteer'*, and then a General, becoming *'Fortress Commander'* at Sile in the Eastern Delta and *'Superintendent of the Mouths of the Nile'*; these latter two ranks brought responsibility for border security with Canaan and the coasts of the Delta. Horemheb had obviously noticed Pramesse's ability as he soon appointed him *'Vizier'* and *'Primate of All Egypt'* (Kitchen 1982: 16, James 2002: 51).

However, Pramesse was destined for even higher things. Horemheb needed to acknowledge a successor, and, childless himself, he was also mindful that a successor with a line of heirs might avoid the problems that had afflicted the throne since the days of Amenhotep III. Pramesse fulfilled this requirement in that he not only had a son, Seti, named after his grandfather, but also a grandson, Ramesses. So Pramesse found himself proclaimed as *'Deputy of His Majesty in the South and the North'* and as *'Hereditary Prince in the Entire Land'*, thus announcing him as heir-presumptive to Horemheb (Kitchen 1982: 17, James 2002: 52).

Upon the death of Horemheb, Pramesse ascended the throne, taking the name Ramesses I. His main disadvantage was his age as he was probably in his mid-sixties on his accession and so he probably only occupied the throne for about two years and during the latter part of this time he appointed his son co-regent and, upon his death in 1294 B.C.E., Seti became pharaoh (James 2002: 54).

Seti I was determined to restore Egypt's empire and repair the damage that had occurred under the Amarna kings, so to this end he inaugurated a major building policy at home and a committed foreign policy abroad (Van Dijk 2000: 295-296). He led a campaign through Syria in the first year of his reign and by Year five had stormed Quadesh itself (Faulkner 1947: 34-39; Kitchen 1982: 25). A record of these campaigns is found on the northern wall of the Great Hypostyle Hall at Karnak, extending onto the eastern half of the eastern wall (Breasted 1906: Vol 3, 37). Whilst Seti I dedicated his victories to Amun he was not slow to liken himself to Seth upon the battlefield, and to also show his Delta roots and the synergy between Seth and Baal that had existed since Hyksos times; thus over the reliefs depicting the battle for Quadesh, he has the following inscription of his full royal titulary:

'Horus: Mighty Bull, Shining in Thebes, Vivifier of the Two Lands, King of Upper and Lower Egypt, Lord of the Two Lands: Menmaatre; Son of Re: Seti-Merenptah; Good God, mighty in strength, brave like Montu, mightiest of the mighty, like him that begat him, illuminating the Two Lands like the horizon-god, great in strength like the son of Nut, victorious, the double Horus by his own hand, treading the battlefield like Seth, great in terror like Baal in the countries.' (Breasted 1906: Vol 3, 72).

By Year six of his reign, Seti I had covered himself in glory with his campaigns abroad and had restored Egypt's empire; thus emulating his ancestor Thutmosis III, he now turned to his other ambition, to be as great a builder as Amenophis III. In addition to his above mentioned building at Karnak, on the West Bank, his memorial temple at Gurnah and his tomb in the Valley of the Kings were under construction. In the north he began new work on the temples of Re at Heliopolis and Ptah at Memphis, and in the eastern Delta he built himself a new palace. It is at Abydos, however, home of the god Osiris, that he constructed a vast temple that poses some interesting questions with regard to Seth.

A sacred building had existed at Abydos from earliest times, and it was added to in the 6th Dynasty. Texts dating to the reign of Pepi II mention a temple dedicated to Khentiamentiu, god of the necropolis at Abydos, whose worship was later fused with that of Osiris (David 1981: 7). Before Seti I, a number of pharaohs had either added to, or replaced the temples; amongst them were Sesostris I, Tuthmosis I and Tuthmosis III, but Seti I produced a new concept.

The temple was built mainly by Seti I; a pair of cartouches discovered by Ghazouli (1964: 167-168) under the first Pylon belong to him even though the decoration was completed by Ramesses II. These cartouches, like all Seti I's others at Abydos, have the Seth figure in the nomen replaced by a figure of Osiris and a *tit*-knot, to write the name cryptographically so as not to offend Osiris by depicting his supposed murderer (Robins 1997: 174 and Brand 2000: 31):

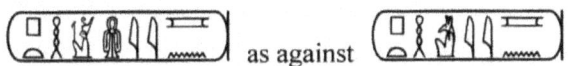

Both translate as '*he of the god Seth, beloved of Ptah*'. Cruz-Uribe (2009: 209-210) suggests that following the Amarna period there was a major reinterpretation of the solar cult and a re-examination of the position of various deities within that scenario, during these discussions Seth's role could well have entered into the picture, especially as the Ramessides worshipped him as a family god. In the Theban area, it may well have been thought that such a northern deity should not take precedence over the local Amun cult and a possible way around this dilemma was to utilise the traditional notion of substitution of deities thus replacing the Seth figure with that of Osiris could be an example of this practice.

The temple at Abydos differs from other Egyptian temples in that most temples are provided with one shrine, dedicated to the chief god as, for example, in the temple of Re at Heliopolis. Sometimes there may be subsidiary shrines dedicated to the god's wife and son, e.g. Amun, Mut and Khons at Karnak, but at Abydos there are seven main shrines in the sanctuary area which are dedicated to two triads: the imperial Ramesside gods, Amun, Re-Harakhte and Ptah; and the Osirian family, Isis, Horus and Osiris. In addition there is a shrine that is dedicated to Seti I (David 1981: 10). A further shrine dedicated to Seti I is also found in the so-called 'Osirian complex'; in this shrine Seti I appears as a dead, deified king and, in a reversal of the usual scenes where he would perform particular rituals in honour of the gods, in this shrine he is shown acting as a god whilst the ritual is performed on his behalf by various deities (David 1981: 141). As David suggests (1981: 146), the scenes in this particular shrine are to do with the installation of Seti I as an Osirian king and the temple is acting as a mortuary temple for the dead king.

However, the first shrine probably represented the coronation and acceptance of Seti I as an earthly king and his ultimate acceptance as a dead king at one with Osiris (David 1981: 87-88; O'Connor 2009: 45). One can imagine therefore the quandary that Seti I faced: he was building a marvellous temple at Abydos the home of Osiris in which he acknowledged the 'state-gods' of Egypt but how to acknowledge his own family god, Seth? One of the usual scenes where this could be done was that representing the uniting of the two lands. Here one would normally expect to see the enthroned king supported by Nekhbet and Wadjet, the two patron deities of Upper and Lower Egypt respectively (Wilkinson 2005: 170 and 258) and with Horus and Seth binding the Two Lands. However, in this shrine Seth has been replaced by Thoth (Calverley and Broome 1935: plate 30; David 1981: 92-94), possibly again to avoid offending Osiris. However, did Seti I really ignore this respect for Osiris and honour his own god? On the west wall of the shrine which would have been the one facing the entrance the reliefs are completely destroyed apart from the one shown on the south side, lower register where the king is depicted wearing the White Crown and the accompanying inscription reads: '*The august Mansion of Millions of Years of the King of Upper and Lower Egypt, Menmaatre, beloved of Osiris, 'Lord of the Necropolis*'' (Calverley and Broome 1935: plate 33; David 1981: 95). Did the opposite lower register show the king wearing the Red Crown and the upper registers depict Seti I being honoured by Seth and Horus as seen on the lintel from Heliopolis shown in Figure 15 and also by Brand (2000: figure 72)? A similar relief at Karnak outside the Temple of Amun is described by Blackman (1998; 191-192). It shows Seti I again being purified by Seth and Horus and the accompanying inscriptions state:

'*Utterance by the Ombite* (i.e. Seth): *I have purified thee with life and good fortune, so that thou are rejuvenated like thy father Re, and celebratest jubilee like Atum, appearing gloriously in gladness of heart.*'

'*Utterance by Horus: I have purified thee with life and good fortune so that thy duration is the duration of Re, and thou celebratest very many jubilees, appearing gloriously.*'

Obviously we will never know if this scene was depicted but the total destruction of the reliefs upon this wall is

*Figure 13: Lintel of Seti I from Heliopolis.
Copyright: L'Institut royal du patrimoine artistique, KIK-IRPA, Brussels, Belgium.*

Figure 14: Offering Table of Seti I. Copyright Photo SCALA, Florence: Metropolitan Museum of Art. New York 2010.

unusual even for Egypt and leads one to conjecture that if it did show that scene, was it obliterated once the power of the Ramesside kings waned? Certainly at other sites Seti I had no hesitation in depicting Seth; apart from the example cited above, there are ones where he is depicted as a Seth-headed sphinx which have been found in Alexandria (Brand 2000: figure 61) and Heliopolis (Brand 2000: figure 62) and on a lintel at Heliopolis (Figure 13) and an offering table where he is depicted worshipping Seth (Figure 14 and also Brand 2000: figures 91 and 92).

On the Karnak reliefs showing the slaying of prisoners before Amun following the campaign against the Hittites, the inscription contains the statement (Breasted 1906: Vol 3: 76):

'I give to thee the possessions of Horus and Seth, and their victories. The portions of the two gods are made thy portions.'

A further scene from the north wall – top register of the hypostyle hall at Karnak depicts a kneeling Seti I wearing the red crown making a bread offering *'to his father Seth, great of strength who dwells in the temple of Seti I in the temple of Amun.'* (Cruz-Uribe 2009: 215).

So by the sixteenth year of his reign, Seti I had ensured that Egypt had returned to her former glories, stable at home and with a considerable empire. Aged approximately fifty, he died suddenly and was succeeded by Ramesses II.

Following the burial of Seti I, Ramesses II became pharaoh and after a time at Thebes to oversee the funeral, he journeyed to Abydos and found that his father's temple, which was still under construction when Seti I died, had been neglected. Usually no pharaoh renewed his father's monuments, preferring to concentrate upon his own but here Ramesses differed and summoning the court he announced (Kitchen 1982: 46):

'See I have had you summoned concerning the matter that is before me. I have considered that it is a worthy deed, to benefit those who have passed away. Compassion is a blessing; it is good that a son should be concerned to care about his father. I am determined to confer benefits on Merenptah (Seti I), such that it will be said forever after, 'It is his son who perpetuated his name!' So may my father Osiris favour me with the long lifespan of his son Horus, according as I am one who does what he did.'

Thus the temple of Seti I at Abydos was completed by Ramesses II.

Ramesses II now turned his attention to the southward advance of the Hittites (Breasted 1906: 123-174; Kitchen 1982: 50-64). Ramesses II named the four divisions of his army after the gods Amun, Re, Ptah and Seth, indicating the respect that he held for these 'state-gods' of Egypt. He also mentions Seth on the so-called 'Marriage stela'. This stela commemorates the marriage between Ramesses II and a Hittite princess to cement the peace treaty that the two nations finally agreed upon. There is a passage where Ramesses II is supposedly concerned that the weather for the princess's journey to Egypt should be good; the inscription states (Kitchen 1982: 86):

'Now His Majesty had pondered in his mind, saying, 'How will they manage, those whom I have now sent to Syria, in these days of rain and snow that happen in winter?' So, he offered a great oblation to his father (the god) Seth, saying, 'The sky is in your hands, the earth is under your feet, whatever happens is what you command – so, may you not send rain, icy blast or snow, until the marvel you have decreed for me shall reach me!'

Then his father Seth heeded all that he said, and so the sky was calm and the summer days occurred in the winter season.'

Seth is also mentioned in the 'Stela of the year 400'. This stela was erected at Tanis by an important official of Ramesses II, named Seti and was intended to honour Ramesses's father Seti I (Breasted 1906: Vol 3, 226). The stela tells how Seti, whilst a general, came to Avaris to do honour to the god Seth and states that the visit was in the four-hundredth year of that god being established there, a reference that is now taken to mean the period of time that had elapsed between the Hyksos building their great temple to Seth and Seti's visit (Newby 1980: 167). The stela depicts, at the top, Ramesses II followed by an official offering two flasks of wine to Seth (Montet 1933: 194-195). Seth is depicted as a robust, stocky man and has both Egyptian and foreign characteristics, probably confirming the way in which the Hyksos depicted him. Following Ramesses II's titular, the inscription reads (Montet 1933: 197-198):

'His Majesty orders a great granite stela to be made, in the mighty name of his fathers, so as to raise high the name of the father of his fathers, the king Menmaat-Re, son of the sun, Seti-beloved-of-Ptah, firmly established for eternity, like Re, every day.

In the year 400, fourth month of summer, fourth day of the King of Upper and Lower Egypt: Seti is all powerful, son of the sun, his beloved. Nubti whom Harakhte desires to be forever and ever; came the hereditary prince, governor of the city, vizier, fan-bearer on the right of the king, chief of bowmen, governor of foreign countries, commandant of the fortress of Tharu, chief of the Medjay, king's scribe, master of horse, chief priest of the Ram-god, lord of Mendes, High Priest of Seth, chief prophet of all the gods, Seti, triumphant, son of the hereditary prince, governor of the city, vizier, chief of bowmen, governor of foreign countries, commandant of the fortress of Tharu, king's scribe, master of horse, Pramesse, triumphant; born of the lady, singer of Re, Tuya, triumphant. He said: 'Hail to thee, O Seth, son of Nut, great in strength in the barque of millions of years, overthrowing enemies in front of the barque of Re, great in terror, grant me a happy life following thy ka, because I am established in ...'

Seth also features on many of the obelisk fragments found at Tanis, described by Leclant and Yoyotte (1957: 43-80): on side 3 of Obelisk XX, the kneeling king is depicted offering two flasks of wine to *'Seth, great god, lord of heaven'* (Leclant and Yoyotte 1957: 45-46). Whereas the god is usually depicted with the 𓁣 hieroglyph, here it is drawn with the Sethian animal lying down 𓃩 as it is on the 'Stela of the Year 400'. Above the god's ears is the formula *'May he grant great life and strength.'*

Obelisk XVIII on side 3 of the pyramidion again depicts the king, this time standing, offering two flasks of wine to Seth who is again described as *'Seth, great god, lord of heaven'*, this time with the more typical hieroglyph 𓁣 (Leclant and Yoyotte 1957: 60-61). Upon Obelisk XIX, one finds a secondary name *'beloved of Seth'* on the lower part of side 2 (Leclant and Yoyotte 1957: 63).

These examples all occur in the vicinity of Tanis where Ramesses II established his capital: *Pi-Ramesse A-nakhtu 'Domain of Ramesses-Great-of-Victories'* near here, probably reflecting his Delta roots, thus honouring his family god, Seth, in this area.

He also honoured Seth in Nubia: a wall relief in the hall of the smaller temple at Abu Simbel depicts Ramesses II being blessed by Seth and Horus (Lepsius 1849: v, 173; Porter and Moss 1975: 113; Davies and Friedman 1998: 14,; James 2002: 227).

The god was well known to the Egyptian populace too: Papyrus Leiden 1, 360 preserves a letter written by the servant Mersuiotef to his mistress, the noble lady, Tel, in which he calls upon many gods, including Seth, to look favourably upon her (Wente 1990: 33). The complete text reads as follows:

'The servant Mersuiotef communicates to his mistress, the chantress of Isis, Tel; In life, prosperity and health (l.p.h) and in the favour of Amon-Re, King of the Gods! I am calling upon Pre-Harakhti, upon Amon of Ramesses-miamon, l.p.h; upon Ptah of Ramesses-miamon, l.p.h; upon Seth, great in virility, of Ramesses-miamon, l.p.h; and upon all the gods and goddesses of Pi-Ramessu-miamon, the great Ka of Pre-Harakhti, to keep you healthy, to keep you alive, to keep you prosperous, and to keep you in the favour of Isis, your mistress, and let me see you in health. And further:

The General is all right; his people are all right; and his children are all right. Do not worry about them. We are all right today, but I do not know our condition for the morrow. Farewell!'

During his long life Ramesses II fathered many sons and daughters, many of whom he outlived (Kitchen 1982: 102), so, as heir-apparent, Set-hir-khopshef *('Seth is with his strong arm')*, in Year 21 of his father's reign, shares in the official greetings being exchanged following the treaty with the Hittites. However, he too dies before his father in Year 53 of the reign (Kitchen 1982: 102) and the succession passes to Khaemwaset *('Appearing in Thebes')*, well known for his devotion to Ptah, for whom he was high priest at Memphis (Kitchen 1982: 103-109). He too dies in Year 55 of the reign and so the succession, changes for the fifth time, passing now to Prince Merneptah *('Beloved of Ptah')*. He eventually succeeded his father who died after a reign of 67 years in c. 1213 B.C.E.

Merneptah had a peaceful beginning to his reign, but in Year 5, the Libyans, in tandem with a loose confederation which the Egyptians referred to as 'the Sea Peoples', attempted an invasion of the Western Delta. A great battle ensued resulting in victory for Merneptah which he commemorated upon the walls of Karnak (Breasted 1906: Vol 3: 240-252; Manassa 2003); the part of the inscription recording the approach of the two armies is described:

'The infantry of his majesty went forth together with his chariotry, Amun-Re being with them, and the Ombite (i.e. Seth) giving to them the hand.' (Breasted 1906: Vol 3: 245).

So here Seth is equated with Amun-Re as one of the state-gods of Egypt, this is continued later, where the triumph is being described, a further passage states:

'Victorious is Re, mighty against the Nine Bows (the traditional enemies of Egypt); Seth giveth victory and might to Horus.' (Breasted 1906: Vol 3: 251).

On the walls of his mortuary temple Merneptah also had carved a further account of this campaign (the 'Victory Stela') within which he describes how Seth has forsaken the Libyans:

'Seth turned his back against their chief, their settlements having been destroyed at his command.' (Manassa 2003: 39).

In all of these passages Merneptah is acknowledging the aggressive side of Seth which helps to defeat the Libyans and Sea Peoples.

Upon the death of Merneptah it appears that his successor, Seti II, was absent and a usurper, Amenmesses, took the throne and buried Merneptah; however, after 3 or 4 years, Seti II seized back the throne and declared a *damnation memoriae* against Amenmesses. His name was expunged from virtually every item and monument that had borne it (Baker 2008: 51). Seti II's declared successor was his son, Seti-Merneptah, indicating that Seth was still regarded fondly by the Dynasty, but unfortunately he died before his father, resulting in his younger brother, Siptah, inheriting the throne as a minor, with the result that his stepmother, Twosret, ruled in his name. Upon Siptah's death, in his regnal Year 6, Twosret declared herself queen, using full pharaonic titulary like Hatshepsut some 300 years earlier (Van Dijk 2000: 304). Twosret probably only reigned for about two years. A limestone stela, now in the Basel Museum, dating to the Nineteenth Dynasty and belonging to the treasurer Seti, depicts him worshipping Seth and Hathor (Gordan-Rastelli 2011: 37). This demonstrates that the worship of the god was not confined to royalty but the general populace also revered him. Te Velde (1967: 135-138) lists 53 different personal names in which Seth is mentioned ranging from ones where the child had been born on a festival day of the god e.g. 'Seth-is born', 'Seth-is-in-his-festival', 'Seth-has-appeared' and 'Seth-is-in-the-ship' to ones which illustrate great devotion to the god e.g. 'servant of Seth', 'worshipper of Seth', 'chosen of Seth', 'son (or daughter) of Seth' and 'I belong to Seth'. At a time when the royal family had Seth as their personal god it is probably not surprising that he was being worshipped by sections of the general population who were naming their offspring after him.

Upon the death of Twosret there appears to have been a short period of anarchy before the accession of her successor, Setnakhte *('Victorious is Seth')*. This man's identity and his eligibility to become pharaoh is the subject of debate. It has been suggested that he was either a son or grandson of Ramesses II and his name may indicate a familial relationship with Seti I or an origin in the east Delta (Baker 2008: 407). Very few attestations of Setnakhte are known and he appears to have died after a rule of just over two years, to be succeeded by his son, Ramesses III.

Ramesses III was arguably the last great pharaoh of Egypt (Van Dijk 2000: 305). During the first years of his reign, he consolidated the throne and stabilised the country from the unrest left at the end of the Nineteenth Dynasty and beginning of the Twentieth Dynasty. Then, in his Year five, the Libyans once again attempted to invade the Delta, but they were routed by Ramesses III, a fact commemorated upon the walls of his mortuary temple at Medinet Habu, together with his other victories against the Sea Peoples in Year eight and the Libyans again in Year eleven. Whilst these victories are dedicated to Amun, these inscriptions also include references to Seth:

'They come bowing down in fear of him, the blooming youth, valiant like Baal (with a Seth figure as determinative)*'* and *'Lo, this Good God, the august, divine youth, who came forth from Re, beautiful as a child, like the son if Isis, Seth, valiant, strong-armed, like his father Montu'* (Breasted 1906: Vol 4: 25 and 61).

Seth is also depicted at Medinet Habu in the central passage of the great temple with Ramesses III censing and libating to him (Lepsius 1849: 208; Porter and Moss 1972: 484). The same scene, with the figure of the king replaced by the deceased, is seen upon a stela of Pa-ahaty, described as *"the follower of Seth,"* discovered within the Sakkara region and dated from this time.This stela is now in the Cairo Museum (inventory number S.1761). Seth is described upon the relief as *"Lord of the southern land."* (Bakry 1962: 7-8). An interesting epitaph as one would expect *"Lord of the northern land,"* to be the title seen if Seth was mainly prominent in the Delta region and this possibly indicates that his worship was uniform throughout Egypt at this time, a situation possibly confirmed by the fact that Ramesses III also had new lintels added to doorways in the temple of Seth at Naqada; one shows Seth and Amun seated back to back over intertwined Nile plants (Petrie and Quibell 1896: Plate LXXIX). On the left side, the priest Userhat is shown worshipping the two gods, accompanied by this inscription:

'Beloved of Amun lord of the thrones of the two lands who is in Karnak. Giving praise to thy ka*, O Lord of the gods, that he may grant long life and a good old age...in Karnak to the* ka *of the prophet of Seth, Userhat, justified'*

On the right side, Userhat is again shown worshipping the two gods, accompanied by the inscription:

'Seth Nubti, lord of the South land, great god, lord of heaven, fair child of Re. Giving praise to thy ka*, Seth, the very valorous that he may give...in Thebes to the* ka *of the prophet of Seth, Userhat'*

Behind the figure of Userhat on the right is the inscription:

'made by his son, who makes his name to live, for the ka *of the prophet of Seth, Userhat'* (Petrie and Quibell 1896: 70).

Interestingly The Yale Egyptological Institute in Egypt has just published upon their website (www.yale.edu/egyptology/qamula_al-barqa.html) details of a rock inscription at Matna el-Barqa, west of Naqada, showing a figure of Seth seated upon a large gold sign on the left and three columns of hieroglyphic text on the right which translate as follows:

'Made by the w'b priest Usherhat for his lord, Seth the Ombite.'

This Userhat, the survey team speculated, is probably the same person represented upon the lintel described above.

Ramesses III also notes his restorations to this Seth temple at Ombos in the Papyrus Harris where he states:

'I restored the house of Seth, lord of Ombos; I built its walls which were in ruin, I equipped the house in its midst in his divine name, built with excellent work, forever. "House-of-Ramesses-Ruler-of-Heliopolis, life-prosperity-health, in-the-House-of-Seth-of-Ombos," was its great name. I equipped it with slaves, the captives and people, whom I created. I made for him herds in the North, in order to present them to his ka as a daily offering. I made for him divine offerings anew, being an increase of the daily offerings which were before him. I gave to him lands, high and low, and islands, in the South and the North, bearing barley and spelt. His treasury was supplied with the things which my hands brought, in order to double the feasts before him every day.' (Breasted 1906: Vol 4: 180-181).

He also made a temple to Seth in what he describes as the 'Residence City' – presumably the capital in the Delta near Tanis; we do not know whether he built a new temple or renovated the existing one that Ramesses II had created. Again, he states:

'I made a great temple, enlarged with labour, in the house of "Seth-of-Ramesses-Meriamon, life-prosperity-health;" built, laid, smoothed, and inscribed with designs; having doorposts of stone, and doors of cedar. "House-of-Ramesses-Ruler-of-Heliopolis, life-prosperity-health, in-the-House-of-Seth," its name was called forever. I assigned to it serf-labourers of the people whom I created, male and female slaves whom I carried off as captives of my sword. I made for him divine offerings, full and pure, in order to offer them to his ka every day. I filled his treasury with possessions without number, with granaries of grain by the ten-thousand, herds of cattle like the sand, in order to offer them to thy ka, O thou great in might.' (Breasted 1906: Vol 4: 182).

These two statements give some idea of the respect that Ramesses III had for Seth and the amount of slaves, cattle and lands that a temple could call upon to raise its income and provide the temple with the necessary items for the daily offerings.

In his temple at Karnak Ramesses III is depicted upon a relief in the Hypostyle Hall offering a *nemset*-vase to Seth and Nephthys (Chicago Reliefs 1936: Plate 42). Although the temple is dedicated to Amun, this once again illustrates that Seth at this time was not viewed in a negative fashion. Continuing this theme, Cairo Museum has a triad, found in the king's Temple at Medinet Habu, showing Ramesses III being crowned by Horus and Seth (Porter and Moss 1972: 526), probably representing Upper and Lower Egypt respectively.

Ramesses III died in 1153 B.C.E. after a reign of 32 years. He appears to have been the victim of a conspiracy; certainly the Harem Conspiracy Papyrus describes this scenario, and although surviving the initial attack, he died three weeks later (Baker 2008: 315). He was succeeded by his son, Ramesses IV.

The later part of the Twentieth Dynasty covers a period of 81 years and sees eight pharaohs (Ramesses IV to XI) reign. The exact relationship of these to one another is complicated (Van Dijk 2000: 308), and due to some of the pharaohs dying with no heirs, four of Ramesses III's sons ascend to the throne at various times (Ramesses IV, V, VI and VIII). Seth appeared to still have an important role among the state gods at this time, e.g. in the inner part of the hypostyle of the Temple of Khons at Karnak, Ramesses IV is depicted kneeling upon a *sma*-symbol being bound by Seth and Horus (Porter and Moss 1972: 235). He was also worshipped by the general populace as can be seen by the incorporation of his name into those of the general public at this time. Thus cartouches of Ramesses IV are shown upon a stela being adored by a royal butler named Ramesses-set-hirwenemef:

(Porter and Moss 1964: 776).

Ramesses VIII succeeded to the throne because his predecessor's chosen successor, his only child, Ramesses, had died before his father (Baker 2008: 329). He was originally named Sethirkopshef, (*'Seth is with his strong arm'*) but followed the now seemingly ingrained principle of taking the nomen Ramesses. He reigned for only about one year before being succeeded by Ramesses IX, who may have been a grandson of Ramesses III. He was faced with yet more unrest throughout the kingdom: Libyan raiders in the Western Desert, tomb robberies, labour strikes and the increasing power of the priesthood of Amun. This latter problem came to a head when the high priest of Amun, Amunhotep, had himself depicted on two reliefs at Karnak on the same scale as the pharaoh (Baker 2008: 331).

Dating to the reign of Ramesses IX is Papyrus Valencay No 2 which consists of a letter from the stable master Pahen and the chief of police Sahnufe to a person whose name and titles are unfortunately lost. The letter is concerned with the finding of a fugitive. In the course of the letter the two writers refer to the fact that they visited one Setsankh, the prophet of Seth in the town of Sheneset to consult with the god Seth as to the whereabouts of the fugitive. They report that Seth indicated that the fugitive was to the south of them and would be found (Wente 1990: 130). This passage is significant not only because the prophet included Seth in his name but also because the god is used as an oracle. The use of gods as oracles is well attested in the New Kingdom and is discussed by Luiselli (2010: 70).

Ramesses X succeeded Ramesses IX but his relationship to his predecessor is not known; although he reigned for ten years, virtually nothing is known about him and his tomb in the Valley of the Kings has never been properly explored (Van Dijk 2000: 308).

The Dynasty was brought to a close with the twenty-eight year long reign of Ramesses XI, who may have been a son of either Ramesses IX or X. Whilst he ruled from his capital Pi-ramesse in the north, the south of the country was effectively controlled by the High Priests of Amun, culminating in Herihor, who also adds the titles 'Viceroy of Kush' and 'Vizier' to that of 'High Priest of Amun'. This gave him a position of such unassailable power in the south that he put his name in cartouches within the Karnak Temple complex. This suggests that there was a tacit understanding between Ramesses and Herihor that one ruled in the north and one in the south of the country (Van Dijk 2000: 309). Following the death of Ramesses XI in 1069 B. C. E., the Third Intermediate Period began.

The last ruler of Egypt to be buried in a pyramid-topped tomb was Ahmose I; his son and successor, Amenophis I, separated his mortuary temple and tomb and may well be the pharaoh who set up the royal tomb workers' village at Deir-el-Medina (Bierbrier 1982: 14). Certainly Amenophis I and his mother, Ahmes-Nefertari, were worshipped as patrons by the royal workmen in later times (Friedman 1994: 111). The community was certainly in existence under his successor, Thutmosis I, who was the first pharaoh who chose to be buried in the hidden valley now known as the Valley of the Kings (Bierbrier 1982: 15-16). Little is known of how the workmen were organised at this period, and the village fell into disuse when Akhenaten transferred the capital to Amarna, but it was re-established by Horemheb, and from the time of the reign of Seti I we have a great deal of information concerning the village and its inhabitants (Bierbrier 1982: 6).

In theory, all the artisans of the tomb, and definitely their foremen and scribes, were appointed by the vizier. The two foremen, one for each of the 'crews', called the Right and the Left (presumably from the side of the tomb they worked upon) had direct control of the daily working and, together with at least one scribe, they were regarded as the administrators of the tomb workers (Lesko 1994: 18). From early times religion appears to have played an important part in the life of the villagers; this may reflect their jobs i.e. building the pharaoh's tomb or perhaps that this is the best preserved village that we have to study and that all Egyptians were just as pious. Several large temples stood to the north and north-east of the village and the cliff face near the village was dotted with chapels to various gods (Bierbrier 1982: 85). In these chapels and the houses of the village have been discovered many stelae amongst which is that of Aapehty, now in the British Museum (acquisition no: 35630), see Figure 15.

Aapehty translates as 'great of strength' and is one of the epithets of Seth, which is probably why Aapehty is shown on the stele in the act of adoration in front of a standing figure of Seth. Aapehty was the deputy of the right hand gang and the son of its foreman, Paneb. Whilst there were many foreign workers present in Deir-el-Medina, presumably brought in for their particular expertise, (Ward 1994: 61-85) it is unlikely that the foreman was one of these, so here we have a stele, dedicated to Seth, in one of the holiest places that existed in Egypt at that time, in the sense that the workers were involved in the construction and decoration of the king's tombs, this surely indicated that the god was an accepted part of the pantheon.

Figure 15: Limestone stela of Aapehty (British Museum 35630). Copyright: British Museum.

An ostracon, also from Deir el-Medina, and now in the Cairo Museum, depicts Seth as a human figure with the Seth animal head seated upon a throne. In one hand he holds an ankh and the other probably had a was-sceptre (Cruz-Uribe 2009: 213).

In 1928 a assemblage of religious, magical, documentary and literary papyri was discovered at Deir el-Medina (Szpakowska 2003: 67). The assemblage belonged to a scribe named Qehherkhopshef and included a 'Dream Book', this explicitly described the dreams of at least two categories of individuals, the final section beginning with the heading: 'Beginning of the Dreams of the followers of Seth (Szpakowska 2003: 73). This is preceded by a description of the personality and physical characteristics of this type of man. Whilst parts of the papyrus are missing it has been possible to construct the following description:

A man with curly hair, possibly naturally red in colour who is potentially violent, decadent and debauched and is a womaniser. He often drinks to excess and when he does, his Sethian character takes control. Whilst he may be a member of the royal classes, his tastes and manners are unrefined, unrestrained and earthy, like those of a commoner. One can recognise here many of the characteristics that we have seen attributed to the god Seth in the Pyramid, Coffin and Book of the Dead texts but the Dream Book although placing the man of Seth outside the norms of Egyptian society does not suggest that this is necessarily a bad thing. It is regrettable that the first portion of the papyrus which is missing possibly contained a description of the opposite individual to the 'follower of Seth' that of a 'follower of Horus', presumably an individual who would have been described in a more amiable manner.

The Chester Beatty papyrus dates from the reign of Ramesses V and comes from Thebes. It was first published by Gardiner in 1931. Good translations can be found in Simpson (1973), Lichtheim (1976), and Morgan (2005).

When Horus came to manhood, he presented himself before the Company of the Gods and requested his birthright, i.e. the throne of Osiris (Simpson 1973: 109; Lichtheim 1976: 214; Morgan 2005: 304). Then Shu, the son of Re spoke and said, *"Give the kingly office to Horus."* On hearing this, Isis gave a great cry of joy and requested that Osiris may hear the news but Re-Harakhti said that the decision should not have been made without him and withdrew in a fit of pique, as he would rather like to have given the throne to Seth. So Seth said *"Let Horus be cast forth with me so that I may defeat him before the Company of Heaven, this is the only way to sort it."* At this Thoth said, *"How will that help us to discern the guilty one, shall we give the throne to Seth whilst his son* (i.e Osiris's son) *Horus is still alive?"*

Re-Harakhti was very annoyed at this and the Company of Heaven appeared to be at an impasse, so Atum suggested that they refer the matter to the great ancient god Banebdjedet, in order that he may pronounce judgement on the two contenders (Simpson 1973: 110; Lichtheim 1976: 215; Morgan 2005: 304). Banebdjedet rather than making a decision, suggested that they should write a letter to Neith and whatever she decided they should do. So the Company requested that Thoth write to Neith stating that for the past eighty years the two men had been before the tribunal but none of the gods knew how to pronounce judgement upon them, so would she write and tell them what to do?

Neith replied (Simpson 1973: 111; Lichtheim 1976: 215; Morgan 2005: 305) saying, *"Give the office of Osiris to his son Horus or else I shall be angry and the heavens will crash to the ground."* She also requested that Re-Harakhti doubled Seth's possessions and that he gave him his two daughters, Anat and Astarte, as an inducement to abide by the decision. When this letter reached the Company of Heaven, Thoth read it out and everyone agreed that the goddess was correct in what she had written. Re-Harakhti again appeared to take this badly and said to Horus *"Thou art feeble in thy limbs, and this kingly office is too great for you, child, the taste of whose mouth is bad",* (Simpson 1973: 112; Lichtheim 1976: 216; Morgan 2005: 306). This last comment perhaps suggested that Horus still had the bad breath of an infant and, therefore, was much too young to take on the throne. Re-Harakhti then went off in a sulk which was only lifted when his daughter, Hathor, exposed herself to him, a strange thing for a daughter to do before her father, but it obviously worked as he once again sat down with the Company of Heaven and addressed Seth and Horus saying, *"Speak concerning yourselves"* (Simpson 1973: 112; Lichtheim 1976: 216; Morgan 2005: 306). Seth then stated that his strength was great and that he daily killed Apophis, the enemy of Re, with his harpoon whilst standing in the front of Re's barque as it journeyed through the underworld and that no other god could do this and therefore he was entitled to the office of Osiris. This swayed many of the gods to support Seth, but once again Thoth cried aloud *"Shall the office be given to a brother on the side of the mother, while a son of the body is yet alive?"* An opposite view to this was given by the god, Banebdjedet, who stated, *"Shall the office be given to this child, while Seth, his elder brother is yet alive?"* (Simpson 1973: 113; Lichtheim 1976: 216; Morgan 2005: 306). Isis was very annoyed at this and threatened to recount their words to Atum and to Khepra, at which the Company of Heaven, in yet another about face, said to her: *"Be not vexed, Horus will get what is rightly his."*

At this it was now Seth's turn to be annoyed and he threatened each day to kill one of the gods in the Company of Heaven with his sceptre weighing 4,500 pounds and he also stated that he would take no further part in the tribunal whilst Isis was present.

Re then told the Company to cross over to an island where they could debate the issue in peace and ordered the ferryman not to let Isis cross. The Company did this and sat down to eat, but Isis disguised herself as an aged woman and approached the ferryman, Nemty, bent over as though with arthritis and wearing a ring of gold upon her finger. She requested that Nemty ferry her over to the island using the ploy that she had some food for a child who had been looking after the cattle there who was hungry. Nemty said he had been told not to ferry any woman across but also asked what she would give him if he broke his word. At this Isis said she would give him a loaf of bread. Nemty was unimpressed with this so Isis promised him the gold ring which he took and subsequently ferried her across to the island (Simpson 1973: 114-5; Lichtheim 1976: 217; Morgan 2005: 307).

Isis then changed her appearance once again to that of a beautiful young woman and walked near where the gods were eating lunch and Seth noticed her and was immediately attracted to her. So he left the picnic and approached Isis. Isis then spun him a story that she was the widow of a herdsman who had only one son and that when her husband died and the son came to tend the cattle a stranger told him to go away because he was going to take the cattle of the son's father and Isis requested that Seth become her son's protector. Seth, falling into the trap, then said, *"Shall the cattle be given to the foreigner, while the son of the good man is alive."* (Simpson 1973: 115; Lichtheim 1976: 217; Morgan 2005: 308).

This, of course, was just what Isis wanted to hear and Seth had to admit to Re what he had said, to which Re said, *"You have been judged by yourself and the White Crown shall be placed upon the head of Horus and he shall be promoted to the place of his father Osiris."*

Although Seth was annoyed, the Company of Heaven asked him why this was, as all they were doing was complying with the wishes of Atum and Re-Harakhti. So they gave the White Crown to Horus, and Seth then demanded that it be removed and that Horus should be cast into the water, where he and Seth could fight over the office of ruler. Re-Harakhti agreed to this.

Seth then said to Horus, *"Let us change into hippopotamuses and let us plunge into the waters and whoever emerges within three months then shall this office not be given."* Presumably this was meant to imply that the loser would be the one who could not hold his breath longest and had to emerge from the waters first. They both plunged into the water leaving Isis weeping certain that Seth would kill Horus (Simpson 1973: 117-8; Lichtheim 1976: 218; Morgan 2005: 309).

So Isis took a quantity of twine and made a rope which she attached to a harpoon and threw it into the water. Her aim was obviously not good as she succeeded in hitting Horus, who cried out in pain and asked his mother to recall the harpoon which she did. She tried a second time and this time hit Seth, who in his pain cried out saying, *"What have I done against thee, my sister Isis? Recall this harpoon for I am your brother on the side of your mother."* At this, Isis took pity on Seth and recalled the harpoon, whereupon Horus in turn was annoyed with his mother and taking a swing at her with a chopper in his hand struck off her head (Simpson 1973: 118; Lichtheim 1976: 219; Morgan 2005: 310). In the course of this battle Horus also lost an eye and Seth his testicles. Isis meanwhile had changed herself into a flint statue with no head and Re-Harakhti asked Thoth who this headless female that had appeared was, and when Thoth told him that it was Isis and that it was Horus who had decapitated her, Re-Harakhti told the Company of Heaven that they must inflict a great punishment upon Horus for this act. Thus, the gods searched for Horus who had taken refuge in the Oasis country. He was found there by Hathor, who bathed his injured eye with milk from a gazelle and then sought out Re-Harakhti and told him that she had found Horus who had been injured, that she had restored him and here he was (Simpson 1973: 119; Lichtheim 1976: 219; Morgan 2005: 310).

At this the Company of Heaven requested that both Horus and Seth be summoned in order that a judgement may be made between them (yet again). So, once they had been summoned Re-Harakhti told them to eat and drink together and to be at peace with one another and cease wrangling every day. At this Seth said to Horus, *"Let us pass a happy day together in my house,"* and Horus agreed to this (Simpson 1973: 119-20; Lichtheim 1976: 219; Morgan 2005: 310).

There then comes an unusual passage where Seth attempted to bugger Horus but the latter managed to catch Seth's semen in his hands and he takes it to Isis to show her what Seth has attempted. Isis is so shocked that she cuts off Horus's hands and casts them into the water and fashions new ones for him. She then got Horus to ejaculate into a pot and taking the resultant semen she asked a gardener what herb it was that Seth eats, to which he replied he eats lettuces, so Isis smeared Horus's semen over the lettuces and Seth unknowingly ate it (Simpson 1973: 120; Lichtheim 1976: 220; Morgan 2005: 310-311). The lettuce is associated with the ithyphallic god, Min, and as such may be regarded as an aphrodisiac (Simpson 1973: 120).

Seth and Horus then came before the tribunal once again, and Seth told them that he had buggered Horus as one does to a defeated foe. This caused much merriment amongst the Company of Heaven and they began to tease Horus, but he told them that Seth was lying and they would see for themselves if they requested that the semen of Seth be summoned and that they also summoned his own (Simpson 1973: 121; Lichtheim 1976: 220; Morgan 2005: 311).

Thoth placed his hand upon Horus's arm and called for Seth's semen to come forward whereupon it answered him from the water. He then placed his hand on the arm of Seth and requested that Horus's semen comes forward. It answered by saying, *"where would you like me to come forward from?"* and Thoth initially requested from Seth's ear but the semen declined to do this so Thoth requested that it emerged from Seth's forehead which it did as a disk of gold, which Thoth placed upon his own head as an ornament (Simpson 1973: 121; Lichtheim 1976: 220; Morgan 2005: 311-312). This became the disk of the moon seen on Thoth's head and, according to Te Velde (1967: 44), may be equated to the eye of Horus.

Then the Company of Heaven were persuaded that Seth had been lying and he, once again in anger, stated that Horus should not receive the office and that the two of them should fashion two ships of stone and that they should sail them and that whoever wins should be given the throne. Horus went away and built a ship from cedar wood that he disguised to appear as stone whilst Seth went to a mountain top and fashioned a ship of stone which, of course, sank whilst that of Horus floated. Seth then changed himself into a hippopotamus and sank Horus's ship and they began to fight once again but this time the Company of Heaven told them to stop (Simpson 1973: 121; Lichtheim 1976: 221; Morgan 2005: 312).

So Horus went to see Neith and asked for judgement to be given, stating that they had been in contention for eighty years and that Seth kept ignoring what the Company of Heaven said and that he, Horus, had on a number of occasions been declared the rightful heir to his father. So Thoth said to Re-Harakhti, *"Send a letter to Osiris that he may pronounce judgement."* This they agreed to do and Thoth penned the letter requesting that Osiris write to them saying what they should do to Horus and Seth (Simpson 1973: 123; Lichtheim 1976: 221; Morgan 2005: 313).

Osiris, as one would imagine, replied quickly, supporting Horus and stating that it was he himself who made the gods strong and supplied them with their barley and spelt which nourished them. So the Company of Heaven went to the 'Island-in-the-Midst' and Horus was declared in the right over Seth and Atum requested that Seth be brought before them as a prisoner which Isis did. Atum asked Seth why he had not allowed judgement to be made against him and why he had taken for himself the office of Horus? Seth, in an amazing about face, replied to this saying that it was not true, and that Horus should be summoned so that he could be given the office of his father Osiris. This was done and the White Crown was set upon the head of Horus and he was told that he was the king of Egypt and the good lord of every land for infinity. Ptah then asked what they should do with Seth and Re-Harakhti said that Seth should be given to him so that he could live with him as his son and he would be the thunder in the sky and that men would fear him (Simpson 1973: 123-5; Lichtheim 1976: 222; Morgan 2005: 313-314).

What was the significance of this myth? Gardiner thought the myth's function was primarily to lift and divert the spirits of its first audiences through humour (Oden 1979: 359). Griffiths also takes this view, stating that "its aim is merely to divert" (Griffiths 1970: 199), certainly the gods are not portrayed in any great light being inclined to petty squabbles and bandying insults around like children in the playground, but perhaps this made the myth and its characters more understandable to a general audience in a similar way to the Medieval Passion Plays. Frankfort (1948: 22) describes Seth and Horus as the antagonists per se – the mythological symbols for all conflict. Strife is an element in the universe that cannot be ignored and the Ancient Egyptians had a tendency to understand the world in dualistic terms as a series of pairs of contrasts (Te Velde 1967: 75). In the myth Seth is subdued by Horus but never destroyed, both are wounded in the struggle, Horus in his eye and Seth in his testicles, but in the end there is reconciliation and the harmony of the universe is established. Whether to the Egyptians of the Ramesside age this myth was regarded as having an historical basis relating to the predynastic conflicts or was just regarded as an enjoyable bawdy tale where the gods could be perceived as having some of man's foibles we unfortunately will never know.

The collection of spells that became the Book of the Dead began to take shape not long before the beginning of the New Kingdom (Kemp 2007: 5). Many of the spells were based on earlier versions the occurred in both the Coffin Texts and the Pyramid Texts and the whole of the Book of the Dead was designed to prepare for life after death and to help the spiritual parts of the body on their journey to the underworld, where they would hope to reside in the Egyptian version of Paradise. They would be written on a roll of papyrus and placed within the coffin, hence the modern name of Book of the Dead (Figure 19). The Egyptian name was 'Going Forth by Day' and reflected their desire to return from wherever the hereafter was located, to visit familiar places that they had known whilst alive.

For the spells to work effectively special conditions had to be observed. As a consequence often the spells were accompanied by instructions specifying such things as the time and place where the spell should be recited, whether certain objects needed to be present, and the material that these needed to be made of (Taylor 2010a: 31-32).

There are approximately 192 numbered spells and Allen (1974: 2) has estimated that all but 79 (i.e. just under sixty percent) of them can be traced back to the Coffin Texts. Not all spells are found in all versions of the Book of the Dead and the examples quoted come from translations by Faulkner (1972) and Allen (1974). Seth is mentioned in 51 of the spells (26.6% of total); once again he is depicted in negative (26), positive (13) and neutral (12) roles. Full translations of these spells mentioning Seth are given in Appendix 3.

Within the negative texts many are concerned with the harm that Seth did to Osiris and Horus's subsequent revenge, including reference to the damage done to Seth's testicles and Horus's eye (spells 9, 19, 20, 23, 28, 65, 78, 80, 83, 86, 90, 99, 112, 134, 137a, 137b, and 173). Spell 112 is of interest as it is identical to Coffin Text 157 where Re likens the damage done to Horus's eye to a black pig. Spell 60 refers to the battle between Horus and Seth: 'this day when the Two Lands raged.'

Spell 175 refers to the fear that Seth (his soul in the spell) causes even when he is in the solar barque and has the deceased asking Atum whether Seth's soul has been sent to the west, to which Atum replies that he has put Seth's soul under guard so that Osiris should not fear.

Spells 20 and 189 refer to the confederacy of Seth and its subsequent defeat.

We have seen in the above section that fear of Seth's power and might led to him being portrayed in a negative manner, these same qualities could also be applied to identifying him in a positive manner. Thus, spells 32, 39, 50, 54, 62, 108 and 111 are all concerned with the power of Seth used to benefit the deceased. Spells 39, 108 and 111 are to do with Seth defeating Apophis and other snakes that threaten the sacred barque of Re during its journey through the hours of darkness (see figure 16).

Spell 140 has Seth with other gods and goddesses rejoicing in the defeat of Apophis. Spell 8 has Seth among the gods in Heliopolis and spell 38A associates Seth with Horus and refers to them as 'the Two Lords'. Spell 153A is similar to Coffin text 769 and is concerned with ascending a ladder to heaven with both Horus and Seth assisting in this process.

Figure 16: Stela of Taqayna from 19th Dynasty showing Seth spearing Apophis. Copyright: Rijksmuseum van Oudheden, Inventory No AP60.

The neutral spells are ones in which Seth is referred to in an oblique manner, e.g. the deceased's back is identified with Seth (spell 42), the messenger of the earth-god (presumably Osiris) is said to be with Seth (spell 94). The deceased rejects faeces and urine (i.e. he does not wish to be turned upside down and made to eat these abominable things) in the same way that Seth rejects them (spell 178). Two further spells (182 and 183) refer to the fact that the rival gods (i.e. Horus and Seth) have been pacified and now fraternise with each other.

In spite of the scarcity of evidence during some other periods it is fair to state that this particular period probably shows Seth at his most popular. As the Ramesside pharaohs originated from the Delta, they worshipped Seth as their family god, and because of this they were prepared to honour him not only in this region but throughout Egypt. They admired his strength and wished to be likened to him when they were called upon to lead their armies against foreign invaders, although conversely at the same time they could recognise Seth as being the god within the Egyptian pantheon that represented these foreigners! This apparent conflict in Seth's position can also be recognised in the fact that, whilst the Chester Beatty papyrus which describes the conflict between Horus and Seth dates to this period, and whilst Seth is frequently described in a negative sense within the Book of the Dead spells, he could also be described within these same spells as a positive force e.g. when he is defending Re's solar barque against the snake Apophis. This more positive side to the god's character was also reflected in his name being incorporated not only with those of the pharaohs but also with those of the general populace, indicating that not only was he a state-god but that people also worshipped him as a local or personal god.

8. THE THIRD INTERMEDIATE PERIOD 1069-656 B.C.E.

As mentioned at the end of the previous chapter, the steadily increasing power of the priesthood of Amun at Thebes had culminated with Herihor ruling alongside Ramesses XI for some six years. Following both his death and that of Ramesses, a continued state of co-rulership appears to have existed, with the High Priests ruling the southern part of the country from Thebes and Dynasty 21, based at Tanis, ruling the northern part. Outside influences became more evident resulting in both Libyan (22nd/23rd) and Nubian (25th) ruling Dynasties and eventually conquest by the Assyrians, who established vassal kings. Seth during this period has few mentions but those on the Dakhleh stelae establish that his worship was important at this oasis, and the inscription on the Shabaka Stone gives another take on the dispute between Horus and Seth.

Herihor was succeeded by his son-in-law, Piankh, for a short time, subsequently to this, Pinedjem, Piankh's son, became High Priest. Unlike his predecessors, he did not give himself regnal years but used those of Smendes I who was ruling in the Delta (Clayton 1994: 176). Pinedjem appears to have exerted control over an area extending from Aswan in the south to el-Hiba, just south of the Faiyum. He cemented relationships with the rulers in Tanis by marriage, taking for his wife one Henuttawy, a daughter of Ramesses XI, by whom he had several sons and daughters. One son became Psusennes I, the third king in the 21st Dynasty at Tanis, whilst two other sons, Masaherta and Menkheperre, became his next two successors as High Priests at Thebes (Clayton 1994: 177). These in turn were succeeded by Smendes II, the son of Menkheperre and Pinedjem II, another son of Menkheperre, this time by his wife, Isiemkheb, the sister of Psusennes I.

Following the death of Ramesses XI, Smendes proclaimed himself king. His origins are obscure but he appears to have cemented his claim to the throne by marrying one of the daughters of Ramesses XI, named Tentamun (Dodson and Hilton 2004: 194). Smendes moved the capital from Pi-Ramesse to Tanis and the links between Thebes and Tanis were further strengthened by the building of a temple at Tanis dedicated to the Theban trio of Amun, Mut and Khonsu (Taylor 2000: 333). Within the precincts of this temple were found the burial chambers of the 21st Dynasty kings (Hawass and Janot 2008: 80) including the tombs of Psusennes I, his wife, Mutnodjmet and his son and successor, Amenemope.

Following the death of Amenemope there appears to have been a ruler named Aakheperre Setepenre, usually referred to as Osorkon the Elder, who reigned for approximately 6 years. He, in turn, was succeeded by Siamun, who reigned for almost 20 years. He built extensively at Tanis, where he enlarged the temple of Amun (Taylor 2000: 333). The dynasty ended with the reign of Psusennes II, about which little is known. His successor, Sheshonq I, legitimised his claim by marrying Maatkare, Psusennes' daughter and was the founder of the 22nd Dynasty.

The priests and priestesses of Amun were buried, like the pharaohs, on the West Bank at Thebes. In 1891 Grebaut and Daressy (Daressy 1900: 141-148; Porter and Moss 1964: 635) discovered a cache of coffins belonging to these burials at Deir-el-Bahri. Amongst these coffins was one attributed to Hori:

who was described as being: "*A Prophet of Seth* Sepermery." At first sight it appears surprising that this man's coffin should be included with those of the priests and priestesses of Amun, but it could well indicate that during this period Seth was certainly not held in contempt. Certainly, a priesthood dedicated to Seth was active at the Dakhleh Oasis at this time and continued in existence until the 2nd century C. E. (Kaper 1962: 63). A statue dedicated by the High Priest of Seth, Penbast, was found in the temple of Deir el-Haggar during restoration work between 1992 and 1995 (Kaper 1997: 231-241). It has been dated to the Third Intermediate Period.

The 22nd Dynasty is usually referred to as the Libyan or Bubastite Dynasty. Manetho lists the kings as all being from Bubastis in the eastern Delta (Manetho 2004: 159). Sheshonq I was initially the commander-in-chief of the army and had the title: '*Great Chief of the* Meshwesh'. The *Meshwesh* were a police force originally recruited from amongst the Libyan tribes (Taylor 2000: 334). Sheshonq was able to bring the divided factions at Thebes and Tanis once more into a united Egypt. He did this by appointing his sons to certain key positions, for example one son, Iuput, was both 'Governor of Upper Egypt' and 'High Priest of Amun' and also the chief of the armies (Dodson & Hilton 2004: 219); another, Djedptahaufankh, was 'Third Prophet of Amun', and a third, Nimlot, acted as the military commander at Herakleopolis (Dodson & Hilton 2004: 221). From the point of view of Seth's role at this time his reign is important as the Dakhleh Stela may be dated to it. This stela is one of two found at Dakhleh and presented to the Ashmolean Museum, Oxford by Sir Henry Lyons (Breasted 1906 (4): 359-361; Gardiner 1933: 19; Kaper 2001: 71; Whitehouse 2002: 2-3). The stela records the official visit of a group sent by Sheshonq to Dakhleh Oasis to *'restore order and central government control of the oasis after a period of war and turmoil'* (Teeter & Johnson 2009: 88). The group of officials surveyed all of the water sources in the oasis in order to determine which belonged to the pharaoh and which to individuals. They determined that one particular well that had belonged to a woman named Tayuhenut now belonged to her sole legitimate heir, Nysu-Bastet, who was the owner of the stela and also the priest of Seth at the oasis. Their decision was confirmed by an oracle from the god Seth, presumably by his cult statue moving in response to questions being put to it (Gardiner 1933: 28; Whitehouse 2002: 3). The fact that Seth was used as arbitrator in this case suggests that he was the prime god at Dakhleh, a fact that we will encounter later in Dynasty 25 (Janssen 1968: 166) and during Graeco-Roman times (Kaper 1962: 45).

Seth's name on this earlier stela is spelt out using the Seth-animal hieroglyph indicating that, certainly in the oases region, he was still the principal deity and he is referred to as 'the Lord of the Oasis' (Kaper 2001: 72)

Osorkon I succeeded his father, he replaced his brother as High Priest of Amun with one of his sons, Sheshonq II, whom he also named co-regent in 890 B.C.E. However, Sheshonq pre-deceased his father (Dodson & Hilton 2004: 210), who on his death was succeeded by a minor son, Takelot I. He, in turn, was succeeded by Osorkon II at much the same time as his cousin, Harsiese, succeeded his father, Sheshonq II, as High Priest of Amun. Problems began in year 4 of Osorkon's reign when Harsiese declared himself king in the south (Taylor 2000: 337). On the death of Harsiese, Osorkon appointed his son, Nimlot, as High Priest (Clayton 1994: 187). Osorkon was in turn succeeded by his son, Takelot II. When his half-brother Nimlot died, he ignored the claims of one Harsiese, a grandson of the original of the same name to be High Priest and instead installed his son Prince Osorkon. This led to a ten-year civil war between these factions (Assmann 1996: 313).

When Takelot II died he should have been succeeded by Prince Osorkon but instead his younger brother Shesonq III seized power. Whilst he reigned for 53 years (Taylor 2000: 345), he had to contend with splits between Tanis and Thebes, and also between the east and central Delta (Tanis and Leontopolis).

At Leontopolis one Pedibastet had himself declared as pharaoh and proclaimed a new dynasty- the 23rd. His successors ruled from here for a number of years concurrently with the latter kings of Dynasty 22 at Tanis. Towards the end of this time a third power, *'the Princedom of the West'*, based at Sais in the Delta came to prominence, so that by Year 36 of Shosenq V a man named Tefnakhte was the ruler here. He extended his influence as far south as Lisht in the Nile Valley, later being forced to retreat by the Kushite king, Piye. However, once Piye had returned south, Tefnakhte declared himself king and founded the 24th Dynasty (Taylor 2000: 338).

Piye was the founder of the 25th Dynasty. He originated in Napata, a state that had formed at the extreme southern tip of Kush in Nubia in the vicinity of the Fourth Cataract (Assmann 1996: 317). Whist Napata can trace its origins back to 850 B.C.E., it appeared that the fallout from the civil war mentioned above during the reign of Takelot II had caused many of the Theban priests of Amun to flee to Napata, where Amun was also the state god. As a consequence of this, Napata broke off relationships with the 22nd Dynasty and the subsequent generations of rulers in Napata saw themselves as the legitimate inheritors of the throne of Egypt (Assmann 1996: 320). This led Piye to have his sister adopted as heir to the ruling 'God's Wife of Amun', Shepenwepet, the daughter of Osorkon III. In about 727 B.C.E., Piye moved against the coalition of four Egyptian kings in Year 21 of his Nubian reign (Taylor 2000: 353). He was successful in this campaign but rather than punish the kings he made them vassal governors and returned to Napata (Dodson and Hilton 2004: 234). To his reign may be dated the Smaller Dakhleh Stela (Janssen 1968: 165-172). This stela was discovered, together with the larger one by Captain Lyons in Dakhleh Oasis and was also presented to the Ashmolean Museum, Oxford. The stela is dated to year 24 of Piye's reign, and tells that a certain official in the Oasis, called Harentbia, donated in a temple of Seth a daily offering of five loaves in memory of his father. The maintenance of this offering was entrusted to a priest, the son of Ankhor (Janssen 1968: 171). At the top of the stela is depicted, on the left, the figure of Seth as a falcon-headed god with a sun disc upon his head (see Plate XXV in Janssen 1968). In front of him is written:

'Utterance by Sutekh, great of strength, the son of Nut.'

Whereas the earlier Dakhleh stela had used the Seth-animal hieroglyph in the spelling of the god's name this later stela avoids its use (Kaper 2001: 74). The image of

Seth on this later stela shows the god with the head of a falcon and wearing the Double Crown, thus making him resemble Horus. This possibly is indicative of the changing attitude towards Seth at this time, wheras in the Nile valley all mention of Seth appears to have ceased here in the oases wher he was the principal god a more subtle change appears to have taken place (Kaper 2001: 74).

Following Piye's death, he was succeeded by his brother, Shabaka, who took up residence at Memphis and was obviously so taken with this city that he wished to return it to its former glories. This is shown by the text translated from the so-called Shabaka Stone.

This stone is a heavy black slab of Green Breccia from Wadi Hammamat. It was given to the British Museum by the second Earl Spencer in 1805. The provenance of the stone is unknown. Upon it are three horizontal rows of hieroglyphs and 61 columns. The inscription claims to be the rendering of an ancient papyrus text, of which Shabaka says:

'His Majesty had this book written anew in the house of his father Ptah. His Majesty had found it as a work of his ancestors, worm-eaten, and one did not know it from beginning to end. So His Majesty had it rewritten so that it is more beautiful than it was before'. (Assmann 1996: 345-346).

Whilst Shabaka alleged that he had copied an ancient work, modern Egyptologists believe that this is just propaganda to justify his accession to the throne (Sellers 1992: 85).

The subject of the text for the most part is Memphis, its mythic and political significance as the location where creation emerged from the primal waters, and as the seminal locus of pharaonic kingship (Assman 1996: 346). It begins by proclaiming Ptah-Tatenen, the primordial deity, self-created creator of the gods, and ruler over the unified kingdom as king of Lower and Upper Egypt. Of interest to us is that the text then refers to the legal dispute between Horus and Seth, and is written as if the gods were speaking to one another:

'*Geb says to Seth: "Go to the place in which you were born."*

Seth: "Upper Egypt."

Geb's words to Horus: "Go to the place in which your father was drowned."

Horus: "Lower Egypt."

Geb's words to Horus and Seth: "I have separated you."

Then it seemed wrong to Geb that the portion of Horus was like the portion of Seth. So Geb gave Horus his inheritance, for he is the son of his firstborn son (i.e. Osiris, Horus's father was the son of Geb).

Geb's words to the Ennead: "I have appointed Horus, the firstborn."

Geb's words to the Ennead: "Him alone, Horus, the inheritance."

Geb's words to the Ennead: "To his heir, Horus, my inheritance."

Geb's words to the Ennead: "To the son of my son, Horus, the Jackal of Upper Egypt."

Geb's words to the Ennead: "The firstborn, Horus, the Opener-of-the-ways."

Geb's words to the Ennead: "The son who was born, Horus, on the birthday of the Opener-of-the-ways."

Then Horus stood over the land. He is the uniter of this land, proclaimed in the great name: Tenen, south-of-his-Wall, Lord of Eternity. Then sprouted the two 'Great in Magic' upon his head. He is Horus who arose as 'King of Upper and Lower Egypt', who united the Two Lands in the Nome of the (White) Wall, the place in which the Two Lands were united.

Reed (heraldic plant for Upper Egypt) *and papyrus* (heraldic plant for Lower Egypt) *were placed on the double door of the House of Ptah. That means: Horus and Seth pacified and united. They fraternized so as to cease quarrelling wherever they may be, being united in the House of Ptah, the "Balance of the Two Lands" in which Upper and Lower Egypt have been weighed.*'

As Assmann (1996: 348) points out, the relevance of this myth to Shabaka is obvious: he too was faced with a divided land. Piye in returning to Napata had not really united the kingdom, and it was only when Shabaka had ended the Libyan polyarchy that a return to the classical pharaonic monarchy could occur.

After a 14-year reign, Shabaka died and was succeeded by his two nephews, Piye's sons, first Shebitku for 12 years and then Taharqa in 690 B.C.E. (Clayton 1994: 192).

When the latter of these succeeded to the throne of Egypt he was confronted with the Assyrians, whose power had been growing over the last few years. In 673 B.C.E. Esarhaddon, the Assyrian king, was repulsed at Ashkelon on the Egyptian/Palestinian border by a combined force of Egyptians and Palestinians. However, two years later Esarhaddon was back and this time he was successful and struck deep into Egypt itself, capturing Memphis together with the majority of Taharqa's family. The pharaoh fortunately managed to escape to Thebes; a good account of this can be obtained in Morkot (2000: 259-272). Esarhaddon now attempted to make the part of Egypt that he controlled, i.e. Memphis and the Delta, part of the Assyrian empire. Many new Assyrian officials were appointed, but the cities were left under the rule of their dynasts, so Bakennefi at Athribis at the base of the Delta, Pakrur at Per-Soped in the eastern Delta and Nekau at Memphis (Morkot 2000: 274). When trouble once again broke out in Egypt in 669 B.C.E. Esarhaddon returned, but died on the road and was succeeded by his son, Ashurbanipal, who, probably to validate his claim, withdrew back to Assyria (Kitchen 1973: 392).

Egypt's reprieve was short lived, however, and within two years Ashurbanipal's army had defeated the Egyptians at Karbaniti (Morkot 2000: 277-278). All the nobility of the Delta who had sided with Taharqa were executed except for the future Necho I of the 26th Dynasty who was appointed chief vassal king in Egypt (Assmann 1996: 336). Taharqa had retreated to Napata where he died in 664 B.C.E. and was succeeded by his nephew Tantamani who immediately re-invaded Egypt, stormed Memphis and retook the Delta, where Necho I, who had been the sole resistance to him, was executed (Kitchen 1973: 393). Ashurbanipal once again reacted and the Assyrians quickly regained Memphis, but this time they pursued Tantamani to Thebes and looted the city (Kitchen 1973: 394). The Assyrians appointed Necho's son, Psamtik I, as their vassal king: he, as we will see in the next chapter, was able to reunite the country under one ruler.

Whilst the majority of the Nile Valley and the Delta regions were vying for prominence at this time within the oasis region, Seth appeared to be the major god, as may be seen in the text of the Dakhleh stela. The smaller Dakhleh stela possibly has clues to the perception of Seth in the 25th Dynasty compared to earlier times even in the oases region. The Shabaka stone text, whilst ultimately recognising Horus as the ruler of Upper and Lower Egypt, does mention that Horus and Seth had been pacified and united. This possibly refers back to the early dynastic struggle between the supporters of these two gods, or perhaps it suggests that Shabaka wished to be seen as embodying the best characteristics of the two gods in his role as pharaoh.

9. THE LATE PERIOD 664-332 B.C.E.

The Saite Period saw a return to stability and the old religious values. Art forms looked back to the Middle and Old Kingdoms for inspiration, but the Assyrian invasion of Egypt had affected the Egyptians greatly, probably due to the sacking of Thebes and the laying waste of its huge temple treasury. Whereas in the aftermath of the Hyksos invasion Seth saw his role as god of things foreign enhanced; now in this role he was abhorred and blamed for the atrocities committed by the Assyrians. Surprisingly, however, we shall see that beautiful depictions of him from this period survive, illustrating the fact that in some parts of the country (possibly the oases again) he was not vilified.

Psamtik on being appointed vassal king under the Assyrians had initially to control the petty kings of the Delta region, but he harboured thoughts of reuniting Egypt under his rule. He was helped in establishing himself by the preoccupation of the Assyrians with the threat of a resurgent Babylon to their south (Dodson and Hilton 2004: 242), and as their power withered, so his own grew. He achieved reconciliation with Thebes in the ninth year of his reign by having his daughter, Nitokris I, recognised by Shepenwepet III, as the successor to the 'Divine Adoratrice of Amun'; the office of governor of the south was uncoupled from that of mayor of Thebes and conferred instead on the major-domo of the 'God's Wife of Amun'. Psamtik ensured that the holders of this office came from the north and also placed the local militia under his supreme command, which he achieved by use of a mercenary force comprising many Greeks, Carians, Jews and other foreigners. In 653 B.C.E. he drove the remaining Assyrian garrisons from the country and successfully reunited the whole country under his rule (Assmann 1996: 338).

Psamtik ruled for 54 years and oversaw a return to stability and the old religious values. We have already seen that under the Kushite kings Memphis was returned to some of its former glory and the legal dispute between Horus and Seth was placed at the heart of their policy of religious renovation (Assmann 1996: 389). Now, under Psamtik, the Horus and Seth myth is taken up and rewritten. Seth is once again tried and found guilty, he is punished, and the lament of his cities is described in terms of a political defeat in British Museum Papyrus 10252 (dating from the fourth century B.C.E.) and Papyrus Louvre 3129 (a Ptolemaic copy) (Jay 2007: 95). The extract forming part of an anti-Seth cursing ritual for the temple of Osiris at Abydos:

'*Su wails*, Wns *is in mourning,*

Grieving plaints are heard throughout Oxyrhynchos.

The oases Khargeh and Dakhleh cry out their woe,

misfortune roams through their centres.

Kynopolis keens, for its lord is not in it.

Hypselis is a barren place, Ombos torn down,

their houses destroyed, all their inhabitants annihilated.

Their lord is no more, who planned rebellion is no more,

for he has fallen into captivity' (Schott 1930: 14-16).

This passage is interesting as it illustrates the number of towns that were associated with the worship of Seth at this time; it is no surprise to see the oases of Khargeh and Dakhleh included or, indeed, Ombos. The other places mentioned cover much of Egypt. *Su* was in the Heracleopolitan nome (Gardiner 1947: vol 2, 117) and *Wns* in the Delta near Buto (Gardiner 1947: vol 2, 31), Oxyrhynchos was the major town of the nineteenth nome of Upper Egypt located upon the left bank of the Nile south of the Faiyum; Kynopolis on the opposite bank was that of the seventeenth nome, and Hypselis, near Assyut, was the capital of the eleventh nome (Wilson 1955: 229).

All of this was part of what some authors have termed archaism (Assmann 1996: 343). During this period the art of the past became a model to be copied: tomb reliefs depicted the individual dressed in the style and clothing of the Old Kingdom and inscriptions on tombs and coffins were modelled on the ancient Pyramid Texts. The various versions of the Book of the Dead, which until this period had consisted of an individual choosing whatever 'spells' he or she thought appropriate, now yielded to a much more definitive edition, although, somewhat surprisingly given the demonization of Seth that was taking place elsewhere, within the Book of the Dead Seth was still depicted in negative, positive and neutral ways. Dr Marcus Muller of the Totenbuch-Project, Bonn kindly examined 32 passages in late versions of the Book of the Dead where Seth is mentioned on my behalf and is broadly in agreement with my classification of the negative, positive and neutral spells. Thus he concluded that in 16 cases Seth was portrayed negatively. Not surprisingly, these were associated mainly with the Horus/Osiris and Seth conflict, i.e. spells 9, 17, 18, 19, 28, 60, 73 (which is identical to spell 9 (Allen 1974: 65),

78, 83, 86, 90, 110, 134, and 149 (see previously). Muller also includes here spells 113 and 149 which I interpreted as neutral (see previously). In eleven spells he was portrayed positively, including three where he is still the opponent of Apophis, namely spells 39, 108 and 111 (see previously); in eight other spells the positive aspects of Seth are noted (spells 8, 32, 42, 50, 54, 62, 99 and 140), I am in broad agreement here except with regard to spell 42, which I classified as neutral, and spell 99, which I classified as negative (see previously). The five remaining passages, which Muller did not specify, he classified as portraying Seth neutrally (personal communication).

However, the Assyrian invasion of Egypt had scarred the inhabitants greatly, especially due to the sacking of Thebes, and Seth, due to his association with 'things foreign', becomes embroiled in the resentment this engendered. He now appears as a foreign ruler who has been defeated and driven out, but unlike his association with the Hyksos there is now no attempt at reconciliation. In the passage quoted below from Papyrus Louvre 3129 in Urkunden VI (Schott 1930: 18-24), he is depicted as attempting a new invasion: with his allies he returns to Egypt and wreaks havoc amongst its temples (presumably mirroring what the Assyrians had done during their march south to Thebes in pursuit of Taharqa, the penultimate pharaoh of the Nubian Dynasty 25), forcing Isis to accuse him before Re:

'O Re-Horakhty, Sole Lord, whose like is not,

who gives commands, whose word is complied with,

whose judgment one cannot escape:

Remember what you ordained when the decrees were created!

Therein you gave guidance, that is to say: steps for men,

cult regulations for the gods,

instructions for the king in his palace [...]

Behold, Seth, the rebel, has come on his way,

he has turned once more to Egypt,

to plunder with his hand.

He is in the course of appropriating the land by force,

in keeping with the way he behaved before

when he destroyed the holy sites,

when he tore down their chapels,

when he made uproar in the temples.

He has inflicted suffering, he has repeated injury,

he has made unrest rise up anew.

He has brought suffering to the sanctuary,

he has planned rebellion in Memphis.

Behold, he penetrates into the Serapeum,

he has brought injury to the house of Opet.

He has hewn wood in Iusaas,

he has caught fish in Lake Moeris.

He has hunted game, he has caught fowl,

in the temple precinct of the First of Houses.

He has set foot [in the Pure House],

he has made uproar to the Ennead.

He has planned battle, he has roared

to the gods of Menset.

He has inflicted new suffering

on the banks of This.

He has made uproar in Mendes/Busiris;

the city and nome of Busiris/Mendes are in sore distress.

He has approached the House of Bas;

he has done violence in its walls.

He has taken wood from Sais of Neith;

he has done bad deeds in the embalming house.

He has made unrest arise anew in the Imhet cave

and strife in Kher-Aha.

He has brought what Atum abhors into the temple of the Ennead.

He has devised contumely and made uproar

in the temple of Amun-Wer in the Imhet cave.

He has bethought himself of battle; he has set fire

in the temple of the eastern Bas.

He has neared Saft-el-Henna, he has entered the walled quarter,

he has done sacrilege to the holy Nebes tree

- when it greens, the earth greens –

He has neared that sacred chamber of Iusaas

with the acacia, which contains death and life.

He has planned to eat the mafdet *[the sacred panther]*

before the countenance of Mut and Bastet.

Behold, he has eaten the Abdu fish [a sacred fish]

at the places of the ba of the east.

He has set foot on the land near Khefthernebes

before the countenance of Re in heaven.

He has fed the sacred ram

in the temple of Amun the great.

He has laid hands on the Mnhp *plant*

before the countenance of the ram of Mendes.

He has organised a massacre of the people in Busiris

before the countenance of Wennefer, the Justified.

He has fed of the Abdu fish

and eaten of the 'dw fish

in the great hall of Heliopolis.

He has cut off supply, he has stolen the offerings

from the place of the Sole Lord, whose like is not,

[so that wailing reigns in his two houses to all gods,

and the rites are not performed at the established times].

He has caught the hawk and the itn *fish*

before the countenance of Shu and Tefnut.

Behold, he has bound the Apis bull

before the countenance of him who made all that is.

He has let the milk of Sekhat-Hor dry away,

he has thrown down the htmt *cow, the mother of god.*

He has cut off supply on the lake of the Tm trees,

he let the lake of the htmt *cow dry up.*

He has planned to stand up as a robber,

he has sought to elevate himself.

Suffering reigns in the place where he abides.

Destruction is in what you [Re-Horakhty] have commanded'.

(Assmann 1996: 390-392).

This leads one to believe that worship of Seth at this time was something to be abhorred, and this is illustrated by a statue initially of Seth in the Copenhagen Museum (Hill 2007: 34-37; Schorsch and Wypyski 2009: 177-200). Whilst the statue initially dates to the 19th or 20th Dynasty, during the Late Period Seth's upright ears were removed and replaced by ram's horns (Schorsch and Wypyski 2009: 185) in an attempt to cause the statue to depict either Khnum or Amun. Conversely, the British Museum (acquisition number 13403) possesses an ivory sceptre head 3.8 cm in length depicting Seth, which is of exquisite workmanship. The object is pierced at the back so that it could be worn as a pendant. It was found at Sakkara and is dated to the 26th Dynasty. The workmanship of this object would certainly suggest that Seth was still regarded in some quarters with reverence.

Following the death of Psamtik in 610 B.C.E., his son, Nekau, continued his father's policies, forming an Egyptian navy by recruiting displaced Ionian Greeks (Clayton 1994: 196). Nekau was succeeded in turn by his son, Psamtik II, who reigned for only 6 years and is best known for a campaign against the still-powerful Kushites in Nubia. Wahibre (Apries), his successor, mounted a failed campaign against Libya, which resulted in him being displaced by one of his generals, Ahmose II (Dodson and Hilton 2004: 243).

The civil war had involved native Egyptians turning against the many foreign mercenaries, including Greeks amongst their number, that were in the army. Ahmose attempted to settle matters by declaring specific trading rights and privileges for foreigners settled in Naukratis in the Delta, making it a free zone for Greek trade. This caused the city to become very Hellenised and, no doubt, aided Alexander's later conquest of Egypt (Clayton 1994: 197).

The latter years of Ahmose's reign were concerned with the rise of the Persians, who as a new power in the Middle East were slowly advancing towards Egypt's borders. Within a few years of succeeding to the throne, Psamtik III was defeated by them at Pelusium; he fled to Memphis, but was captured and taken to Susa, the Persian capital, where he was initially allowed to live but, when discovered plotting against the Persians, was put to death (Dodson and Hilton 2004: 243).

The success of Cambyses, the Persian king, resulted in Egypt's incorporation into the Persian Empire; from the outset the Persian kings took the role of pharaohs, and indeed Cambyses had an Egyptian titulary composed for him (Lloyd 1982: 166-180). This titulary occurs as part of an inscription on a statue of an official named Udjahorresnet, who appears to have served under both Cambyses and his successor, Darius. In the inscription, which is concerned with the expulsion of foreigners from the temple complex of the goddess Neith at Sais, Cambyses is described as *ḥm n nsw-bity Kmbtt*, *'the Majesty of the King of Upper and Lower Egypt Cambyses'*. The text claims that some of the religious activities described were motivated: *m wd n ḥm.f* 'at the command of His Majesty'. This would all appear to indicate that the native Egyptians had accepted the Persian conquest and now regarded the Persian kings as legitimate pharaohs. However, as Lloyd points out (1982: 176), there are two parts in the inscription where Udjahorresnet may have allowed his true feelings to show. In lines 33 and 34 he states:

*'I was a man good in his city, saving its people from monstrous cataclysm (*nsn*) when it happened in the entire land, the like of which had not happened in this land.'*

Continuing this theme, lines 40 to 42 state:

*'I did for them everything beneficial as a father would have done for his son, when the cataclysm (*nsn*) befell in this nome in the midst of the monstrous cataclysm which happened in the entire land.'*

The use of the term *nsn* is of interest as it undoubtedly has Sethian implications, often being translated as rage, madness or storm, frequently with a figure of Seth as its determinative. Lloyd suggests (1982: 177) that here the Persian invasion is being depicted as an eruption into Egypt of chaotic forces which were believed to pose a constant threat to the preservation of the ordered universe, and which were always personified as followers of Seth.

Lloyd also suggests that what we are seeing here is that initially, certainly by Udjahorresnet, Cambyses was seen as a:wr '3 n h3st nb(t), *'The Great Chief of Every Foreign Land'*, and as such, was an enemy of Egypt potentially endowed with the role of Seth, but that he is able to throw off that role and become the *'Great Ruler of Egypt'*, thus assuming the role of Horus (Lloyd 1982: 177). Whether the rest of the Egyptian populace were prepared to take this course of acceptance is, of course, debatable, and one can only assume that many of them would have still viewed the Persians as hated foreign invaders which would result in the subsequent backlash against Seth. Certainly, the period is marked by a number of revolts against the Persians by native Egyptians (Dodson and Hilton 2004: 248-249). From 404 to 343 B.C.E. three native Dynasties (the 28th, 29th and 30th) ruled until the last native pharaoh, Nectanebo II, was once more defeated by the Persians, who ruled for 10 years until Egypt became part of the Empire of Alexander the Great.

This period saw a return to stability and old religious values. In the preceding years of the Third Intermediate Period the idea of Egypt as a unified kingdom had been severely eroded due to such factors as the power of the Amun priesthood in Thebes, the Libyan and Nubian dynasties and the eventual conquest by the Assyrians (Lloyd 2000a: 371). Following the reunification under Psamtik a return to religious values was prominent amongst his desired aims. As part of this aim the Book of the Dead spells were much more rigorously defined in their sequence. Interestingly, as we have seen, this did not include expunging the more positive and neutral spells that referred to Seth. However, there is a backlash against Seth where his association with things foreign is seen as a bad thing in the context of the Assyrian invasion. The subsequent Persian invasion did not help this state of affairs and from this time onwards, certainly within the Nile valley, Seth was demonised.

10. THE GRAECO-ROMAN PERIOD 332 – 30 B.C.E.

Seth during this period was for the most part still viewed as the god associated with foreign things and as we have seen in the Late Period (see above, Chapter 9), he suffered from this association. The Egyptians probably thought that Seth had once again sided with the foreigners in permitting the Persians not only to invade the country but also to plunder the temples (Lloyd 2000a: 390); it was as though he had put the foreigners' desires first rather than those of Egypt. This is reflected in his representation in contemporary papyri, for example, in Papyrus Jumilhac, where Seth is portrayed as the enemy of Anubis, the main character in this papyrus. The reliefs upon the walls of the temple at Edfu also show Seth as the enemy of Horus and portray the struggle between the two gods and the subsequent victory of Horus. It all seems a far cry from the days when Seth was seen as the defender of Re against Apophis in the sacred barque.

Alexander the Great entered Egypt in 332 B.C.E. He was looked upon as a divine saviour by the Egyptians and as such had himself confirmed as the son of the god at the oracle of Amun in the Oasis of Siwa. This was an astute piece of work by Alexander as he recognised that a legitimate pharaoh needed two fathers: a divine one (Amun) and a real one – a reigning king who also fulfilled these conditions. Consequently Alexander made it known that his mother, Olympia, had slept with Nectanebo in the guise of Amun after he had been driven out by the Persians and accepted at the Macedonian court as a magician (Assmann 1996: 377-378). He now possessed a divine father (Amun), a real father (Philip II of Macedonia) and a father (Nectanebo II of Egypt) to legitimise his claim to the throne of Egypt. Crowned at Memphis, Alexander then journeyed to Thebes to have his accession approved by Amun. Though Alexander was not in Egypt for any great length of time, he did found Alexandria and ordered that the temples devastated by the Persians be rebuilt (Lloyd 2000b: 395-396).

Following Alexander's death in 323 B.C.E., Egypt was taken over by his general Ptolemy, who was crowned as Ptolemy Soter in 305 B.C.E. He tried to ensure the loyalty of the native Egyptian population by setting himself within their ancient religious traditions (Ellis 1992: 11) and his heirs maintained this stance with extensive temple building, for example at Edfu, Denderah and Kom Ombo. Nevertheless the Ptolemies maintained a strong Greek identity, always adopting Greek names and titles, and none of them spoke Egyptian with the exception of the last ruler, Cleopatra VII (Peacock 2000: 422).

Prior to Alexander's conquest there had been Greeks present in Egypt, either as members of the military or as traders, living mainly in Naukratis or in Memphis, but these Greeks only numbered some thousands at most, and were always aware that they were living in a foreign land (Bowman 1986: 22). Alexander's conquest changed all that and opened up Egypt to many more emigrant Greeks, who took up official positions; a relatively small number of native Egyptians could also aspire to government careers under this new regime, provided that they were competent in the Greek language (Bowman 1986: 61). However, the majority of the native populace, who could not understand Greek, were left to their own devices (Lewis 1986: 8-9). By establishing Alexandria on the Mediterranean coast, Alexander emphasised that Egypt was now part of the Greek world and established a Greek counterpart to the rival Memphis, the Egyptian capital for so many years previously (Lewis 1986: 9). From the early days of the Ptolemies, preservation of the traditional institutions of Egyptian religion was a fundamental requirement (Bowman 1986: 169). Many of the great temples in Egypt that are now on a modern visitor's itinerary were extensively embellished or indeed constructed during this Graeco-Roman period.

To the Egyptians their native culture seemed to be under threat and this was reflected in an increasing rewriting from the Saite Period onwards of Seth's role in the murder of Osiris (Gunn and Gardiner 1918: 45; Te Velde 1969: 143-144). This articulated a nationalistic reaction to the foreign rule of the Persians, the Greeks and eventually the Romans (Assmann 2001: 367). An example of this can be seen in Papyrus Jumilhac, which dates from the early Ptolemaic era (approx 300 B.C.E.). This papyrus was acquired by the Louvre in 1945 from Count Odet de Jumilhac (James 1962: 177). This text from the eighteenth nome of Upper Egypt, the Prefecture of the Jackal, is claimed to be a rewriting by priests of documents dating to the Old Kingdom that had been eaten by worms and mice! That said, the style of writing is definitely of the Ptolemaic period so whether the claim is true or was an attempt at 'authenticity' is debatable. Much of the text not surprisingly deals with Anubis (Kay 2007: 97), as he is the local god, but the papyrus also deals with attempts by Seth and his followers to destroy or despoil the body of Osiris (Pinch 2002: 80). Although it differs from the *'Contendings of Horus and Seth'* as written down in the Chester-Beatty papyrus some parallels can be drawn between the two. A number of the stories contained within P. Jumilhac are concerned with the 'Eyes of Horus', which were damaged (as were Seth's testicles) during the battles recounted in the Chester-Beatty Papyrus. Further stories, as we shall see below, expose Seth's sexuality to ridicule: in one, he is likened to Baba (see below for description) and in another he is portrayed as himself, lusting after Isis.

The papyrus begins with the 'Myth of the Horus chests' (Vandier 1961: 73-74): first, the exact position of the chests is given- they are found in the south of the district of Hout-Nesout, in eastern Gebel, north-east of Per-Benen. The chests are stolen by Seth's men because they contain the 'Eyes of Horus' (the *wedjat* eyes); Seth then personally puts them in the mountain and turns himself into a crocodile, an animal associated with Seth (Te Velde 1967: 26), and installs himself in a house which in the text is called Per-Benen.

Anubis learns of Seth's crime and decides to recover the chests. To better achieve this aim, he turns himself into a winged serpent. His wings and hands are armed with knives and from his body leap six serpents, three on each side, who throw flames all around him. In this guise he establishes himself upon a hill, called the "hill of the serpent". He succeeds in re-capturing the chests by night without having to fight Seth. With the knives he causes the chests to jump and he removes the *wedjat* eyes, putting each one into a woven casket with a papyrus and then he flees and buries them north of this place (presumably Per-Benen).

Anubis then returns to Per-Benen and Seth attacks him; two of the serpents that sprang from Anubis's body put out the eyes of the crocodile (the papyrus labels this *'a just punishment for the crime that Seth has committed against the eyes of Horus'*). The serpents then destroy Per-Benen.

The story continues (Vandier 1961: 75) with Anubis again encountering Seth and his allies, this time at Letopolis. Anubis is once again transformed into a great serpent precisely named in the text as "Benen". Thoth supporting Anubis utters the words: *"Benen comes against you, in his manifestation as Khentikhem* (the god of Letopolis), *and he will prevail against you."* This occurs and Anubis returns with the two chests to the 18th nome. The text continues: *"Anubis placed the two chests in this mountain, and from then on they are known as 'the chests of Horus'"*.

Isis now visits the chests, accompanied by Horus, here somewhat confusingly referred to as Horus-Anubis in spite of the fact that Anubis has rescued the two 'Eyes of Horus'. Subsequently only Horus is referred to and as Vandier states: *"such contradictions never seem to worry the Ancient Egyptians."* (Vandier 1961: 76). Derchain in his paper on the possible authorship of the papyrus suggests that the author had interwoven different legends in order to strengthen Anubis's role in these matters (1990: 21) and twinning him with Horus may have helped achieve this aim; alternatively the fact that the twinning of the two deities only occurs once could indicate a copying error by the author.

On arriving where Anubis had placed the chests, Isis and Horus observe that the eyes have caused a vineyard to spring up. Isis requests that Horus create a sanctuary near this spot, so that the *wedjat* eyes could be watched over.

The next few pages of Papyrus Jumilhac are concerned with a large number of myths that refer to Anubis (Vandier 1961: 88-91). The sixth of these myths concerns Thoth and Baba, the latter was a god of the erect phallus, he was identified as a dangerous god who murdered on sight, this hostile aspect led to him being identified with Seth (Hart 1986: 52), a view also expressed by Manetho (1940: 188-191). Vandier in this particular myth also identifies Baba as just another manifestation of Seth (1961: 93). Thus this myth is just another version of the continual struggle that was supposedly occurring in the 18th nome between Seth and his supporters and those of Osiris.

The myth begins with an unflattering description of Baba; whilst he is normally described as a red dog, in this text he is seen as a baboon, the scribe insisting upon this animal's characteristic eyes and terrifying look. The choice of the colour red is significant as it represents evil (Wilkinson 1994: 106-107; Reiblein 2011: 33). The baboon is more normally associated with the god Thoth (Wilkinson 1992: 73) and perhaps the scribe here is taking the frequent fights that take place between members of this species as representative of the dispute between Thoth and Baba. The alleged discord between Thoth and Baba initially takes place in a strictly legalistic manner: Thoth is the accuser, and Baba the accused. Whilst the complaints are not made clear in the papyrus, they are to be examined by Re assisted by the two Enneads, presumably not including Seth in their number, whose members are both witness and jury. The Enneads, encouraged by Re to speak, remain silent. Encouraged by this, Baba sets out to discredit Thoth: the god would have eaten Re's meal and stolen what belonged to the universal master. This causes the jury to react strongly, and as one they declare Baba's words to be lies. Thoth thus cries out: *"O, great! Go far away, because you are in the wrong"* (Vandier 1961: 93). The first act of this myth ends with Re delivering the verdict that Thoth is right, and Baba wrong.

The second act is quite different and resembles light comedy. The story seeks to show the libertine aspects of Baba. The god is surprised by Thoth, sleeping by the side of a woman, after having abandoned himself to the pleasures of love. On waking he realises that Thoth, due to his magical powers, has rendered him impotent. Witnesses to this scene are Re and the members of the Two Enneads, whom Thoth had ensured to call before performing his magic trick (Vandier 1961: 94).

Baba, as one would expect, reacts furiously to his predicament and takes up arms and marches against Thoth, but as Vandier (1961: 94) puts it: *"What can brute force do against magic power?"* Thoth uttered some secret spell, and Baba, at the very moment that he was going to strike his enemy, suddenly turned his weapon against his own head. The Ennead, still present, comment like an ancient chorus in an Athenian tragedy, on the surprising turn of events in the fight. *"His weapon is against himself,"* they cry.

The story ends, as it began, with a judgement: Re abandons Baba to Thoth and the latter sacrifices him (Manniche 1987: 105-106). We conclude that Baba is not dead and the myth ends with the sentence: *"Know the meaning of the red dog: it is Baba, and Baba is Nebedj."* *Nebedj* is a well known name for Seth (Kees 1924: 69-79), which proves, in this myth at least, that Baba and Seth should be identified as one and the same god, as Vandier has suggested.

After more myths concerned solely with Anubis, the papyrus then considers the myth of 'Anubis and Djesertep opposing the criminal doings of Seth and Demib' (Vandier 1961: 103-105). The first part of this story confines the action to an underling, Demib, chief amongst Seth's companions. Demib has been charged by Seth with a secret mission, which would lead him into the crypt, where probably an Osirian relic might be found. Alerted by Djesertep, whose job was to keep an eye on Demib, Imakhouemankh, leader of Osiris' protecting genies, takes hold of Demib and cuts his head off. Seth then intervenes himself, and taking the form of Anubis, he searches for his subordinate; on failing to find him he fulfils the mission himself and manages to steal the *ḥt-m-ḥ ftjw* of the divine body. Vandier believes that this obscure phrase probably meant either cult objects usually found in front of the god, or little statues of bound enemies, made according to a magic formula. This latter suggestion could explain why Seth wanted to get hold of them, to break the magic circle they created round him

(Vandier 1961: 103-104). The story continues: Seth is fleeing with the *ḥt-m-ḥ ftjw* so Anubis and Thoth once more unite, Thoth using magic spells throws Seth to the earth and there Anubis ties his arms and legs and Seth becomes Osiris' chair. Isis now joins in by tearing his back with her teeth and Re lends his authority to the decision already taken by declaring that from now on Seth should serve as Osiris' seat. However, this is not the end of the story as Seth succeeds in fleeing to the region of the Gebel, which, according to the story, is to the east of the "castle of humours".

After fleeing, Seth transforms himself into a panther, but Anubis manages to get hold of him and Thoth, again uttering a magic spell, causes him to remain on the ground long enough for Anubis to once again bind his arms and legs and then to burn him. The smell from the burning body rises in the sky and was considered by Re and the gods surrounding him to be good. Anubis had probably flayed Seth before putting him on the pyre because the text states that Anubis took Seth's skin and put it on his shoulders before making an offering to Osiris. Vandier suggests that this is why the priest in the Opening of the Mouth ceremonies wore a panther skin (Vandier 1961: 104). The story continues by saying that Seth's companions, worried by his absence, came south to the district of Dounaouy/Hardai to find him. Anubis marched against them and slew them all.

The papyrus now continues with a similar myth but this time the main protagonists are Seth and Anubis alone (Vandier 1961: 105). Seth learns that Anubis is away so he once again disguises himself as Anubis to deceive the gate guardians and easily succeeds in carrying off the *ḥt-m-ḥ ftjw*. Anubis learns of the swindle and pursues Seth, who has already crossed the Nile and come into the region of Saka. In order to escape Anubis, Seth turns himself into a bull, but the ruse does not work and Anubis seizes him, binds him tightly and punishes him by chaining him up. Anubis puts the sacred objects back in their place and changes himself into a falcon with outstretched wings to protect them.

The papyrus then relates a tale concerning Horus and Seth (Vandier 1961: 106-109). First, Seth is accused by Isis and Horus. Cleverly, they do not complain directly; they accuse the god of committing many bad deeds against the universal master, Re, who is presiding over the tribunal. Because Re needs to be seen as impartial, he orders Thoth to judge the dispute between Horus and Seth. Surrounded by gods, members of the jury, Thoth sits on a mat and lists all Seth's crimes. The latter appears to have no defence and utters no word to justify his actions. Thus he is condemned and Thoth establishes all the rights of Horus: that all Egypt with everything produced therein must return to the son of Osiris. This judgement is written down and sent to Re for ratification. The jurors demand that Horus receives his father's inheritance, and that Seth should be sent off into the desert. Re agrees.

Seth reacts violently. He assembles his allies, with a view to a great battle and marches against Thoth. The text at this point is damaged so Vandier proposes two translations of which he prefers the second (Vandier 1961: 107-108). The bold sections in the two translations highlight the differences between them.

First translation:

*"Then Seth marched against Thoth. He went with a knife and cut **off the arms of his enemies**; then he stole Thoth's books and threw them into the river. But Thoth then uttered incantations and put back **his shoulder to their place and weighted it down** with his brush in such a way that they were firmly fixed in their place."*

Second translation:

*"The Seth marched against Thoth's **cult objects**. He went with his knife and cut **the strings of** Thoth's books and threw them into the river. But then Thoth uttered incantations and put his **new books** back into the place of the **old ones** and fixed them exactly there with his brush."*

Fortunately, the papyrus is less damaged in the subsequent section which deals with Seth's capture and punishment.

Seth changed into a red dog and hid in a bush, but he was quickly tracked down and he was pierced by the hunter's spears: *"All those who saw him cried out: "Here he is! Here he is!", and they threw him over with what was in their mouth, and massacred him with what was in their hands."*

Vandier suggests that 'what was in their mouth' meant the shouts they made and 'what was in their hands' were their weapons (1961: 108). Horus then appeared as king of Upper and Lower Egypt on the throne of his father, Osiris, with Thoth taking on the functions of vizier. Horus was surrounded by a court of gods and goddesses and he himself took on the task of halting the war and slashing the rebels to pieces. The myth concluded by stating that Horus destroyed Seth's allies, destroyed his towns and districts, and pulled off his *ḥps*, i.e. his front paw, so that watched over by genies it may be placed in the middle of the sky, becoming the Great Bear, whose stars if joined by a continuous line approximate the shape of Seth's leg. *"Seth's leg in the northern sky was held by the 'Great Sow' i.e. Taweret"* (Vandier 1961: 108). Seth, being a prisoner in the northern sky is now condemned to no longer wander among the gods, and thus he gets a just punishment for his crimes. The papyrus goes on to state that, to keep alive the memory of these events, a red dog is sacrificed every year upon Thoth's feast day. Te Velde (1967: 146-147) suggests that the passage describing the destruction of Seth's towns and districts represents the condemnation of the cult of Seth in every form and may reflect the actual situation within the Nile valley at this time.

The papyrus then moves on to a story involving Isis and Seth (Vandier 1961: 109-110). Up to now, Isis has played a minor role in the various myths but here it is she, and she alone, who acts against Seth. The latter, as usual, has gathered his gang to attack the 18th nome of Upper Egypt. In response, Isis takes the role of Sekhmet, the lioness-headed goddess, more qualified than Isis to struggle successfully against her enemies. In her new shape the goddess hides in the Gebel which is south of Dounaouy/Hardai, and when her enemies pass by, without being aware of her, she spits flame at them, and kills everyone. Thus, she was called *"Hathor, mistress of the two blazing fires"*, because it was by fire that she triumphed over her enemies. Here, she set up a sanctuary from where it was easy to watch the comings and goings of Seth and his gang. A footnote by Vandier (1961: 109, footnote 6) points out that whilst the text has Sekhmet (Isis) killing everyone, Seth, of course, had escaped and in any case only part of his gang had been with him!

When Seth saw Isis installed within the sanctuary, he changes himself into a bull. Isis then takes the shape of a female dog whose tail ended in a knife, and begins to run before the Seth bull. So swift was she that her enemy could not overtake her. Whilst pursuing her, Seth's semen spread over the ground. At that moment Isis, who must have halted, cries out: *"what an abominable thing, oh bull, to have spread your seed!"* This seed caused watermelons to grow in the Gebel. Then Isis went right into the Gebel, doubtless to hide herself. The action then moves to the north. Seth, having decided that he could not possibly attain his objective in the south, in the region of Dounaouy/Hardai, intends to go northwards into the 18th nome of Upper Egypt. But Isis, realising his plan, hurries herself northwards to defend this area of territory against the expected incursion of Seth. A wise precaution; hardly installed, Isis sees that Seth's companions, coming from the 19th nome (Oxyrhynchus), have crossed the Nile and are coming towards the eastern Gebel. She turns into the uraeus and plunges her venom into her enemies. All die; their blood spreads over the mountain, and according to the papyrus, that is why red lead is found at Geheset.

The common trait amongst all these myths is that Seth is depicted in a negative manner, and as suggested by Te Velde (1967: 146-147) may reflect the situation within the Nile Valley at this time, with Seth being blamed for the atrocities that had occurred following the invasions of the Assyrians and Persians. Certainly Papyrus Jumilhac (Vandier 1961: 10-11) has no qualms in describing the sad condition of the towns and nomes associated with Seth:

"He (Horus) defeated Seth and annihilated his gang. He destroyed his towns and his nomes and he scratched out his name in this land, after he had broken his statues in pieces."

This implies, certainly from a religious text point of view, the condemnation of the cult of Seth in every form and certainly legitamises it from a theological aspect. Whether this was translated into an actual destruction of his temples and his images or whether these disappeared due to neglect is a moot point. Certainly the hatred displayed towards Seth in these times can be seen in the many terms of abuse with which he is indicated (Te Velde 1967: 148-151). Some of these names illustrating that the abhorrence of Seth can be interpreted as an outcome in the religious field of feelings of fear and hatred towards foreign conquerors who were identified with Seth. Alexander and the subsequent Ptolemies were not viewed in this negative way which may be explained by the fact that they sought to re-establish the Egyptian religion rather than sacking its temples.

Papyrus Berlin is a demotic text dated to Year 35 of a Ptolemy whom Gaudard (2005: 45) believes was Ptolemy VI (180-145 B.C.E.). The text is a dramatic work based on the conflict of Horus and Seth. It was probably performed annually during the Osirian Khoiak festival at Pelusium in the Egyptian Fayum (Kay 2007: 95). Although it is very fragmentary, Gaudard has managed to make some suggestions as to the content (2005: 63-65). It begins with the driving away of Seth from Egypt. Seth is likened to a donkey (Gaudard 2005: 64), an animal (as we have seen frequently), that is associated with Seth and indeed during this late period is frequently used to depict Seth (Te Velde 1967: 14). There then follows a dialogue between the team of Horus and the team of Seth, who speak about the punishment that has been inflicted upon Seth. The men of Seth would like the men of Horus to free Seth. Seth is also said to be copulating, drunk and *'as thirsty as a donkey of the oasis.'* An explanatory gloss attributes this state to the fact that Seth went to the oasis with the 'Eye of Horus' and has swallowed it. All the gods start speaking to him and insist on his failure, saying that he has tripped with his sandals and has fallen. Seth is likened to a 'camel, pig and hippopotamus' (Gaudard 2005: 64), Te Velde (1967: 26) mentions all these animals as being identified with Seth as well as the ass, oryx antelope, gazelle, crocodile and fish. Seth complains that the female donkey, who is his sister and wife, Nephthys, was taken from him when he was about to copulate with her and that he has been deceived. In this story Seth is again shown to be a drunkard and depicted having sex in a similar manner to some of the stories previously discussed that occur in P.Jumilhac. Kay (2006: 95) suggests that this text was designed to provide entertainment as much as any edification.

A third fragment of the papyrus is interesting in that it records a description of the role played in the play by one of the actors (Gaudard 2005: 238-245). In this, the actor describes all that he has done to punish Seth and help Horus (and of course the pharaoh, as he becomes Horus on ascending to the throne) to rule over Egypt, presumably by bringing the story to the populace the majority of whom would be illiterate and therefore dependent upon these plays for their understanding of the story.

A version of the myth of Horus is carved upon the temple walls at Edfu. It was begun during the reign of Ptolemy III Euergetes I and was completed during the reign of Ptolemy VIII Euergetes II in 142 B.C.E. (Watterson 1998: 47-48). It comprises five sets of reliefs and texts called A, B, C, D and E by Fairman (1935, and 1974), and Blackman and Fairman (1942, 1943 and 1944); it is also published in Lloyd (1998: 255-325). The actual reliefs have been published in a series of books by the Institut Français d'Archéologie Orientale (Rochemonteix, Chassinat, Cauville and Devauchelle 1934-1985).

Text A, also known as the *Legend of the Winged Disk*, is dated to the time when the gods ruled upon the earth actually stated as year 363 of Re-Horakhty and shows Horus Behdety (as the great Winged Disk) and his followers fighting in the bark of Re against Seth, depicted as a hippopotamus, and his associates, who take the form of crocodiles and hippopotami (Fairman 1935: 26).

Text B, entitled *'offering grape and water drink'*, describes a fight between Horus, son of Isis, and Seth, the former being assisted by Horus Behdety (Fairman 1935: 26).

Text C is a ritual drama which was enacted annually at Edfu during the Festival of Victory (Gaudard 2005: 2). Act I consists of the ritual harpooning of Seth as a hippopotamus (Fairman 1974: 84-100). In these reliefs the hippopotamus representing Seth is deliberately

*Figure 17: The king spearing Seth as represented upon the walls of the temple at Edfu.
Copyright: Antony E. David.*

*Figure 18: Horus the Behdite stands upon the back of a hippopotamus, representing Seth,
whose head he pierces with his harpoon. Relief depicted upon the walls of the temple at Edfu.*

depicted as a tiny, relatively helpless-looking animal that can be easily defeated by the king, who is represented on a much larger scale (Figure 17).

This small-scale representation was employed by the Egyptian artisans to theoretically diminish the magical powers of Seth (Wilkinson 1994: 44-45). This depiction of Seth as a hippopotamus appears to be used when he needs to be seen as a destructive and terrifying power, presumably because the hippopotamus when roused is seen in this manner. However, the animal could be depicted in a more gentle light as seen in its association with the goddess Taweret, the protectress of women in childbirth (Hart 1986: 211-212), presumably because the female hippopotamus is a good mother (Asheri, Lloyd and Corcella 2007: 71).

Act II is a celebration of Horus' victory and includes his coronation as king of Upper and Lower Egypt (Fairman 1974: 101-108). Act III comprises more celebrations and the dismemberment of Seth (Fairman 1974: 109-118), see Figure 18, and an epilogue proclaims the triumph of Horus, the gods and the king (Fairman 1974: 119-120).

Text D depicts Seth as a red hippopotamus going to Elephantine, the colour red once again being used as the colour to represent evil (Wilkinson 1994: 106-107). He is pursued by Horus, son of Isis, who overtakes him near Edfu, and after the ensuing fight, Seth flees northwards and Horus assumes the office of his father (Fairman 1935: 27).

Text E describes a fight between Horus, 'Lord of Lower Egypt', living in Memphis, and Seth, 'Lord of Upper Egypt', living in Shas-hotep (a metropolis of the 11th Upper Egyptian nome- Gauthier 1928: 107-108). They fight, Horus in the guise of a youth, and Seth in that of a red donkey. Horus triumphs and cuts off Seth's leg (Fairman 1935: 27), echoing the story in P. Jumilhac where Horus is described as pulling off Seth's front paw.

Whilst in the majority of these reliefs and associated texts Seth is shown as the aggressor and the enemy of Horus occasionally he is depicted forgetting his evil aspect and turning into a good spirit (Cauville 2012: 47): *"Seth, bearer of his vessels full of good wine from the vineyards of Bahariya, the kegs in his hand full of the new eye of Horus to rejoice your heart, you drink from it, those who are in your following drink from it as well, you rejoice, their hearts are happy."*

Illustrating once again the dichotomy that the Ancient Egyptians found themselves in when dealing with Seth.

The Bremner-Rhind papyrus dates back to the end of the Thirtieth Dynasty (Kay 2006: 95), it contains four distinct works: the *Songs of Isis and Nephthys*, the *Ritual of Bringing in Sokar*, the *Book of Overthrowing 'Apep* and the *Names of 'Apep, which shall not be* (Faulkner 1936: 121). The first of these, as the name suggests, is concerned with a series of hymns sung by two priestesses representing the goddesses Isis and Nephthys. The hymns that they sing purporting to be the mourning of the two goddesses for the departed Osiris and their summons to the god for him to rise again. Perhaps unsurprisingly, Seth in this section is portrayed in a bad manner he, after all, is the god responsible for the death of Osiris. So phrases such as: *'While Seth is in all the evil which he does,'* (Faulkner 1936: 123) and *'The entire Ennead serve thee, they ward off Seth for thee when he comes,'* (Faulkner 1936: 124) occur. Conversely, in the part of the papyrus concerned with the overthrowing of 'Apep, Seth is here depicted in his role as protector of Re and such phrases as: *'Seth has rendered thy moment of action impotent. Isis repels thee, Nephthys cuts thee up, the Great Ennead which is in the prow of the bark of Re drives thee off, Seth has stabbed at thy neck...* (Faulkner 1937: 169) are used. Once again we have here both sides of Seth's character depicted illustrating that the Egyptians had no problem in accommodating both the dark and light sides of the god.

The myth of Horus and Seth was referred to by several Greek authors, usually using the name Typhon to denote Seth. This was because the Greeks identified many of their own gods with many of the Egyptian gods (Bowman 1986: 176).

Seth was first identified with Typhon by Pherecydes of Syros around 540 B.C.E (Schibly 1990: 82-83). He says that Typhon originally went by the name of Seth and that Seth was the destructive storm-god of the desert and fierce opponent of Horus and Osiris and that Seth's opposition to the falcon-god Horus typified the battle between the forces of good and evil. This is probably Pherecydes' interpretation of the Egyptian conflict between *maat* and *isfet* i.e. order and chaos.

Herodotus may have visited Egypt after 460 B.C.E. Unfortunately, he did not know Egyptian and so was forced to rely upon expatriate Greeks and Greek-speaking Egyptians for his information, which too often led to him being misled regarding translations of the inscriptions that he enquired about (Brown 1965: 60). That said, he gives an account of a sacred combat, part of a festival at Papremis (Herodotus 1999: 2.62-63); Griffiths (1960: 85-93) compared this to the fight between Horus and Seth basing this on the fact that he places Papremis in the north-western Delta, near Khemmis and Buto. Since both of these latter places are connected with Horus, Griffiths states that it would be natural to find an episode from the Horian cycle of legends made the subject of a festive rite there. He does acknowledge that this is speculative, but as the account appears to allude to an attempt by Horus to violate his mother and there are numerous allusions to Seth's attempts to violate Horus as he seeks refuge with his mother in the Delta region, his explanation probably has some validity.

Herodotus also talks of the gods being the early rulers of Egypt and states that: *"The last of them to rule the country was Osiris' son Horus, called by the Greeks Apollo; he deposed Typhon, and was the last divine king of Egypt"* (Herodotus 1999: 2.144, 451). He also mentions that *"Typhon came seeking through the world for the son of Osiris"* (Herodotus 1999: 2.156, 469).

Manetho, an Egyptian priest from Sebennytos in the Delta, lived under the first two Ptolemies and wrote a history of Egypt. Whilst the original is lost, fragments have been preserved by such writers as Josephus, Julius Africanus and Eusebius (Manetho 2004: vii). Manetho mentions that the throne of Egypt passed from Osiris to his brother Typhon, and lastly to Horus (Manetho 2004: 5). He attributes a reign of 29 years to Typhon (Manetho 2004: 17) in one account and 45 years in another (Manetho 2004: 9). He also refers to Avaris being a city which from earliest times had been dedicated to Typhon (Manetho 2004: 125) and to the fact that Bebon (Baba) can be an alternative name for Typhon (Manetho 2004: 189-191; see above, section 12.2).

Strabo in his Geography (1932: 73-74) has the following statement:

"A little above Sais is the asylum of Osiris in which his body is said to lie; but many lay claim to this, and particularly the inhabitants of the Philae which is situated above Syene and Elephantine. For this they tell the mythical story, namely that Isis placed coffins of Osiris beneath the earth in several places (but only one of them, and that unknown to all, contained the body) and she did this because she wished to hide the body from Typhon."

Diodorus, who visited Egypt in 60 or 59 B.C.E., also gives a rendition of the Osiris myth (Oldfather 1933: 67-71). After relating the murder of Osiris, he mentions that Isis, supported by Horus, destroyed Typhon and ruled over Egypt. He also appears to confuse Horus and Osiris as he states that the former was killed by Seth and his followers and was resuscitated by his mother Isis.

The most complete account is that by Plutarch (50-120 C.E.). He undoubtedly visited Egypt (Griffiths 1970: 101), but because he could not speak Egyptian, let alone translate hieroglyphs, he was relying mainly on previous authors and priestly accounts as his sources. This latter point is borne out by the fact that he often uses the phrase *"then they said"* (Power 2010: 87-88). Plutarch undoubtedly utilised Manetho (Griffiths 1970: 78) and knew the accounts of Diodorus and Herodotus. Though he was writing down an Egyptian myth he no doubt wanted it to be read and heard in Greece (Power 2010: 87). Plutarch realises that his primarily Greek audience may not know the names of the Egyptian gods so in common with other contemporary authors he equates them with Greek ones, thus Nut with Rhea, Geb with Cronus, Aroursis (the Elder Horus) with Apollo, and Seth with Typhon (Power 2010: 88). He first mentions Typhon when he describes him as being hostile to Isis and demented by ignorance and deceit (Griffiths 1970: 121). He relates how Typhon was born on the third intercalary day of the Egyptian calendar. The Egyptian calendar consisted of 12 months of 30 days and five intercalary days, known as *ḥryw rnpt* or "the days beyond the year" in Egyptian (von Bomhard 1999: xii). Typhon's birth is described: *"...as not in the right time or place, but bursting through with a blow, he leapt from his mother's side"* (Griffiths 1970: 137).

Plutarch begins the myth proper by telling us that Osiris became ruler of the Egyptians and his first task was to deliver them from their destitute and brutish ways. He achieved this by demonstrating to them the advantages of cultivation, giving them laws and teaching them to honour the gods. Having achieved such success within Egypt he resolved to travel the entire earth and attempt to civilise it. During his absence, Seth (equated in Plutarch's account with Typhon) attempted nothing revolutionary, because Isis, who had remained in Egypt, was vigilant and alert. On the return of Osiris, however, Seth contrived a treacherous plot against him, together with seventy-two co-conspirators (Plutarch 2003: 35, 13).

Seth, having secretly measured Osiris's body, had a richly ornamented chest of corresponding size made. He then threw a magnificent party to which he invited Osiris and his co-conspirators, and whilst the festivities were taking place he had the chest brought into the room where it was greatly admired by all. Seth then jestingly promised that he would present the chest to any man who would exactly fit into it when they lay down. Many of the party tried and all failed until Osiris was prevailed upon to lie in the chest, and, of course, he fitted perfectly. At this stage those who knew about the plot ran forward and slammed down the lid, which they then fastened shut. The chest was then set adrift in the river Nile (Plutarch 2003: 37, 13).

On hearing this news Isis was distraught and travelled far and wide asking for information about the chest and its whereabouts. At one stage she questioned some children who were able to tell her exactly where the chest was launched into the Nile (Plutarch 2003: 37, 14).

Interestingly, Plutarch puts in an aside to the main story here (Plutarch 2003: 39, 14) where he recounts that Osiris, before his death, had mistaken Nephthys for Isis and copulated with her; the result of this illicit union was Anubis, whom Nephthys, fearful of Seth's anger should he discover the illegitimate child, hides in the marshes. Isis hears of this and searches for the child, whom she eventually discovers and raises as her own, and Anubis becomes her guardian and attendant.

This may be a later addition to the story, perhaps added by the priests that Plutarch used as his sources in order to recast the negative view that people may have had of Nephthys in her role as wife of Seth.

Isis subsequently discovered that the chest had been cast up by the sea near Byblos where it had become incorporated into the trunk of a tree. This tree was greatly admired by the ruler of the country, who caused it to be chopped down and the trunk used as a pillar to support the roof of his house. Isis disguised herself and, using her skills, became nursemaid to the king's son until she was discovered by the queen. Isis then requested the pillar (Plutarch 2003: 41, 16) from which she liberated the coffin and opened it to reveal the body of Osiris. She then journeyed back to Egypt with the chest and body, which she hid in the desert. Plutarch (Plutarch 2003: 45, 18) says that Horus, who, was being reared in the vicinity of Buto, helped Isis in this task but later versions of the account (quoted for example by Armour 2001: 60, and Pinch 2002: 80) recount that only at this stage was Isis able to use her magic to warm and breathe life into Osiris's body long enough for her to become impregnated with his seed and eventually to give birth to Horus.

Unfortunately, Seth whilst hunting by moonlight came across the chest and, of course, recognised it. He opened the chest and cut Osiris's body into fourteen parts which he then distributed throughout Egypt. Isis, aided by her sister Nephthys, who appears to have forsaken her husband Seth, then searched for the fourteen parts. She succeeded in locating all but the phallus of Osiris, which Seth had thrown into the river and had been eaten by fishes. Undeterred, Isis made a replica of the phallus from clay (Plutarch 2003: 47, 18).

At this stage Plutarch recounts (Plutarch 2003: 47, 19) that Osiris came to Horus from the other world and exercised and trained him for battle. After a time, he asked Horus what he held to be the most noble of all things, to which Horus replied, *"to avenge one's father and mother for evil done to them."* Osiris now knew that Horus was ready to face Seth and claim his birthright. Interestingly, there is no mention in the hieroglyphic texts of this appearance of Osiris after his death and this appears to be something Plutarch has added in (Griffiths 1960: 104). Power suggests that this is a Greek-inspired section as no Greek story is complete without mention of a battle (2010: 96), a somewhat simplistic view! Plutarch gives only a cursory description (Plutarch 2003: 49, 19) of the battles between Horus and Seth which result in Horus claiming his birthright. A much more detailed account of their contending has already been given in Chapter 8.

This account, in common with other Egyptological work, takes the death of Cleopatra as its endpoint. However, a large body of evidence exists for the continued worship of Seth in Egypt during the Roman occupation. The Heidelberg Festival papyrus refers to a festival of Typhon in the second century C.E. (Youtie 1951: 189-192), and in the Dakhleh and Kharga oases there are abundant references in reliefs and texts to the worship of Seth into later Roman times (Frankfurter 1998: 113 and Ikram - personal communication) and of individuals who were holders of the office of "prophet of Seth" (Cruz-Uribe 2009: 207). The god was also invoked in ritual spells of the third and fourth centuries, for example:

"....this is the chief name of Typhon, at whom the ground, the depths of the sea, Hades, heaven, the sun, the moon, the visible chorus of stars, the whole universe all tremble, the name which, when it is uttered, forcibly brings gods and spirits to it...

The invocation

I call you who did first control gods' wrath

You who hold royal sceptre o'er the heavens,

You who are midpoint of the stars above,

You, master Typhon, you I call, who are

The dreaded sovereign o'er the firmament.

You who are fearful, awesome, threatening,

You who're obscure and irresistible

And hater of the wicked, you I call,

Typhon".

(Frankfurter 1998: 114).

During this period, festivals were held at Busiris and Lycopolis, where the making and eating of cakes with a relief of a bound ass upon them signified the ritual execration of Seth/Typhon (Frankfurter 1998: 54).

The worship of Seth in Egypt during the Roman period offers ample opportunity for further study.

The Ptolemies went to great lengths to preserve the traditional Egyptian religion and indeed either extensively embellished or newly constructed many temples throughout Egypt (Bowman 1986: 168). The major deities Amon, Isis, Re, Horus, Osiris, Anubis and Hathor continued to be ubiquitous and prominent but no doubt in the towns and villages of the country ordinary people continued their worship of their local gods. So, although we have at the present time no evidence to support this, Seth was probably still worshipped in the towns and villages traditionally associated with him e.g. certain Delta sites and Ombos in Upper Egypt. Certainly the aspect of Seth, popular during the New Kingdom, as protector of world order fighting Apophis is clearly seen in the oases but, on the other hand, he is clearly identified with the forces of chaos in the reliefs seen at Edfu (Cruz-Uribe 2009: 208).

This dichotomy may well be due to his association with 'things foreign' which told against him following the Assyrian and Persian invasions, and resulted in the prominence of the myths where he is portrayed as villain of the piece as illustrated by his roles in Papyrus Jumilhac, the Berlin Papyrus and upon the walls of the temple at Edfu. It is therefore not surprising that Plutarch and other Greek writers chose to highlight this aspect of Seth's character. The fact that they could not read hieroglyphs themselves and were reliant upon the tales told to them by the Egyptian priests allowed for accounts that were biased against Seth. One can imagine that a very different account of the god and his role in Egyptian religion may have been given by a priest of Seth hailing from Ombos compared to that given by a priest in Alexandria, Memphis or Thebes, who were probably the ones encountered by Plutarch and his compatriots.

11. SETH AND FOREIGN GODS

We have seen through the course of this account how Seth is associated with foreign gods, and this chapter seeks to expand upon this subject. The ancient Egyptians preferred their life to be an ordered one, one lived by *maat*, this concept that stood for the divinely-appointed order of things, the equilibrium of the universe with the world, the regular movements of the stars, the sun, the moon, the seasons and the sequence of time. *Maat* stood for social and religious order, the relationship between man and man, man and the gods and man and the dead (Watterson 1984: 60). Whilst the Egyptians could attempt to live this ordered life within Egypt, things foreign were a threat to this concept and, as such, were liable to be outside their control. The Seth-animal was imagined to live outside this controlled, inhabited world in the desert (Te Velde 1967: 111), a place that the Egyptians feared. Seth was also the god of other things that threatened *maat*: wind, storms, violent rain; it was an easy step to include things foreign as also belonging to his sphere of influence.

The Egyptians viewed foreigners as barbarians and as living in a miserable part of the world (compared to the land of Egypt), their water supply was wretched, which forced them to live a nomadic existence, and hence they had a restless nature and were always grumbling. Furthermore, their sexual conduct was reprehensible, Seth, of course, was also known as a god whose sexual temperament transgressed taboos (Kemboly 2010: 227) and who could exert his sexual appetite with either female or male as we have seen. Foreigners were also given to drunkeness, and were quarrelsome and murderous (Te Velde 1967: 111). The foreigner is the 'Other', a being that does not speak Egyptian and is a source of danger and disorder (Zivie-Coche 2011: 4).

An example of this attitude may be seen in the Middle Kingdom tale – 'The Story of Sinuhe'. Sinuhe, having fled Egypt due to a misunderstanding, became very successful whilst living in a foreign country, but in spite of this success more than anything he wished to return to Egypt:

"Whichever god decreed this flight, have mercy, bring me home! Surely you will let me see the place in which my heart dwells! What is more important than that my corpse be buried in the land in which I was born? Come to my aid! What if the happy event should occur? May god pity me! May he act so as to make happy the end of one whom he punished! May his heart ache for one whom he forced to live abroad! If he is truly appeased today, may he hearken to the prayer of one far away! May he return one whom he made roam the earth to the place from which he carried him off!"
(Lichtheim 1973: 228-229).

Many of the places associated with Seth, e.g. Ombos and the eastern Delta lay on the borders of the desert, often on caravan routes which would have enabled contact with foreigners to have taken place. One of the first areas where this occurred was at the border of the Libyan desert particularly at the oases located there. The Libyan god of the oases was Ash. He was depicted as a hawk deity, and the Egyptians identified him as the god of the Libu and Tinhu tribes, who were known as the 'people of the oases' (Hart 1986: 33). Ash was also 'Lord of the Desert' and this allowed an obvious identification between him and Seth in what Wilkinson (1999: 282) describes as one of the first examples of syncretism. Religious syncretism is defined as the blending of two or more religious systems into a new system, or, as in this case, the incorporation into a religious tradition of beliefs from unrelated traditions. Once Seth had been thus associated with a foreign god to the west of the country, it is easy to see that in the east, where there would have been contact with the semitic-speaking peoples and the Hittites, a similar situation arose with their gods, Baal and Teshub respectively, who demonstrated properties in common with Seth. We will now take a closer look at these relationships.

The first of these gods that we will examine is Ash. Apart from Ash's role as 'Lord of the Desert', Hart also suggests (1986: 34) that he was the original god of Ombos prior to the arrival of Seth as its major deity. Certainly by Dynasty 2 a seal-impression of Peribsen from Abydos (Petrie 1901: 179, Wilkinson 1999: 263) shows Ash with the body of a human and a Seth-like head wearing the white crown of Upper Egypt and carrying a *was*-sceptre.

The *was*-sceptre quickly became part of depictions initially of, Seth and then of the rest of the Egyptian male gods (it was rarely held by female gods) and eventually of the pharaohs. The sceptre was a symbol of power and dominion. The top part of the sceptre was thought to represent the Seth animal (Wainwright 1932: 171). An immense *was*-sceptre was found in Seth's temple at Ombos (Petrie and Quibell 1896: 68, Gordon, Gordon and Schwabe 1995: 189).

Whilst Seth appears to have taken over from Ash as 'Lord of the Desert and Oases', a single representation of Ash is known from the Ptolemaic (or possibly Roman) period. In the Brighton Museum there is an elaborately decorated cartonnage mummy-case. One of the divinities depicted upon the case is a god with three heads, those of a lion, a serpent wearing the crown of Upper Egypt and a vulture. The accompanying inscription refers to this god as *'Ash with many faces'* (Shorter 1925: 78). It seems surprising that after so many years Ash should be depicted, but a possible explanation is that during the Saite revival, which revered anything that belonged to the Old Kingdom, his cult may have been revived.

Baal was the chief god of the Western semitic-speaking peoples; his cult had spread from Ugarit in Syria where he was a prominent god of the sky and storms (Hart 1986: 50; West 1999: 85). He was initially brought to Egypt by the Hyksos and probably because of his association with storms, a trait he shared with Seth, and the fact that he was a foreign god, he became associated with Seth, so that his name in hieroglyphs was written with a Seth determinative.

From the time of Amenhotep II, there existed a temple dedicated to Baal at Peru-nefer, the harbour city quarter of Memphis (Burkard and Thissen 2003: 61) where he was worshipped by sailors as the vanquisher of Yamm, the god of the sea (Hart 1986: 50). Indeed because Baal was regarded by the Egyptians as a manifestation of Seth, they now endowed Seth with a new function and depicted him fighting the sea (Te Velde 1967: 123). However, Baal as a god of the Western semitic-speakers is not forgotten and Gardiner (1932: 82-85) relates the taking of the town of Joppa by Thutmosis III. In Gardiner's translation of the account Seth functions as the god of the inhabitants of the town, and as such he is expected by the citizens to guarantee their success over the Egyptians. After capturing the town, the Egyptian commander reports to the pharaoh that Amun has delivered Joppa to the Egyptians. Thus the scribe who wrote this report saw Amun as the Egyptian god, 'Lord of Egypt', and Seth in his role as 'Lord of foreign lands' as the god of the Western semitic-speakers. In actual fact, the god of the inhabitants of Joppa would have been Baal.

Baal is not only a god of thunder but is also very strong. He is also the god of the cloud travelling and the 'Lord of the earth', whilst Seth is a 'Lord of strength'. Both are often referred to as strong oxen (Zandee 1963: 149), and it is easy to see the parallels that the Egyptians were able to draw between the two gods.

Teshub was initially the Hurrian god of sky and storm; his Hittite name was Tarhuntas (with some minor variants). He is usually depicted as a man holding a triple thunderbolt and an axe or mace. During the Ramesside period the Egyptians had a great deal of contact with the Hittites, initially fighting for control of modern Syria and eventually, in the time of Ramesses II, concluding a peace treaty (Kitchen 1982: 75-79). In this treaty the Egyptian supreme deity is Re and that of the Hittites, Teshub, who is represented as Seth (Kitchen 1982: 78); moreover, within the treaty the Hittites enumerated several gods who were totally unknown within Egypt, so they are all called Seth e.g. Seth of Zippalanda, Seth of Pittiyark, Seth of Hissaspa (Te Velde 1967: 119). In the Hittite version of the treaty, Re is referred to as Shamash (the Libyan name for Re) and Seth as Teshub (Langdon and Gardiner 1920: 187).

Anat was a warrior-goddess of the Syrians and was first promoted by the Hyksos and then, not surprisingly, by the Ramessides. She was identified (together with her sister, Astarte – see below) as a daughter of Re and wife of Seth. The Ramesside monarchs saw these two goddesses as protectors of the monarch in combat so, for example, Ramesses III uses Anat and Astarte as his shield on the battlefield and Ramesses II's dog was named *"Anat in vigour"* (Hart 1986: 18). Ramesses II also named one of his daughters Bint-Anat ('daughter of Anat') (Dodson and Hilton 2004: 170). The Western Semites identified Anat as the consort of Baal and presumably, once the Egyptians had established the connection between Baal and Seth, this led to the identification of Anat as wife of Seth. Anat features in a homosexual episode with Seth in the Chester Beatty Papyrus VII (Gardiner 1935: 61-63). Here, Anat dressed as a man, is disporting herself in a stream and is seen by the sun-god being taken from behind by Seth. Some of Seth's seed (semen) hits the sun god between the eyes and causes him to be ill, so he lies down upon his bed and when Anat visits him he asks:

What is the matter with you, Anat the divine, you the victorious, woman acting as a warrior, clad as men and girt as women? I came home in the evening, and I know that you have come to free Seth from the seed.
(Manniche 1987: 54).

This homosexual aspect of Seth we have already seen in his encounter with Horus (see previously) and, as homosexuality was generally not encouraged (Manniche 1987: 22), possibly expresses in a different manner the 'otherness' of Seth. Alternatively, it could just be a way of expressing his virility aznd his power and might over others.

Astarte, another warrior-goddess of the Syrians, was primarily associated by the Egyptians with horses and chariots. On a stela set up near the Sphinx, she is described as being delighted with the equestrian skill of Amenhotep II (Hart 1986: 35). She too was a daughter of Re and wife of Seth (Watterson 1984: 115).

In Greek mythology, Typhon was the child of Mother Earth and Tartarus (the place of torture in Hades). He was the largest monster ever born, with an ass' head (an animal often associated with Seth, Te Velde 1967: 26), and immensely long arms that ended in countless serpents' heads; more serpents comprised his legs and he possessed vast wings which blotted out the sun. From his eyes he flashed fire, and from his mouth he belched flaming rocks. After his birth he headed towards Olympus, causing the gods to flee in terror to Egypt where they disguised themselves as animals so that they would not be noticed amongst the Egyptian gods (Watterson 1984: 116-117). Zeus eventually overcame him with his thunderbolts, and the monster then fled to Sicily where Zeus threw Mount Etna on top of him.

So, like Seth, Typhon was associated with violence and turmoil, and he was associated with the colour red due to his having become a volcano, whilst Seth was associated with the colour through his role as god of the desert (*dšrt* - the red land) (Te Velde 1967: 62).

Initially Seth, due to his nature and his murder of Osiris, was seen as a god apart by the Egyptians, and this meant he was ideally placed to have anything that was foreign to them placed under his aegis. At this stage, probably up to the end of the Ramesside period, his role was probably seen as a mediator between things foreign and the Egyptian religion, hence his identification with Ash, Baal, and Teshub. Unfortunately, following the Assyrian and to some extent the Persian invasions of Egypt, things foreign were looked at in a new unfavourable light. The previously self-assured goodwill shown by the Egyptians to foreigners and things foreign turned to hatred (Te Velde 1967: 139). The Egyptians were faced with a situation where the chosen country (*B mri*) could be occupied and plundered by foreigners, and not surprisingly, this dread and discontent were unloaded upon the traditional god of foreigners, Seth (Te Velde 1967: 143; Zivie-Coche 2011: 2).

12. CONCLUDING REMARKS

We have seen that Seth was an ancient god, first worshipped in the region of Naqada at Nebet – 'gold town' – giving rise to the epithet of Seth, *Nebty* – 'he of gold town'. His worship must have also spread to other centres in Upper Egypt, two major sites being Hypselis, the capital of the 11th Upper Egyptian nome which was known to the Egyptians as *Sha-sehetep* – 'the pig-is-pacified', the pig here probably representing Seth (as it was an animal associated with him (Te Velde 1967: 22), and Oxyrhynchus, the capital of the 19th nome of Upper Egypt. All of these places are close to the desert and so one can readily imagine that the worship of a god associated with the desert would have sprung up amongst the inhabitants. The desert was something to be feared and its god would need to be placated.

At the same time as various cult centres were being established in Seth's name, Horus (a falcon god) was also being worshipped in both Lower Egypt at Behdet and Upper Egypt at Nekhen (later called by the Greeks, Hierakonpolis). It is suggested that Horus originated in the Delta and his worship made its way to Nekhen when some of his followers sailed south (Watterson 1984: 99). Nekhen became strong and eventually (as discussed in Chapter 2) under King Scorpion the followers of the hawk (Horus) defeated the followers of Seth.

Once the country as a whole was united under Narmer, then Horus became the royal god and this was remembered in the king's 'Horus Name'. Another part of the titulary was the 'Golden Horus' name, so called because as a monogram it features a hawk sitting upon the hieroglyph for gold:

As discussed earlier it has been suggested either that this represents Horus' victory over Seth, as the hieroglyph for gold (*nebu*) symbolises Seth due to his worship at Nebet, or that it indicates a concept of the king being a falcon made of gold (Watterson 1984: 100.) However, could it be that like the 'Two Ladies' name it was a way of saying that the king was recognised as being the god of both Lower Egypt (Horus) and Upper Egypt (Seth)? Certainly, as we have seen in the Pyramid Texts, there are numerous mentions of the 'Mounds of Horus' and the 'Mounds of Seth', these being taken as representing the two realms of Egypt and the towns and villages of Lower and Upper Egypt respectively, and indicating that even after the unification the Ancient Egyptians still recognised this division of the realm into two. The queens of the early dynasties, as we have also seen, recognised this duality in their titles of: 'She-who-unites-the Two-Lords' (i.e. Horus and Seth) and 'She-who-sees-Horus and Seth.'

It seems to me that the story of the conflict between the followers of Horus and those of Seth got mixed in with the myths of Osiris and Horus. Osiris was originally worshipped as a fertility-god and this can be seen in the fact that he is usually depicted with flesh coloured black or green. The first of these colours being that of the rich dark earth of the Nile valley came to represent the colour of resurrection and eternal life; the second, that of luxuriant vegetation, and thus of life itself (Wilkinson 1994: 116). The ruling king was recognised as Horus during life but became Osiris upon his death, and his successor needed to become Horus in turn. The old king who in life had mediated between his people and the powers of nature now merged with these powers upon his death. As Osiris he is king of the underworld but represented in the growing grain, the rising of the Nile during its inundation and in the earth itself. Much of the Pyramid Texts were concerned with this process and represent the writing down of an age-old oral tradition which presumably ensured that under normal circumstances the eldest son of the previous king would succeed to the throne.

Into this mix the struggles between the followers of Horus and those of Seth get thrown and I believe that the accounts that we have in the Chester Beatty papyrus, and the subsequent Plutarch account that is surely based on this, and the account from the Shabaka stone represent two different views of this struggle. Whilst both of these accounts date to later periods in Egyptian history, the likelihood is that they represent stories that originate from much earlier times. The first seeks to portray Seth in a bad light (although it is of interest that, at the very end, rather than being treated as a defeated foe, Re requests that Seth be allowed to live with him in heaven – presumably paving the way for his role in the nightly defeat of Apophis), and the second seems much more of an account of a legal dispute which is decided by Geb. In this account, rather than the conflict being resolved by a test of strength, it is resolved by law. Initially, Egypt is divided equally between the two protagonists, possibly reflecting the situation when Upper Egypt was mainly associated with Seth and Lower Egypt with Horus. But then, in the account, Geb has a change of heart and awards the whole of Egypt to Horus as the son of his son (i.e. Osiris), but, rather than this resulting in conflict, the account is at pains to stress that Horus and Seth made peace and united to ensure the completeness of Egypt.

To the Egyptians this meant that every king was an embodiment of both Horus and Seth. As we have seen earlier, Hatshepsut put this into the following words:

"I united the two lords, that is, their parts,

by ruling like the son of Isis (i.e. Horus)

and being strong like the son of Nut (i.e. Seth)."

As Assmann (1996: 44) puts it, the contrast between Seth and Horus symbolises a change from old disorder to new stability. In the mythic version of this change, order triumphs over chaos, rule over anarchy and law over force. But this alternative is not cast aside and demonised rather it is seen as a necessary part of the whole. Life must have both positive and negative aspects. The king must demonstrate the guile, cunning and respect for his parents shown by Horus, on the one hand, and also the brute strength, ferocity and bloody-mindedness of Seth, on the other. It is likely that during this early Dynastic Period Seth was regarded as a benevolent god by a large part of the population, certainly around the site of Nebet and also in the Delta, where possibly many of his supporters may have been pushed following the success of the 'Followers of Horus', and also at the oases of the Libyan Desert, where he was known as the 'Lord of the Oases'. Possibly because of his role here, he also became known as the god of the eastern deserts and became associated with all the frightening elements that the Egyptians believed emanated from the desert; wind, rain, storm and thunder. As the Egyptian word for desert (*smyt*) can also stand for foreign land so Seth also added 'Lord of Foreign Lands' to his titles.

I believe that Seth, in this role of 'Lord of Foreign Lands', was still seen very much as an Egyptian god, as Foreign Minister one might say rather than as a Foreign Ambassador. This is important because it means that his first accountability was towards Egypt rather than towards foreigners. It is in this role that Seth was identified during the Hyksos Period and this explains why on their expulsion he was not vilified. To the Egyptians, he had carried out his role as Foreign Minister and, whilst being associated with the foreigners, he had protected Egypt's position within the universe. This probably also explains why the two consorts that the Hyksos had given him, Anat and Astarte, also continued to be worshipped by the Egyptians, achieving particular popularity under the Ramessides.

Certainly, following the Hyksos expulsion, the worship of Seth within the Delta region must have continued because, as we have seen, the Ramessides recognised him as their family god with Seti I and II being named after him and Ramesses II naming one of his army divisions after the god. During the New Kingdom, this dichotomy in Seth's role continued; as we have discussed earlier it can be seen in the reliefs in the tomb of Thuthmosis III depicting the Amduat.

All this appears to me to confirm that the Egyptians could see Seth in two lights. Te Velde (1967: 27-63) sees Seth as an evil figure, citing not only his murder of Osiris but also the circumstances of his birth (when he burst through his mother's side), and his attempted homosexual relationship with Horus as evidence of this, but Kemboly (2010: 244) believes that the Egyptians saw Seth as someone who challenged authority, the establishment, the status quo, social conventions etc. I would tend to agree with this view that suggests that Seth possibly represented a principle through which society kept itself open to criticism and challenges in order to improve and to be able to tolerate a certain amount of disorder.

Much of the demonization of Seth comes in the Late Period of Egyptian history, and I believe that this is due to the fact that following the invasion of the country by the Assyrians, which saw for the first time Thebes itself sacked, the Egyptians believed that Seth had failed in his role of Foreign Minister. He had not put his role as representative of Egypt first and consequently the ravages inflicted by the Assyrians were laid squarely at his door. As Te Velde puts it (1967: 143):

"In late times, the Egyptians were faced with the enigma that the chosen country could yet be occupied and plundered by foreigners. Their dread and discontent were unloaded not upon the whole pantheon, but upon the traditional god of foreigners, who had always had a special and precarious place in the pantheon."

As Gunn and Gardiner (1918: 45) state:

"The persecution of Set during the Saite and later times, when his image appears to have been systematically excised from the monuments, was probably the result of a religious revival, when all old prejudices and hostilities were aroused by a wave of acute nationalism."

The Assyrian invasion may thus be regarded as the historical turning point in the worship and vilification of Seth. This Late Period positioning of the god changed how he was referred to and resulted in the bad side of his character being exaggerated. Thus, when Plutarch was gathering the material for his *Moralia*, the priests that he spoke to would have portrayed Seth solely in this negative light, and as a consequence Plutarch records the murder of Osiris by Seth and the subsequent struggle between Horus and Seth as the only examples of Seth's role in Egyptian religion, something that was to have long-standing effects on how Seth was viewed by early Egyptologists. The identification of his place in the ancient Egyptian pantheon was also not helped by the attempts of early Egyptologists to fit Egyptian religion into a Christian format. In this scenario a Devil was required and to the early Egyptologists Seth fitted that bill! So, to answer the question posed initially by this accounty: Seth – a misrepresented god in the ancient Egyptian pantheon? Yes, by Plutarch, and as a consequence by the majority of Egyptologists even up to modern times; but by the Egyptians themselves? No, they saw Seth as part of the pantheon representing the dualistic thought that is very much part of ancient Egyptian processes. From a 'state-religion' point of view Seth's murder of Osiris is not to be understood as evil, Osiris had to be killed in order for him to become King of the Underworld, Horus had to be challenged for the throne in order to prove the legitimacy of his succession and to restore peace, justice and piety (the whole concept of *maat*) to the land. That the Egyptians understood this can be seen in the fact that Seth's action is judged by the rest of the gods but he is not destroyed, rather he is reconciled with Horus and the attributes of both gods ideally should be embodied within the role of the king.

Te Velde was keen to label Seth as a 'god of confusion', but this is too bald a characterisation. Certainly Seth is a complex character but this probably endeared him to the Egyptians who probably could see aspects of themselves within him. His quarrelsome nature, his strength and his might and, indeed, his liking for drink and sex were all things that they could readily identify within themselves and their families and friends and may well have contributed to his popularity which probably reached its zenith under the Ramessides. Subsequently his popularity waned, certainly in 'state-religion' terms and within the Nile Valley probably due to his identification with 'things foreign' when these were not popular with the Egyptians. But, as I have demonstrated, further from the main centres of religion in, for example, the oases his popularity appears unaffected. Perhaps within the general populace Seth always held a position of particular affection and rather than being a 'god of confusion' perhaps a better epithet would be that of a 'complex god'.

APPENDIX 1: THE PYRAMID TEXTS

In all three appendices the utterance or spell in which Seth is mentioned has been given in full unless it is a lengthy one in which case the relevant section(s) have been extracted and reproduced. Where the meaning of the utterance or spell is not obvious an attempt has been made to give the context in which the particular utterance or spell is involved and an explanation of its contents.

The negative texts that mention Seth number 69 which represent 9.1% of the total texts.

1. Utterance 29

A text for the use of dried incense

"*O King, I have come and I bring to you the 'Eye of Horus'. May you provide your face with it, that it may cleanse you, its perfume being upon you. The perfume of the 'Eye of Horus' is on this King it removes your efflux and protects you from the sweat of the hand of Seth* (Allen translates this as '*defend you from the inundation of the hand of Seth*). *O Osiris the King, may the intact 'Eye of Horus' belong to you, the 'Eye of Horus' being intact, intact!*" (Allen 2005: 254; Faulkner 2007: 6).

2. Utterance 47

This is concerned with the 'Ritual of Offering' – constituents of the preliminary repast – a phrase to utter as the constituent is presented.

"*O Osiris the King, take the 'Eye of Horus' which was wrested from Seth and which you shall take to your mouth, with which you shall split open your mouth – wine, an* ḥȝts-*jar of white* mnw-*stone.*" (Allen 2005: 21; Faulkner 2007: 10).

3. Utterance 54

Virtually identical to Utterance 47 (Allen 2005: 21; Faulkner 2007: 11).

4. Utterance 57F

The following spells were to be recited as weapons; garments and various insignia were presented.

"[lost] *Seth – a* pḏt *bow.*" (Allen 2005: 320; Faulkner 2007: 12).

5. Utterance 57G

"*I give* [lost] *the heart of Seth* – [lost]" (Allen 2005: 320; Faulkner 2007: 12).

6. Utterance 57O

"*O Osiris the King, take the 'Eye of Horus' which he rescued from Seth when he snatched it – an* ḫbzt-*tail.*" (Allen 2005: 318; Faulkner 2007: 13).

7. Utterance 57Q

"*O Osiris the King, take the 'Eye of Horus' on account of which Seth has rejoiced – a* mṯpn(t)-*dagger.*" (Allen 2005: 318; Faulkner 2007: 13).

8. Utterance 57R

"*O Osiris the King, receive the 'Eye of Horus' which he wrested from Seth – a* mȝgsw -*dagger.*" (Allen 2005: 318; Faulkner 2007: 13).

9. Utterance 57S

"*O Osiris the King, receive the 'Eye of Horus' which he rescued from Seth when he snatched it – an* ḫbzt -*tail.*" (Allen 2005: 318; Faulkner 2007: 13).

10. Utterance 59A

"*O Osiris the King, take the 'Eye of Horus' which he saved from Seth when he snatched it – an* ḫbzt -*tail.*" (Allen 2005: 318; Faulkner 2007: 14).

11. Utterance 61

"*O Osiris the King, take the foreleg of Seth which Horus has torn off – four-weave god's linen.*" (Allen 2005: 318; Faulkner 2007: 14).

12. Utterance 64

"*Osiris Neith, you have been swept from him; look you have blinded him.*" (Allen 2005: 318)

"*O Osiris the King, you are secluded because of him; behold, you have brought him to naught – a* ḏsr -*mace.*" (Faulkner 2007: 15).

'Him', in both of these contexts is referring to Seth.

13. Utterance 69

"*O Osiris the King, take the finger of Seth which causes the white 'Eye of Horus' to see – a* smȝ -*staff.*" (Allen 2005: 319; Faulkner 2007: 16).

14. Utterance 70

"*O Osiris the King, take the white 'Eye of Horus' which illumines the tip of the finger of Seth – 2 lumps of electrum.*" (Allen 2005: 319; Faulkner 2007: 16).

15. Utterance 71E

"*O Osiris the King, take the hand of Nephthys, prevent her from putting it on them (? 'the followers of Seth') – a crook.*" (Allen 2005: 319; Faulkner 2007: 16).

16. Utterance 88

Used in the next three instances when placing the offering-table on the ground.

"*O Osiris the King, take the 'Eye of Horus', prevent him (Seth) from trampling it – a tw-loaf.*" (Allen 2005: 23; Faulkner 2007: 20).

17. Utterance 89

"*O Osiris the King, take the 'Eye of Horus' which he (Seth) has pulled out – an* itḫ *-loaf.*" (Allen 2005: 23; Faulkner 2007: 21).

18. Utterance 90

"*O Osiris the King take the 'Eye of Horus', for little is that which Seth has eaten of it – a jar of strong ale.*" (Allen 2005: 23; Faulkner 2007: 21).

19. Utterance 97

Place at his left hand.

"*O Osiris the King, this is the 'Eye of Horus' which he has demanded from Seth.*" (Allen 2005: 259; Faulkner 2007: 22).

20. Utterance 111

Used in the next 12 utterances before the constituents of the 'Presentation of the Repast'.

"*O Osiris the King, take the 'Eye of Horus' which Seth has trampled – a* tw *-loaf.*" (Allen 2005: 24; Faulkner 2007: 24).

21. Utterance 135

"*O Osiris the King, take the 'Eye of Horus' which is in front of Seth – meat of the forepart.*" (Allen 2005: 25; Faulkner 2007: 27).

22. Utterance 136

"*O Osiris the King, take the severed heads of the followers of Seth – a* ro-*bird.*" (Allen 2005: 25; Faulkner 2007: 27).

23. Utterance 145

"*O Osiris the King, take the 'Eye of Horus', for little is that which Seth has eaten of it – 2 bowls of strong ale.*" (Allen 2005: 26; Faulkner 2007: 29).

24. Utterance 160

"*O Osiris the King, take the 'Eye of Horus' which he has rescued from Seth – 2 bowls of* išt-*fruit.*" (Allen 2005: 26; Faulkner 2007: 31).

25. Utterance 161

"*O Osiris the King, take the white 'Eye of Horus' and prevent him (Seth) from wearing it – 2 bowls of white* sšt-*fruit.*"Allen has "*...prevent him from putting it on as a headband.*" (Allen 2005: 27; Faulkner 2007: 31).

26. Utterance 162

"*O Osiris the King, take the green 'Eye of Horus' and prevent him (Seth) from wearing it – 2 bowls of green* sšt-*fruit.*" (Faulkner 2007: 31).

27. Utterance 163

"*O Osiris the King, take the 'Eye of Horus' and prevent him (Seth) from tearing it out – 2 bowls of bruised wheat.*"Allen again has "*...prevent him from putting it on as a headband.*" (Allen 2005: 27; Faulkner 2007: 31).

28. Utterance 164

Faulkner has this as identical to Utterance 163 (Faulkner 2007: 31), but Allen translates it "*Osiris Unis, accept Horus's eye: prevent him (i.e. Seth) from wrenching it away.*" (Allen 2005: 27).

29. Utterance 166

"*O Osiris the King, take the 'Eye of Horus' which they (? 'the followers of Seth') have licked – 2 bowls of* zizyphus-*fruit.*" (Allen 2005: 27; Faulkner 2007: 31).

30. Utterance 168

"*O Osiris the King, take the 'Eye of Horus' and prevent him (Seth) from entrapping it – 2 bowls of carob beans.*" (Allen 2005: 27; Faulkner 2007: 32)

31. Utterance 192

"Take the 'Eye of Horus' which he (Seth) has torn out – I give Horus to you – 2 bowls of npȝt-*cakes."* (Allen 2005: 257; Faulkner 2007: 35).

32. Utterance 219

The king is identified with Osiris. A lengthy text from which the following passage is extracted:

"O Seth, this one here is your brother Osiris, who has been caused to be restored that he may live and punish you; if he lives, this King will live; if he does not die, this King will not die; if he is not destroyed, this King will not be destroyed; if he does not mourn, this King will not mourn; if he mourns, this King will mourn." (Allen 2005: 35; Faulkner 2007: 47).

33. Utterance 222

The king joins the sun-god. A lengthy text where the king is being likened to both Horus and Seth from which the following passage is extracted:

"Provide yourself with the 'Great of Magic', even Seth dwelling in Nubet, *'Lord of Upper Egypt'; nothing is lost to you, nothing has ceased for you; behold, you are more renowned and more powerful than the gods of Upper Egypt and their spirits. O you whom the Pregnant One ejected (gave birth to), you have terminated the night, being equipped as Seth who broke forth violently, even you whom Isis has favoured."* (Allen 2005: 39-40; Faulkner 2007: 50).

The text here is referring to Seth's supposed birth when, rather than being born in the normal manner, *"he broke through his mother's side and leapt forth"* (Te Velde 1967: 27).

34. Utterance 254

The king arrives in the sky and again is likened to both Horus and Seth. A lengthy text from which the following two passages are extracted:

"...she confirms my land in the two 'Fields of Offerings', and I give judgement in the heavens between the two Contestants (i.e. Horus and Seth).....That which appertains to my throne, which I have taken and lifted up, is this which my father Shu gave me in the presence of Seth." (Allen 2005: 43-45; Faulkner 2007: 64).

35. Utterance 260

The king claims his rights as Horus. A medium length text from which the following passage has been extracted:

"I put a stop to the affair in On, for I go forth today in the real form of a living spirit, that I may break up the fight and cut off the turbulent ones." (Allen 2005: 46-47; Faulkner 2007: 69).

This refers to the fight between Seth and Horus where it was said that *"The earth was torn up when the Rivals fought, and their feet scooped out the 'Pool of the God' which is in On"* (Faulkner 2007: 70, note 4).

36. Utterance 356

Horus and Geb support the king against Seth

"O King, Horus has come that he may seek you. He has caused Thoth to turn back the followers of Seth for you, and he has brought them all together. He has driven back the heart of Seth for you, for you are greater than he. You have gone forth in front of him, your nature is superior to his; Geb has seen your nature and has set you in your place. Geb has brought your two sisters to your side for you, namely Isis and Nephthys; Horus has caused the gods to join you, so that they may be brotherly to you in your name of Snwt-*shrines, and not reject you in your name of 'Two Conclaves'. He has caused the gods to protect you, and Geb has put his sandal on the head of your foe* (a typical act of superiority over a conquered enemy), *who flinches from you. Your son Horus has smitten him, he has wrested his 'Eye' from him and given it to you; you have a soul by means of it, you have power by means of it at the head of the spirits. Horus has caused you to lay hold of your foes, and there is none of them who shall escape your name of 'Soul of the King's litter'; Nut has placed you as a god to Seth in your name of God; your mother Nut has spread herself over you in her name of* St-pt; *Horus has laid hold of Seth and has set him under you on your behalf so that he may lift you up and quake beneath you as the earth quakes, you being holier than he in your name of Sacred Land. Horus has caused you to lay hold of him with your hand, lest he get away from you.*

O Osiris the King, Horus has protected you, he has acted on behalf of his spirit in you, so that you may be content in your name of 'Contented Spirit'." (Allen 2005: 72-73; Faulkner 2007: 113-114).

37. Utterance 357

The gods help the king. A lengthy text from which the followings passages are extracted:

"Horus has come that he may recognise you; he has smitten Seth for you whilst he was bound, and you are his fate. Horus has driven him off for you, for you are greater than he; he swims bearing you; he lifts up one who is greater than he in you, and his followers have seen you, that your strength is greater than his, so that they cannot thwart you....Horus has wrested his 'Eye' from Seth and has given it to you...and it is Horus who will make good what Seth has done to you." (Allen 2005: 73-74; Faulkner 2007: 114-115).

38. Utterance 359

The king crosses to the 'Beyond'. A lengthy text from which the following passages have been extracted:

"Horus has cried out because of his 'Eye', Seth has cried out because of his testicles, and there leaps up the 'Eye of Horus', who had fallen on yonder side of the 'Winding Waterway', so that it may protect itself from Seth. Thoth saw it on yonder side of the 'Winding Waterway' when the 'Eye of Horus' leapt up on yonder side of the 'Winding Waterway' and fell on Thoth's wing on yonder side of the 'Winding Waterway'. O you gods who cross over on the wing of Thoth to yonder side of the 'Winding Waterway', to the eastern side of the sky, in order to dispute with Seth about this 'Eye of Horus': I will cross with you upon the wing of Thoth to yonder side of the 'Winding Waterway', to the eastern side of the sky, and I will dispute with Seth about this 'Eye of Horus'... for I am bound for yonder distant castle of the owners of doubles who worship Re there in the 'Mounds of Horus' and the 'Mounds of Seth'.

My face is washed by the gods, male and female; Imsety, Hapy, Duamutef and Kebhsenuf are at my right side, on which is Horus who smote Dndrw in front of his two pillars; Nephthys and Hnt-n-irty are at my left side, on which is Seth." (Allen 2005: 76-77; Faulkner 2007: 116-117).

39. Utterance 372

Horus restores the king.

"O Osiris the King, awake! Horus has caused Thoth to bring your foe (i.e. Seth) to you, he has set you on his back that he may not thwart you; take your place upon him, go up and sit on him, do not let him escape from you. Go down, being holier than he, and set danger against him. Horus has cut off the strong arms of your foes and Horus has brought them to you cut up, Horus has driven off their doubles from them." (Allen 2005: 83; Faulkner 2007: 123).

40. Utterance 427

An address to the sky-god Nut.

"O Nut. Spread yourself over your son Osiris the King that you may conceal him from Seth; protect him, O Nut. Have you come that you may conceal your son? I have indeed come that I may protect this great one." (Allen 2005: 103; Faulkner 2007: 141).

41. Utterance 437

A long 'resurrection' text from which the following passages have been extracted:

"Awake for Horus! Arise against Seth! If you walk, Horus will walk; if you speak, Seth will speak. Seth is brotherly toward you as the 'Great One of On'." (Allen 2005: 105-106; Faulkner 2007: 144).

42. Utterance 455

A 'purification' text.

"The canals are filled, the waterways are flooded by means of the purification which issued from Osiris. O you sm-priest, you patrician, you ten great ones of the Palace, you ten 'Great Ones of On', you 'Great Ennead', sit down and see the purification of my father this King as one purified with zmn and with natron, the saliva which issued from the mouth of Horus, the spittle which issued from the mouth of Seth, wherewith Horus is purified, wherewith the evil which was on him, which Seth did against him, is cast out on the ground; wherewith Seth is purified, and the evil which was on him, which Horus did against him, is cast out on the ground; wherewith the King is purified, and the evil which was on him is cast out on the ground, being what Nwt.k-nw did against you in company with your spirits." (Allen 2005: 110; Faulkner 2007: 151).

43. Utterance 477

Osiris is raised from the dead.

"The sky reels, the earth quakes, Horus comes, Thoth appears, they raise Osiris from upon his side and make him stand up in front of the 'Two Enneads'. Remember, Seth, and put in your heart this word which Geb spoke, this threat which the gods made against you in the 'Mansion of the

Prince' in On because you threw Osiris to earth, when you said, O Seth: 'I have never done this to him', so that you might have power thereby, having been saved, and that you might prevail over Horus; when you said, O Seth: 'It was he who attacked me', when there came into being this his name of 'Earth-attacker', when you said, O Seth: 'It was he who kicked me', when there came into being this his name of Orion, long of leg and lengthy of stride, who presides over Upper Egypt. Raise yourself, O Osiris for Seth has raised himself, he has heard the threat of the gods who spoke about the god's father. Isis has your arm, O Osiris, Nephthys has your hand, so go between them. The sky is given to you, the earth is given to you, and the 'Field of Rushes', the 'Mounds of Horus', and the 'Mounds of Seth'; the towns are given to you and the nomes assembled for you by Atum, and he who speaks about it is Geb." (Allen 2005: 129-130; Faulkner 2007: 164).*

44. Utterance 482

A 'resurrection' text, which includes the following passage:

"He smites him (Seth) who smote you, he binds him who bound you, he sets him under your eldest daughter who is in Kdm." (Allen 2005: 130-131; Faulkner 2007: 169).

45. Utterance 485B

The dead Osiris is sought and found.

"The 'Two Enneads' have found a protector who is at his side, the 'Two Enneads' have not found someone who lags behind him. Geb comes with his power upon him and his yellow eyes in his face that he may smite you and examine the lands in search of Osiris, and he has found him thrown down upon his side in Ghsty. O Osiris, stand up for your father Geb that he may protect you from Seth; Nu I have protected Osiris from his brother Seth, I am he who bound his legs and bound his arms and who threw him down on his side in T3-rw." (Allen 2005: 133; Faulkner 2007: 172).

46. Utterance 497

A 'resurrection' text.

"O King, stand up and sit down, throw off the earth which is on you! Get rid of these two arms behind you, namely Seth! The 'Eye of Horus' will come to you at the ten-day festival while you yearn after it." (Allen 2005: 144-145; Faulkner 2007: 176).

47. Utterance 519

A number of texts including the following phrase:

"..I will stand up when I have taken possession of my blessedness in your presence, just as Horus took possession of his father's house from his father's brother Seth in the presence of Geb." (Allen 2005: 161; Faulkner 2007: 193).

48. Utterance 524

A text concerning the 'Eye of Horus' which includes the following phrases:

"I am not Seth who carried it off...I have blocked the roads of Seth...I found it in On, I took it from the head of Seth in that place where they fought." (Allen 2005: 162-163; Faulkner 2007: 196-197).

49. Utterance 532

An 'Osirian text' which includes the following phrases:

"...they have found Osiris his brother Seth having laid him low in Nedit...and Seth will never be free of carrying you, O Osiris. Wake up for Horus, stand up against Seth..." (Allen 2005: 165; Faulkner 2007: 199-200).

50. Utterance 534

A lengthy spell for the king's tomb which includes the following phrases:

"May there be benefited the tomb of him whom Horus respects and Seth protects. May Seth not come with this his evil coming; do not open your arms to him, but let there be said to him this: his name of 'Hare'. Go to the 'Mountains of Blackness'; go northward, go to Hnt." (Allen 2005: 166; Faulkner 2007: 200-201).

51. Utterance 535

Includes the following phrase:

"You have relieved Horus of his girdle, so that he may punish the followers of Seth. Seize them, remove their heads, cut off their limbs, disembowel them, cut out their hearts, drink of their blood, and claim their hearts in this your name of 'Anubis Claimer of hearts'!" (Allen 2005: 102-103; Faulkner 2007: 203).

Does this text hearken back to PreDynastic times when cannibalism was practised and reflect some of the struggles between the followers of Horus and Seth? Or, does the text refer to the sacrifice of some animal representing Seth as Eyre (2002: 170-171) suggests?

52. Utterance 541

This is one of a series of spells from the funerary ritual.

"O you children of Horus, Hapy, Duamutef, Imsety, Kebhsenuf, spread the protection of life over your father Osiris the King, since he was caused to be restored by the gods. Smite Seth, protect this Osiris the King from him at dawn. Mighty is Horus, he of himself protects his father Osiris the King. Whoever shall act on behalf of the King, you shall worship him." (Allen 2005: 171-172; Faulkner 2007: 210).

53. Utterance 562

A short text concerning the king joining with the gods and which concludes with this sentence:

"This King has come safely to you, O Horus; the 'Eye of Horus' belongs to you, it will not be given over to the rage of Seth." (Allen 2005: 173; Faulkner 2007: 218).

54. Utterance 574

An address to a sacred tree which includes the following sentence:

"Your tomb O Osiris, your shade which is over you O Osiris, which repels your striking-power O Seth." (Allen 2005: 181; Faulkner 2007: 229).

55. Utterance 576

A 'resurrection' text that begins:

"Osiris was laid low by his brother Seth, but He who is in Nedit *moves, his head is raised by Re; he detests sleep and hates inertness, so the King will not putrefy, he will not rot, this king will not be cursed by your anger, you gods."* (Allen 2005: 182; Faulkner 2007: 231).

56. Utterance 587

A long address to the sun-god which includes the following:

"It is he who saved them from every ill which Seth did to them." (Allen 2005: 274; Faulkner 2007: 239).

57. Utterance 593

A variant of Utterance 366 which includes the following:

"...they have put Seth under you on your behalf that he may be burdened with you, they have warded off his evil influence which he spat out against you. Horus brings Seth to you he has given him to you bowed down under you, for your strength is greater than his." (Allen 2005: 217; Faulkner 2007: 243-244).

58. Utterance 606

The king is reconstituted by his son and becomes assimilated with the sun-god; the text includes the following two phrases:

"..I have smitten him who smote you...he to whom ill was done by his brother Seth comes to us say the 'Two Enneads'." (Allen 2005: 226-227; Faulkner 2007: 250-251).

59. Utterance 652

The king assumes authority

"O Osiris the King, take the 'Eye of Horus' which I rescued from Seth when he had snatched it." (Allen 2005: 318; Faulkner 2007: 268).

60. Utterance 658

A text that includes the following:

"Horus has rescued his 'Eye' from Seth and has given it to you. Seth is driven back for you." (Allen 2005: 243; Faulkner 2007: 270).

61. Utterance 667A

An 'ascension' text which includes the following sentence:

"When the season of Inundation comes, provide the efflux which issued from Osiris, that Horus may be cleansed from what his brother Seth did to him, that Seth may be cleansed from what his brother Horus did to him, that this King may be cleansed from every evil thing on him, and that there may be cleansed those who watched for Horus when he sought his father Osiris." (Allen 2005: 325; Faulkner 2007: 281).

62. Utterance 670

A variant upon Utterance 482 that includes the following sentence:

"He has smitten for you him who smote you as an ox, he has slain for you him who slew you as a wild bull, he has bound for you him who bound you and has set him under your eldest daughter who is in Kdm, that mourning may cease in the 'Two Conclaves' of the gods."
(Allen 2005: 267; Faulkner 2007: 285).

63. Utterance 686

The king is anointed.

"O Ointment of Horus! O Ointment of Seth! Horus has taken possession of his 'Eye' and has saved it from his foes and Seth has no rights over it. Horus has filled himself with unguent, and Horus is pleased with what he has done, Horus is equipped with what is his. The 'Eye of Horus' cleaves to him, its perfume is on him, its wrath falls upon his foes. Ointment belongs to this King, this King fills himself with it, its perfume is joined to him, and its wrath falls upon his foes." (Allen 2005: 292; Faulkner 2007: 296).

64. Utterance 691B

The king as Horus calls upon Osiris to wake.

"Wake, wake, O my father Osiris for I am your son who loves you, I am your son Horus who loves you. Behold, I have come that I may bring to you what he took from you. Has he rejoiced over you? Has he drunk blood from you? Has Seth drunk blood from you in the presence of your two sisters? The two sisters who love you are Isis and Nephthys, and they will support you. Do not pass me by, for I have provided you; may you not suffer, may your wisdom judge Horus who is in his house. Quell Seth as Geb, as the being who devours entrails, for your front is that of a jackal, your hinder-parts are the 'Celestial Serpent', your spine is the door-bolt of the god. I have cultivated barley, I have reaped emmer, which I have prepared for your yearly sustenance, so wake, wake, O my father, for this bread of yours."
(Allen 2005: 333; Faulkner 2007: 301-302).

65. Utterance 695

A damaged 'resurrection' text that includes the following phrases:

I have driven off Seth from the north of the sky, the arms of Seth are loose; ...just as she guides Seth."
(Allen 2005: 284; Faulkner 2007: 303-304).

66. Utterance 696

A damaged 'ferryman' text that includes the following phrase:

"...the 'Eye of Horus' there, who runs against the fingers of Seth." (Allen 2005: 284; Faulkner 2007: 304).

67. Utterance 715

Allen (2005: 260) translates this as *"She has acquired all the gods, acquired Horus and his 'Great of Magic' crown as well, and acquired Seth and his 'Great of Magic' crown as well."* Faulkner (2007: 307) describes the passage as damaged text that includes the words *"Seth took it."*

68. Utterance 724

A damaged variant of Utterance 524; which includes the name Seth (Faulkner 2007: 311).

69. Utterance 752

A text concerned with presentation of insignia.

"O Osiris the King, take the 'Eye of Horus' which Seth had hidden – an imnt -vulture." (Allen 2005: 253; Faulkner 2007: 317).

The texts that mention Seth in a positive manner number 20 which represent 2.6% of the total texts.

1. Utterance 21

This is concerned with the ritual of 'Opening the Mouth' of the dead pharaoh to enable him to reacquire his earthly functions.

"...Horus has opened the mouth of this King, Horus has split open the mouth of this King with that wherewith he split open the mouth of his father, with that wherewith he split open the mouth of Osiris, with the iron which issued from Seth, with the adze of iron which split open the mouths of the gods." (Allen 2005: 252; Faulkner 2007: 3-4).

2. Utterance 81

A hymn for awakening the dead king, adapted to presentation of napkins. The king is likened to both Horus and Seth.

"..O you who receive the working women and who adorn the Great One of the carrying-chair, cause the Two Lands to bow to this King even as they bow to Horus; cause the Two Lands to dread this King even as they dread Seth.." (Allen 2005: 22; Faulkner 2007: 19).

3. Utterance 213

"O King, you have not departed dead, you have departed alive; sit upon the throne of Osiris, your sceptre in your hand, that you may give orders to the living; your lotus-bud sceptre in your hand, that you may give orders to those whose seats are hidden. Your arms are Atum, your shoulders are Atum, your belly is Atum, your back is Atum, your hinder-parts are Atum, your legs are Atum, your face is Anubis. The 'Mounds of Horus' serve you, the 'Mounds of Seth' serve you." (Allen 2005: 31; Faulkner 2007: 40).

Faulkner (41, note 4) makes the point here that the 'Mounds of Horus and Seth' signify the two realms of the gods represented by the tells (mounds) on which human settlements were often sited.

4. Utterance 217

The king joins the sun-god. A lengthy text from which the following passage is extracted:

"O Seth and Nephthys, go and proclaim to the gods of Upper Egypt and their spirits: 'This King comes indeed, an imperishable spirit. If he wishes you to die, you will die; if he wishes you to live, you will live.'" (Allen 2005: 33; Faulkner 2007: 44).

With regard to the gods of Lower Egypt, Osiris and Isis are charged with the proclamation later in this Utterance.

5. Utterance 218

The king assumes authority in the 'Beyond'. A lengthy text from which the following passage is extracted:

"See what Seth and Thoth have done, your two brothers who do not know how to mourn you." (Allen 2005: 34; Faulkner 2007: 46).

6. Utterance 268

The king is crowned and enthroned in the 'Beyond'. A medium length text from which the following passage is extracted:

"This King washes himself when Re appears, the Great Ennead shines forth, and 'He of Ombos' (i.e. Seth) is high at the head of the Conclave." (Allen 2005: 49; Faulkner 2007: 76).

7. Utterance 271

An 'ascension' text.

"I have inundated the land which came forth from the lake, I have torn out the papyrus-plant, I have satisfied the Two Lands, I have united the Two Lands, I have joined my mother the 'Great Wild Cow'. O my mother, the 'Wild Cow' which is upon the 'Mountain of Pasture' and upon the 'Mountain of the ẓḥẓḥ -bird', the two ḏd-pillars stand, though the broken rubble has fallen and I ascend on this ladder which my father Re made for me. Horus and Seth take hold of my hands and take me to the Netherworld. O you who were winked at, beware of him to whom command has been given; O you to whom command has been given, beware of him who was winked at. The face of the god is open to me, and I sit on the great throne beside the god." (Allen 2005: 50; Faulkner 2007: 79).

8. Utterance 385

This spell is concerned with protection against snakes and other dangers, it concludes with the following sentence:

"Horus has felled you (i.e. the snake) and you will not live; Seth has cut you up and you will not rise up." (Allen 2005: 90; Faulkner 2007: 127).

9. Utterance 478

This is an invocation to the 'Ladder to the Sky'. A lengthy text which includes the following passages:

"Hail to you, 'Ladder of the God'! Hail to you, 'Ladder of Seth'! Stand up, 'Ladder of the God'! Stand up, 'Ladder of Seth'! Stand up, 'Ladder of Horus' which was made for Osiris so that he might ascend on it to the sky and escort Re! You have come seeking your brother Osiris, for his brother Seth has thrown him down on his side in yonder side of Ghsty. Horus comes with you, his power upon him and turns his face to his father Geb: "I am your son, I am Horus; you begot me just as you begot the god, the 'Lord of the Ladder'. You have given to him the 'Ladder of the God', you have given to him the 'Ladder of Seth', that he may ascend on it to the sky and escort Re. Now let the 'Ladder of the God' be *given to me, let the 'Ladder of Seth' be given to me that I may ascend on it to the sky and escort Re as a divine guardian of those who have gone to their doubles......He who shall see and he who shall hear shall guard and protect himself when I ascend to the sky upon the 'Ladder of the God'; for I appear as the* uraeus *which is on the vertex of Seth."* (Allen 2005: 279-280; Faulkner 2007: 166).

Whilst the text does contain a 'negative aspect', namely the passage that refers to Seth throwing Osiris down, the overall impression is a positive one as the deceased's spirit ascends to the *Akhet*.

10. Utterance 510

A miscellany of spells including the following passage:

"My strength is the strength of 'Seth of Nubet'; ...Horus lifts me up, Seth raises me." (Allen 2005: 153; Faulkner 2007: 186-187).

11. Utterance 511

The king goes to the sky in an earthquake. A lengthy text which includes the following phrase:

"The sky thunders for me, the earth quakes for me; the hailstorm is burst apart for me, I roar as does Seth." (a passage possibly referring to Seth as the 'god of thunder'?) (Allen 2005: 153; Faulkner 2007: 187).

12. Utterance 539

A lengthy 'ascension' text which describes the various body parts and includes this sentence:

"My shoulders are Seth; I will ascend and rise up to the sky." (Allen 2005: 169; Faulkner 2007: 207).

13. Utterance 570

A lengthy text concerned with king and his various functions which includes the following sections:

"I escape my day of death just as Seth escaped his day of death. I escaped my half-months of death just as Seth escaped his half-months of death. I escape my months of death just as Seth escaped his months of death. I escaped my year of death just as Seth escaped his year of death. .. I am the uraeus *which went forth from Seth, which moves incessantly ....which was born before the 'Eye of Horus' was gouged out, before the testicles of Seth were torn off...Open, O Horus; stand guard, O Seth, that I may rise in the eastern side of the sky like Re who rises in the eastern side of the sky."* (Allen 2005: 178-179; Faulkner 2007: 224-225).

Another text that, although containing some negative aspects, overall has a positive sense as the sun is invoked at dawn.

14. Utterance 571

A text concerned with the king being the son of Atum and a star which includes the following:

"...the King escapes his day of death just as Seth escaped his day of death." (Allen 2005: 179; Faulkner 2007: 226).

15. Utterance 575

The king arrives in the 'Beyond' and announces that a number of gods have caused him to come, including:

"I caused him to come; I caused him to come, says Seth." (Allen 2005: 181; Faulkner 2007: 230).

16. Utterance 615

The king crosses to the 'Beyond'.

"The 'Eye of Horus' is placed on the wing of his brother Seth, the ropes are tied, the ferry-boats are made ready for the son of Atum, for the son of Atum is not boatless. This King is bound for the son of Atum, and the son of Atum is not boatless." (Allen 2005: 234; Faulkner 2007: 256).

17. Utterance 683

The king is greeted by the gods and this text records their speeches, including amongst them is this sentence:

"This is Horus who came forth from the Nile, this is the long-horn which came forth from the stockade, this is the viper which came forth from Re, this is the uraeus *which came forth from Seth."* (Allen 2005: 290; Faulkner 2007: 293).

18. Utterance 717

A variant upon Utterance 666 which includes the phrase *"throw away your fetters as Seth who is in Hnhnt."* (Allen 2005: 247; Faulkner 2007: 308).

19. Utterance 719

An 'ascension' text that includes the phrase:

"...and Seth ferries you over the 'Winding Waterway'." (Allen 2005: 248; Faulkner 2007: 309).

20. Utterance 723

A 'resurrection' text.

"O King, raise yourself upon your iron bones and golden members, for this body of yours belongs to a god; it will not grow mouldy, it will not be destroyed, it will not putrefy. The warmth which is in your mouth is the breath which issued from the nostrils of Seth, and the winds of the sky will be destroyed if the warmth which is in your mouth be destroyed; the sky will be deprived of its stars if the warmth which is in your mouth be lacking. May your flesh be born to life, and may your life be more than the life of the stars when they live." (Faulkner 2007: 311).

The neutral texts that refer to Seth number 44 and represent 5.8% of the total texts.

1. Utterance 25

A 'libation' spell

"Someone has gone with his double, Horus has gone with his double, Seth has gone with his double..." (Allen 2005: 19; Faulkner 2007: 4)

Faulkner here uses the term 'double' as an alternative to the expression *ka* (see his Preface: vii).

2. Utterance 34

A 'purification' text, Allen suggests that *zmin* is condensed milk, Faulkner suggests that it is something that can be spat out, possibly a cream and that it calms the quarrelling Horus and Seth.

"Zmin, zmin which splits open your mouth! O King, taste its taste in front of them of the 'God's Booth'. What Horus spits out is zmin, what Seth spits out is zmin, what reconciles the Two Gods is zmin. Recite four times: You are purified in the 'Company of the Followers of Horus' – Upper Egyptian natron of Nekheb, 5 pellets." (Allen 2005: 19; Faulkner 2007: 7).

3. Utterance 35

A further 'purification' text.

"Your purification is the purification of Horus, your purification is the purification of Seth, your purification is the purification of Thoth, your purification is the purification of dwn-ꜥnwy, *and your purification is also among them; your mouth is the mouth of a sucking calf on the day it was born – Lower Egyptian natron of* St-pt, *5 pellets."* (Allen 2005: 19-20; Faulkner 2007: 7).

4. Utterance 36

Virtually identical to Utterance 35 (Allen 2005: 20; Faulkner 2007: 8).

5. Utterance 210

"Awake, O Wpiw! *Be high, O Thoth! Awake, you sleepers! Rouse up, you dwellers in* Kenzet, *who are before the Great Egret who went up from the cultivation and the* Wepwawet-*jackal which emerged from the tamarisk-bush. My mouth is pure, the 'Two Enneads' cense me, and pure indeed is this tongue which is in my mouth. What I detest is faeces, I reject urine, I detest my own detestableness. What I detest is these two, and I will never eat the detestableness of these two, just as Seth rejected the poison. O you two Companions who cross the sky, who are Re and Thoth, take me with you, that I may eat of what you eat, that I may drink of what you drink, that I may live on what you live on, that I may sit on what you sit on, that I may be strong through that whereby you are strong, that I may sail in that in which you sail. My booth is plaited with rushes, my drink-supply is in the 'Field of Offerings', my food-offerings are among you, you gods, my water is wind like that of Re, and I go round the sky like Re, I traverse the sky like Thoth."* (Allen 2005: 30; Faulkner 2007: 39).

6. Utterance 215

The king ascends to the sky as a star and is likened to both Horus and Seth. A lengthy text from which the following relevant passages have been extracted:

"..There is no star-god who has no companion, have you your companion? Look at me! You have seen the shapes of the children of their fathers, who know their speech, the 'Imperishable Stars'; see now those who are in the Castle, who are Horus and Seth. Spit on the face of Horus for him, that you may remove the injury which is on him; pick up the testicles of

Seth, that you may remove his mutilation; that one is born for you, this one is conceived for you.

"You are born, O Horus, in your name of 'Him at whom the earth quakes'; you are conceived, O Seth, in this your name of 'Him at whom the sky trembles'. If this one has no mutilation and if that one has no injury – and vice versa – then you will have no injury and you will have no mutilation."

"You are born, O Horus, for Osiris, and you have more renown than he, you have more power than he. You are conceived, O Seth, for Geb and you have more renown than he, you have more power than he." (Allen 2005: 31-32; Faulkner 2007: 42).

7. Utterance 224

The king becomes the universal governor.

"Rouse yourself, O King! Turn yourself about, O King! Go, that you may govern the 'Mounds of Horus'; go that you may govern the 'Mounds of Seth'." (Allen 2005: 28; Faulkner 2007: 52).

Once again representing the towns of Upper and Lower Egypt upon their tells.

8. Utterance 225

This utterance is a variant of Utterance 224 that once again mentions 'the Mounds of Horus and Seth'. (Allen 2005: 263; Faulkner 2007: 53).

9. Utterance 247

The officiant addresses the king. A medium length text from which the following passage is extracted:

"O you who were in Nedit! Your good bread is prepared in Pe, take your power in On, for it is Horus who commanded that men help his father. As for the 'Lord of the Storm', the slavering of Seth (possibly an envisioning of rain?) is forbidden to him. He raises you up, and it is he who will raise up Atum." (Allen 2005: 41-42; Faulkner 2007: 60)

10. Utterance 306

This utterance is an 'ascension' text which again mentions the 'Mounds of Horus and Seth'. (Allen 2005: 58; Faulkner 2007: 94).

11. Utterance 308

The king greets the gods.

"Hail to you, Horus in the 'Horite Mounds'!

Hail to you, Seth in the 'Sethite Mounds'." (Allen 2005: 58; Faulkner 2007: 96).

12. Utterance 322

An 'ascension' text

"The sky is opened, the earth is opened, the doors of sȝt(y) are opened for Horus, the lotus-doors are thrown open for Seth. Turn yourself about for me, O you who are in your fortress; I have passed by you as Atum, I am hʿy-ɞw who dwells in Lebanon." (Allen 2005: 67; Faulkner 2007: 102).

13. Utterance 327

The king is fed.

"The messenger of Horus loves me and has brought his eye; the messenger of Seth loves me and has brought his testicles; the messenger of Thoth loves me and has brought his arm, and the 'Two Enneads' have trembled at them. These are indeed my messengers whom I love and who will bring me to a meal, and they will bring me to a meal." (Allen 2005: 69; Faulkner 2007: 104).

14. Utterance 386

"I have come to you, O corrupt one, and you shall pass me in R-Psny. If you drive me away, I will drive you away. Horus fell because of his 'Eye', Seth suffered because of his testicles. O Serpent whose head is raised, who is in the n3wt-bushes, fall down, crawl away!" (Allen 2005: 90; Faulkner 2007: 127).

15. Utterance 390

"The King is pure, his double is pure. How hale is the king! How hale is the King! Horus is hale of his body. How hale is the King! How hale is the King! Seth is hale of his body and the King is hale of his body between you. I am he who draws the bowstring as Horus and pulls the cord as Osiris. That man has gone and this man has come. Are you Horus? Down on your face! Be turned upside down! Are you Seth? Down on your face! Be dragged off! This foot of mine which I put on you is the foot of Mafdet; this hand of mine which I lay on you is the hand of Mafdet who dwells in the 'Mansion of Life'. I strike you on your face so that your venom may fail." (Allen 2005; 90; Faulkner 2007: 128-129).

16. Utterance 413

A 'resurrection' text designed to send the king's spirit to the sky.

"Raise yourself, O King! You have your water, you have your inundation; you have your milk which is from the breasts of Mother Isis. Raise yourself, you child of Horus, child who is in ḏbꜥwt-p, as Seth who is in ḥnḥnt. This 'Great One' spends the night fast asleep; awake, O King, raise yourself, receive your head, gather your bones together, shake off your dust, and sit on your iron throne, so that you may eat the foreleg, devour the haunch, and partake of your rib-joints in the sky in company with the gods." (Allen 2005: 87; Faulkner 2007: 136).

17. Utterance 419

The king is addressed by his son on the occasion of his funeral. A medium sized text from which the following passage has been extracted:

"Horus has dispelled the evil which was on you in your four days, Seth has annulled what he did against you in your eight days." (Allen 2005: 95; Faulkner 2007: 138). The first of these in an additional note states that he believes that the four and eight days are concerned with two major stages in the mummification process (Allen 2005: 95, note 31).

18. Utterance 424

A miscellany of short spells including a reference to 'the Mounds of Horus and Seth.' (Allen 2005: 102; Faulkner 2007: 140).

19. Utterance 443

An utterance concerned with the sky-goddess, Nut.

"O Nut, the eyes have gone forth from your head, you have carried off Horus and his greatly-magical, you have carried off Seth and his greatly-magical. O Nut, you have mustered your children in your name of 'Lady of On'. Assign this King to life, lest he perish."
(Allen 2005: 107; Faulkner 2007: 148).

20. Utterance 447

The king departs to the 'Beyond'; the text begins with the following sentence:

"Someone has gone to his double, Osiris has gone to his double, Seth has gone to his double, Mḫnt-irty has gone to his double, you also have gone to your double." (Allen 2005: 108; Faulkner 2007: 148).

21. Utterance 450

A variant on Utterance 447 beginning with a similar sentence including the phrase *"Seth has gone to his double."* (Allen 2005: 108; Faulkner 2007: 149).

22. Utterance 459

The king is restored to life.

"O King, receive this pure water of yours which issued from Elephantine, your water from Elephantine, your bd-natron from 'Irw, your ḥzmn-natron from the Oxyrhynchite nome, your incense from Nubia. May you sit on your iron throne, your forepart being that of a jackal and your hinder part being that of a falcon; may you devour the haunch from the slaughter-block of Osiris and the rib-pieces from upon the slaughter-block of Seth. Your bread is the god's bread which is in the Broad Hall; may you strike with the 'bꜣ-sceptre, may you govern with the i33t-sceptre, may you give orders to the gods, may you grasp for yourself the hand of the 'Imperishable Stars', may you ascend from the Thinite nome, may you descend into the Great Valley. Stand up! Raise yourself!" (Allen 2005: 119-120; Faulkner 2007: 153).

23. Utterance 470

A collection of spells, which include the following:

"I am going to the sky that I may see my father that I may see Re, say I. To the High Mounds or the 'Mounds of Seth'? The High Mounds will pass me on to the 'Mounds of Seth'." (Allen 2005: 126; Faulkner 2007: 159).

24. Utterance 474

This is a variant upon Utterance 306 which includes reference to 'the Mounds of Horus and Seth.' (Allen 2005: 128; Faulkner 2007: 162).

25. Utterance 475

A 'ferryman' text.

"Ahoy, Ferryman! Bring this Horus, bring his 'Eye'; bring this Seth, bring his testicles! There leaps up the 'Eye of Horus' who fell in the east side of the sky, and I will leap up with it, I will travel in the east side

of the sky, I will go and escort Re in the place of the gods who have gone to their doubles, who live in the 'Mounds of Horus' and who live in the 'Mounds of Seth'. Behold, I have come and gone, for I have reached the height of the sky, and I have not been opposed by the 'Great Ones of the Castle of the Mace', who are on the Milky Way. The Day-bark is summoned for me, and I am he who bales it out, for Re has set me as a possessor of life and dominion." (Allen 2005: 128; Faulkner 2007: 163).

26. Utterance 480

This is another variant of Utterance 306 that once again mentions 'the Mounds of Horus and Seth'. (Allen 2005: 281; Faulkner 2007: 168).

27. Utterance 483

Another 'resurrection' text which includes the following passage:

"...may you mount up the god and may Seth be brotherly to you..." (Faulkner 2007: 170-171).

28. Utterance 572

An 'ascension' text which again makes reference to the 'Mounds of Horus and Seth'. (Allen 2005: 180; Faulkner 2007: 227).

29. Utterance 577

A text entitled *'Osiris and the king are associated'* which consists of a long list of gods and goddesses who are *'content'* and includes:

"Content are Seth and Neith." (Allen 2005: 183; Faulkner 2007: 232).

30. Utterance 580

The dead king is addressed in a text in which the described sacrificial ox represents Seth (Allen 2005: 185; Faulkner 2007: 234-235).

31. Utterance 581

A text in which the king is identified with Osiris and which includes the following sentence:

"Seth is offered up, (possibly appertaining to an ox sacrifice once again?) *Osiris is in the right."* (Allen 2005: 185; Faulkner 2007: 236).

32. Utterance 591

A text dealing with the king assuming the *szmt*-apron, which includes the following:

"Seth has adorned himself with his szmt-*apron which has travelled over his land completely "* (Faulkner 2007: 242).

33. Utterance 600

A text concerned with a prayer for the king and his pyramid, which includes the following:

"O you Great Ennead which is on On, *(namely) Atum, Shu, Tefnet, Geb, Nut, Osiris, Isis, Seth and Nephthys."* (Allen 2005: 269; Faulkner 2007: 247).

34. Utterance 601

Similar to Utterance 600 but this time stating that Seth is in Ombos (Allen's version) or Nubet (Faulkner's version). (Allen 2005: 199; Faulkner 2007: 248).

35. Utterance 610

A variant of Utterance 437 in which the king is requested to: *"Awake for Horus!* and *Stand up for Seth!"* (Faulkner 2007: 253).

36. Utterance 612

The king is summoned to live again and the text includes reference to the 'Mounds of Horus and Seth'. (Allen 2005: 195; Faulkner 2007: 255).

37. Utterance 665

A text concerned with the dead king being summoned to rise again and which includes reference to the 'Horite and Sethite Mounds' and a phrase that states:

"Thoth comes to you with the knife which came forth from Seth." (Allen 2005: 323 and 328; Faulkner 2007: 275).

38. Utterance 666A

A 'resurrection' text that again mentions the knife that went forth from Seth and the 'Sethite Mounds'. (Allen 2005: 323; Faulkner 2007: 278).

39. Utterance 66

A text concerned with the king going to the sky which refers to him as *"his face being that of the Seth-animal"* (Allen 2005: 324; Faulkner 2007: 280).

40. Utterance 674

A text concerned with the king assuming royal status in the 'Beyond' and including a reference to *"the sharp knife which came forth from Seth."* (Allen 2005: 122; Faulkner 2007: 288).

41. Utterance 681

The king assumes his kingship in the 'Beyond'; the following sentence is included:

"The King is followed by the Brewers, the chiefs of sky and earth come to him bowing, even the two Guide-serpents, the jackals and the 'Spirits of Seth' who are above and below, who smear on ointment, who are clad in fine linen, who live on offerings." (Allen 2005: 289; Faulkner 2007: 292).

42. Utterance 690

A miscellany of short utterances, which includes reference to the 'Sethite Mounds' and the fact that Seth has spread out his awnings (Allen 2005: 294; Faulkner 2007: 298-299).

43. Utterance 718

This is a partial duplication of Utterance 666A which includes reference to *'Sethite Mounds'*. (Faulkner 2007: 309).

44. Utterance 734

This is a 'resurrection' text which includes the phrase *"Seth who is in ḥnḥnt"* (Faulkner 2007: 314).

APPENDIX 2. THE COFFIN TEXTS

The negative texts that refer to Seth number 72 and represent 6.0% of the total texts.

1. Text 9

The deceased is introduced to Thoth and the members of the judgement tribunal.

"Hail to Thoth and his Tribunal. Hail to you, O Thoth, in who is the peace of the gods, and all the Tribunal who are with you! Command that they shall come forth at the approach of N (standing for Osiris N i.e. the owner of the coffin), *that they may hear all that he has to say that is good on this day, because to you belongs this plume which arose in God's-land, which Osiris brought to Horus, that he might set it on his head as a reward, being vindicated against his foes, male and female. It was he who tore off the testicles of Seth; he neither perished nor died, for you are that star which the West bore, which neither perished nor was annihilated; this N shall neither perish nor be annihilated; and no evil impediment shall be imposed against N – so says Atum. As for anything evil which they may say or do against N in the presence of Geb, they are against them and they will be against them."* (Faulkner 2004: I, 5-6).

2. Text 11

The deceased is vindicated and introduced to the gods.

"Welcome, welcome! The statue is brought to you; so say I. Welcome, welcome! The great statue is brought to you. Encompass N, do all that he shall say, give him praise, you gods. Come, you gods, that you may see him, he having come forth safely and having been vindicated against his foes; he has taken possession of the crown, he has mounted the thrones of Geb, he has taken and destroyed the other (i.e. Seth)." (Faulkner 2004: I, 7).

3. Text 12

Following his vindication the deceased is urged to travel as Re does safe in the knowledge that the gods will act on his behalf.

"O N, go forth great and mighty even as Re went forth great and mighty on the east side of the sky (i.e. the side associated with the living as the west was associated with the dead). *The gods who spoke on behalf of Horus and overthrew Seth for him, they shall speak on behalf of N and overthrow his foes for him."* (Faulkner 2004: I, 8).

4. Text 13

Title: To be recited: The spells for causing a spirit's tomb to flourish in the necropolis; the spell for opening the tomb for the double of the blessed N.

"Ho N! Go forth from your house, from your seat and from any place where you are, as Horus was vindicated when he inherited the inheritance and had acquired power; go forth vindicated from the presence of this Tribunal of the gods of Pe, Dep and On, even as Horus went forth vindicated against Seth from the presence of this 'Tribunal of the Lord of Suffering'" (presumably Osiris who suffered at the hands of Seth). (Faulkner 2004: I, 8).

5. Text 37

A lengthy text which was meant to be recited over a wax image of one's foe inscribed with his name and then the image to be trodden under foot. It contains the following passage:

"..O Osiris, see that foe who is among men and who is in the necropolis has come having joined with Seth. He has disturbed your weariness, and he has said that your wounds are hidden, he has said: 'Sore be the pains of your suffering which are on you.' May your soul be strong against him, see the others who are rebellious at heart, that they may show forth your power and make report of your majesty. May you break and overthrow your foes and set then under your sandals." (Faulkner 2004: I, 28).

6. Text 50

A lengthy text which contains the following passage:

"..See, Seth has come in his own shape and has said: I will cause the god's body to fear, I will inflict injury on him, I will slaughter him." Presumably referring to when Seth mutilated and murdered Osiris. (Faulkner 2004: I, 47).

7. Text 60

A lengthy text which contains the following passage:

"..The ill-disposed are warded off for you, Seth is afraid when he sees you, he discards his strife-making on earth, for the fear of him has fallen on his own body." (Faulkner 2004: I, 60).

8. Text 73

A text that refers to the occasion when the goddesses Isis and Nephthys helped to resurrect Osiris, hoping that they will also do the same for the deceased.

"The djed-pillar of the Day-bark is released for its lord the djed-pillar of the Day-bark is released for its protector. Isis comes and Nephthys comes, one of them from the west and one of them from the east, one of them as a kite and one of them as a screecher, they prevent you from rotting in this your name of Anubis; they prevent your putrefaction from dripping to the ground in this your name of 'Jackal of Upper Egypt'; they prevent the smell of corpse from being foul in this your name of 'Horus of Khati'; they prevent 'Horus of the east' from putrefying, they prevent 'Horus of the Netherworld' from putrefying; they prevent 'Horus Lord of the Two Lands' from putrefying. Your speech is heard by Geb, the impediment is removed for you by Atum, you are vindicated by the Ennead; indeed they will not permit Seth to be free of bearing you aloft forever, O Osiris." (Faulkner 2004: I, 68).

9. Text 74

A lengthy text that contains the following passage: "Live, Osiris! The Great Inert One stands up from his side. I am Isis, I am Nephthys; raise yourself, O my brother, so that your heart may live and that Seth may not exult over you, even he who is subject to this hindrance of you when you are placed on his back for him and he has run beneath your feet, when he supported you on his shoulders, like what your father Geb did for you." (Faulkner 2004: I, 69).

10. Text 113

This text was designed to prevent a man's heart from bearing witness against him in the realm of the dead.

"O Eye-breaker!' says Osiris. He has seen Seth, who has been turned back behind the Wretched One; he waged war against the Double Lion when his heart sat down, and he wept on his own account. His staff is in his hand; complete Osiris, I beg of you. There is given to me <...> and there is allotted to you the <...> in the Broad Hall. Would that the sand had taken this heart of mine, and that it might ask for help from Atum and that it might control the gardens of Seth, for the maker of hearts has not given to him." (Faulkner 2004: I, 107).

11. Text 118

"I have come as the Double Lion so that I may go up into the Night-bark and that I might go down into the Day-bark, that I may judge in the crew of Re in these evenings.

See, you have come, spirit-like and equipped. By what path did you go? By the great path which the Sole One inherited, which men do not know, and upon which the gods never go, but upon which the Foremost Ones went that they might act as guides on the paths to the Great God.

See, you have come, spirit-like and equipped. By what path did you go? By the great path which the Sole One inherited, on which Seth could not go down after the fight.

See, you have come, spirit-like and equipped. By what path did you go? By that path upon which the 'Opponent' went to the west and east, to the secret place of the sky". (Faulkner 2004: I, 110).

12. Text 131

This text relates to the sealing of a decree concerning the family; the giving of a man's family to him in the realm of the dead.

"Horus Great and Mighty, 'Lord of the Field of Rushes'.

Geb, chiefest of the gods, has decreed that there be given to me my family, my children, my brethren, my father, my mother and all my servants and my dependants, they being saved from the acts of Seth and from the numbering by 'Isis the Great' beside Osiris, 'Lord of the West'. Geb, chiefest of the gods, has spoken of causing that there be released to me immediately my family, my children, my brethren, my father, my mother, all my servants and all my dependants, they being saved from any god or goddess, from any spirits male or female, or from any dead man or woman." (Faulkner 2004: I, 113-4).

13. Text 148

A lengthy text that includes the following passages:

"...what he shall kill is Seth the enemy of his father Osiris." And later: "The Contender (i.e. Seth) has not attained my first flight, my place is far from Seth, the *enemy of my father Osiris."* (Faulkner 2004: I, 125-6).

14. Text 157

A medium sized text that includes the following explanation why the pig came to be abhorred by the ancient Egyptians:

"And Re said: "Look again at yonder black pig". And Horus looked at this black pig, and Horus cried out because of the condition of his injured 'Eye', saying: "Behold. My 'Eye' is like that first wound which Seth inflicted on my 'Eye'", and Horus became unconscious in his presence. And Re said; "Put him on his bed until he is well". It so happened that Seth had transformed himself into a pig and had projected a wound into his Eye. And Re said; "The pig is detestable to Horus"."
(Faulkner 2004: I, 135).

15. Text 158

This is a text referring to the mythical description of Isis cutting off Horus's hands and the fashioning of new ones for him. It contains the following passage:

"They are with me", you shall say, and they will end up with you until Seth knows that they are with you and complains." (Faulkner 2004: I, 37).

16. Text 227

A text concerned with Seth becoming the counterpart of Osiris, it contains the following passage:

" ..My son Horus and his mother Isis have protected me from that foe (i.e. Seth) he who would harm me; they have put cords on his arms and fetters on his thighs because of what he has done to me."
(Faulkner 2004: I, 179).

17. Text 303

A text that refers to the dismemberment of Osiris by Seth and the subsequent revenge that was taken by Horus upon him.

"O Falcon, come to Djedu and go all over my mansion – so says Osiris – that you may see it, this new state which I have attained. My paternal brother (Seth) has taken action; he has struck me, and none can speak to me, none of my members can come to me.

O my father Osiris, here am I; I have come to you, for I have smitten Seth for you, I have slain his confederacy, I have smitten them who smote you, I have cut down them who cut you down. I am one who overcomes with strength, the heir of everything; I myself have guarded my body, I have felled my foes, and I have created it, this new state in which I am.

Here am I; I have come, having seen my father; allotment has been made to me, and I have gone out from him, I have guarded him from those who would rob him, and my name has come into being because my power of protection has gone forth." (Faulkner 2004: I, 222-223).

18. Text 310

A text that includes the phrase

"...when he judged between Horus and Seth..." (Faulkner 2004: I, 228).

19. Text 312

A text for transforming the deceased into a divine falcon, which contains the following passages:

"I say: How mighty is Horus! I cause them to know that the terror of him is great and that his horn is sharp against Seth;"

"...may I tell the affairs of his son whom he loves, while the heart of Seth is cut out."

"Let your heart jubilate, for you triumph over Seth, and your son Horus has been placed on your throne." (Faulkner 2004: I, 231-2).

20. Text 315

Osiris welcomes the deceased to the Netherworld.

"The sound of rejoicing is in the realm of the dead, and those who are in the Netherworld have come in peace – so say they to N. Those who are in their tombs are glad because of N, for you are the great god who is in the sky among the gods. Come down to me, O N, for the doors of the paths of the Netherworld are opened for you; I have put fear of you in Djedu and your oblations in Memphis, I will repast your festivals in Abydos. I have felled your foes for you, I have driven off for you those who rebelled against you, I have warded off Seth for you, I have spat on his confederacy for you, I have given you vindication in the 'Two Conclaves', I have set a fair remembrance of you in the 'Castle of the Great Ones' who are in the 'Great Shrine', I have set the love of you in the Netherworld among the spirits, just as Re commanded me to do it for you." (Faulkner 2004: I, 237).

21. Text 316

A lengthy text that includes the following passage:

"... and Seth has fallen because of me, I have made his confederacy slip because of that on account of which he wandered. I have stood on his bonds, the monthly festival was fashioned for me." (Faulkner 2004: I, 239).

22. Text 335

An extremely lengthy text which includes the following passages:

"I restored the 'Eye' after it had been injured on that day when the Rivals fought. What is the fighting of the Rivals? It means the day in which Horus fought with Seth when Seth inflicted a wound on the face of Horus and when Horus carried off the testicles of Seth."

"As for that god who takes souls, who laps up corruption and lives on putrefaction, he is Seth." (Faulkner 2004: I, 263-5).

23. Text 349

A text for preventing a man's magic being taken from him in the realm of the dead.

"Your son Horus has acted on your behalf and the 'Great Ones' tremble when they see the knives which are in your hands when you ascend from the Netherworld. Hail to you, O 'Wise One'! Geb has created you, the 'Ennead' has borne you. Horus is pleased with his father, Atum is pleased with his years, the gods of West and East are pleased with the Great One who came into being in the arms of 'Her who bore the god'.

O N! O N! See and behold! O N! Hear and be yonder! O N raise yourself on your side, and do my command. O you who hate sleep but who were made limp, arise, O you who were in Nedit! Your good bread is prepared in Pe, take your power in On, for it is Horus who commanded that men should help his father. As for the 'Lord of Storm', the slavering of Seth is forbidden to him. He raises you, and it is he who will raise up Atum." (Faulkner 2004: I, 282-3).

24. Text 356

A text that requests power over water.

"The Great One is opened to Osiris, the doors of the firmament are thrown open to Thoth and to the Nile-god, 'Lord of the Horizon' in this his name of Pns. May you grant that I have power over water as over a limb of Seth the rebellious." (Faulkner 2004: II, 1).

25. Text 358

A text that twice contains the following passage:

"May you grant that N have power over the water today as over the food of Seth the rebellious on that day of the storm over the 'Two Lands'." (Faulkner 2004: II, 2).

26. Text 359

A text that likens the deceased to the heir of Osiris and the power the heir has over Seth.

"I am that oar of Re with which he rows his old ones, and I will not be destroyed nor scorched. I am Babi, the eldest son of Osiris, who assembled every god within the circuit of his eye in On; I am the heir of Osiris, the despoiler of the 'Great One' who himself grew weary; I have despoiled the 'Great One' who himself grew weary; I have power through him, and I have taken away the power of the other one (i.e. Seth) from him." (Faulkner 2004: II, 3).

27. Text 376

"The bleared eyes of the 'Great One' fall on you and Maat will examine you for judgement."

The expression 'bleared eyes' may well be an allusion to the damage done by Seth to the 'Eye of Horus'. (Faulkner 2004: II, 11).

28. Text 397

A lengthy text that includes the following three passages:

"O Ferryman, bring me this; bring Horus to me for his 'Eye', bring Seth to me for his testicles. There leaps up the 'Eye of Horus' which fell in the eastern side of the sky so that it may protect itself from Seth."

"Her finials are the tuft which is on the tail of Seth;"

"It is the cloth which issued from the swtyw, which Horus and the Ombite (i.e. Seth) kissed on New Year's Day." (Faulkner 2004: II, 24-5).

29. Text 398

A lengthy text that includes the following two passages:

"O Ferryman, bring Horus to me for his 'Eye', bring Seth to me for his testicles; bring me the 'Eye of Horus' which fled and fell in his garden and which was rescued from Seth."

"Her bulwarks are Horus wrestling with Seth on the plains of Nedit." (Faulkner 2004: II, 33-4).

30. Text 405

A lengthy text that contains the following two passages:

"It has been made from the skin of the Mnevis-bull and from the sinews of the 'Ombite'."

"I am the <...> which fights stubbornly and fells the confederacy of Seth." (Faulkner 2004: II, 54-6).

31. Text 424

A text for driving away crocodiles which includes the following passage:

"I am Seth, and I have trodden down her who was pregnant by you, O Osiris (presumably meaning Isis)." (Faulkner 2004: II, 70).

32. Text 441

A text concerned with protecting a man's soul from monsters who would take it away from him, which contains the following passage:

"I have smitten Seth and I have fettered him on the bank of those who are constricted." (Faulkner 2004: II, 78).

33. Text 444

The deceased is likened to the 'Lord of Eternity'.

"I am a glad-hearted spirit, I have swallowed the kny-garment, I have demolished my portal, I have smitten Seth on the bank of the ibis-gods. I will not give away my power, I will not give away my magic to those two mrwt, the companions of Re; They have found me equipped with my magic in front of the great ones, I have taken the panoply of the 'Lord of Eternity'. I am Nu, I was inert when the 'Two Lands' were complete, (but) I was not gripped and my magic was not attacked; I was not gripped and my foot was not repelled, and those two mrwt, the companions of Re, did not control me. I passed upon the way, I controlled my appearing, and praise was given to me in front of Khem by the 'Great ones of the First Generation'. The fear of me in in the bodies of the mrwt, and I am the 'Lord of Eternity'." (Faulkner 2004: II, 81).

34. Text 445

A badly damaged variant of text 444 which again contains the line: *"I have smitten Seth on that bank of (damaged)."* (Faulkner 2004: II, 81).

35. Text 446

A text from a woman's coffin which contains in its midst the following passage:

"...she has smitten Seth upon the bank of 'I-have-found-him-on-it'." (Faulkner 2004: II, 82).

36. Text 531

A text that contains the following passage:

"May you make him to be a spirit, may you subdue his foes for him, may you guide him to the fair places of the realm of the dead, may you smite the 'confederacy of Seth' for him." (Faulkner 2004: II, 154).

37. Text 532

A spell for giving a man's head to him in the realm of the dead:

"My head is knit on for me by Shu, my neck is made firm for me by Tefenet on that day when the heads of the gods were knit on to them. My eyes have been given to me that I may see with them, I have received my spinal cord through Ptah-Sokar, my mother has given me her hidden power, my son has extended his arms over me, in order to put an end to the injury which Seth did in the secret thing he did against me in this my name of N." (Faulkner 2004: II, 155).

38. Text 568

The deceased has power over Seth.

"Stand up, O Power, and meet Geb, for your faces are spirits, and the power of Seth is brought to naught." (Faulkner 2004: II, 171).

39. Text 587

The deceased affirms that he will not do abhorrent things.

"I am the 'Bull of Offerings', possessor of five loaves in the temple; three loaves are in the sky and two

loaves are on earth. I bathe in the pools of the 'Netherworld'. I ascend to the place of Shu belonging to the sky. What Seth detests is the 'Eye of Horus', and I will not eat faeces; what I detest is urine, and I will never drink it, just as Seth detested the 'Eye of Horus' after the judgement in the great 'Prince-mansion which is in On'. If one gives him to you, fighting will not be stopped, uproar will not be suppressed, the mottled cattle will not move about for themselves. Seth will swallow the 'Eye of Horus' for himself after the judgement in the great 'Prince-mansion which is in On', and if you give this to me, there will be no coming into being or existing." (Faulkner 2004: II, 190).

40. Text 595

"I have set a limit to the 'confederacy of Seth', I have effected their slaughtering, I have put them in the place of execution south of Sepa and north of Hnn." (Faulkner 2004: II, 92).

41. Text 607

A lengthy text that contains the following passage:

"This is the 'Great One' who went forth from the earth, who was loosed from the Abyss, who went forth from Nut; the 'Great Power', born of Geb, who repelled Seth in his rage and who was set over the foreign lands, when they departed." (Faulkner 2004: II,1 95).

42. Text 646

A text for the staff which opens (unfortunately the object has been lost), which contains the following passage:

"Stand up, stand up behind Osiris, stand up, O staff, behind Osiris that he may smite the contentious ones, the 'confederacy of Seth'." (Faulkner 2004: II, 221).

43. Text 666

A lengthy text that contains the following passage:

"..N will not give his powers to the messengers of Seth who live by their thefts." (Faulkner 2004: II, 238).

44. Text 681

A medium sized text that contains the following passages:

"O my son, they will save you from the stroke of Seth in the great storm."

"May you display your noble rank, may he establish your permanence. May you be saved from the stroke of Seth at the shrine."

"O Thoth, son of the Harpooner, brother of Horus and Seth, who are on your throne, silence Seth." (Faulkner 2004: II, 246).

45. Text 693

A medium sized text that contains the following passage:

"May you make fast for yourself the bonds of Seth and his siste (Faulkner 2004: II, 258).

46. Text 775

A text that opens with the following passages:

"The ferry-boat is ferried across...run, O you who are in the 'suite of Horus', run, O you who are in the 'suite of Seth'. He cannot reach him, though he has run before Re to the great city, he has found a ferry-boat in yonder side, having been boatless.

Horus: He is angry with me and he attacks me – so says Horus the boatless. I wish that that mother of mine would speak to me, because I am very much afraid; I am stranded on yonder side because the 'Outcast' (i.e. Seth) is angry with me." (Faulkner 2004: II, 303).

47. Text 790

The deceased claims that he has come to protect Osiris from Seth.

"Words spoken by N: See, I have come that I may open up the Netherworld and that I may see my father Osiris who has flown up. I am a son beloved of my father; I have come so that I may protect Osiris from Seth. I open all the paths which are in the sky, I open all the paths which are on earth, I open all the paths which are in the Netherworld, and I have entered into the horizon, for I know my way and I am one who equips his spirits." (Faulkner 2004: III, 1).

48. Text 837

A medium sized text that contains the following passage:

"Remember, Seth, and put in your heart this word which Geb spoke against you, this threat which the gods made against you in the 'Mansion of the Prince which is in On*' when you felled Osiris to earth in* Nedit, *when you said, Seth, 'I did not do this', so that you might have power over him, that you might be saved and that you might have power over Horus; when you said, Seth, 'It was he who attacked me', when there came into being his name of 'Earth-attacker'; when you said, Seth, 'It was he who kicked me', when there came into being his name of 'Osiris as Orion, long of leg and lengthy of stride, who presides over Upper Egypt.'*

Rise up, Osiris, on your side in Gehesty*; Isis has your arm and Nephthys has your hand, so go between them. Sky and earth are given to you, the 'Field of Rushes' is given to you; go all over the 'Mounds of Horus', travel about the 'Mounds of Seth' in the presence of the two gods, the two lords who give judgement."* (i.e. travel the whole length and breadth of the country) (Faulkner 2004: III, 3-4).

49. Text 838

A text that contains the following passage:

"May you stand up at the head of the 'Conclave of Upper Egypt' as Horus, for the Nine Gods come to you bowing as to Min who is in his house and Seth of Hnt. *Smite him in his name of 'Bull of the Sky', kick him in your name of Orion, for Horus will capture Seth in order to raise up your corpse bearing this staff."* (Faulkner 2004: III, 26).

50. Text 839

A lengthy text that includes the following passage:

"I have come, O my father Osiris, for I am your son, I am Horus, I have come that I may bring to you this foe of yours (i.e. Seth) *and the 'Enneads' have put him beneath you for you <...> a long-horn <...> in this his name of <...>; Atum has <...> him for you as one who is evil. He will be bound, the sun-folk being with him, in this his name of 'Sacrificial Bull'. I bring him to you as a bull with a duct in its neck. Eat it, taste its head at all your meals belonging to you, for your heritage belongs to me; I am your heir upon your throne....may your bonds be cut as Horus who is in his house and your cords hewn asunder as Seth who is in* Hnt.*"* (Faulkner 2004: III, 27).

51. Text 855

The deceased is presented with the 'Eyes of Horus'.

"Ho N! Take the water which is in the 'Eye of Horus', do not let go of it. O Horus who is N, I bring to you the bodily 'Eyes of Horus'; seize them and join them to yourself. Oh N, I bring to you those things which expand the heart of Seth; seize them." (Faulkner 2004: III, 36).

52. Text 856

The deceased protects the 'Eye of Horus' from Seth.

"O N, take the 'Eye of Horus'; prevent him (i.e. Seth) *from consuming it. O N, take the 'Eye of Horus', the garment of which the gods are afraid. O N, Horus has attached his 'Eye' to your forehead for you in its name of 'Great of Magic'. O N, take that of which the gods are afraid just as they are afraid of Horus.*

O N, take the 'Eye of Horus', against which Seth acted. O N, take the 'Eye of Horus', the half of which he saw in the hand of Seth when he snatched it. O N, take the white of the 'Eye of Horus' which he rescued from Seth when he snatched it. O N, take the 'Eye of Horus', some of which he (i.e. Seth) *stole. O N, let him* (i.e. Seth) *be far from you. O N, take the 'Eye of Horus' which hung from the hands of his children. O N, take the water which is in the 'Eye of Horus', do not let go of it."* (Faulkner 2004: III, 36).

53. Text 862

A lengthy text that includes the following passage:

"O N, take the 'Eye of Horus', prevent him (i.e. Seth) *from consuming it."* (Faulkner 2004: III, 40).

54. Text 876

A text designed to make Osiris's neck firm for him; it is somewhat fragmentary but includes the following passage:

"Re'-Atum in the place in which your brother Seth set you <...>at the riparian land, whom Horus smote at the back-land of 'Andjet." (Faulkner 2004: III, 45).

55. Text 900

"I am the maiden <...> and enduring, who fought Seth and his confederacy." (Faulkner 2004: III, 56).

56. Text 935

The deceased is given the 'Eye of Horus'.

"O N, I give you the 'Eye of Horus', because of which the gods were merciful.

O N, I give you the 'Eye of Horus'; betake yourself to it.

O N, I give you the 'Eye of Horus' which they guarded.

O N, I give you the lesser 'Eye of Horus', of which Seth ate.

O N, I give you the 'Eye of Horus', with which your mouth is opened.

The pupil which is the 'Eye of Horus', eat it.

O N, I give you the 'Eye of Horus', and you will not be ill." (Faulkner 2004: III, 70).

57. Text 936

A lengthy text concerned with the 'Table of Offerings', which contains the following passages:

"...may you cause the Two Lands to fear N just as they fear the 'Outcast' (i.e. Seth);"

"O N, I give you the 'Eye of Horus' which was wrested from Seth and your mouth is opened with it."

"...and I give you the 'Eye of Horus' which he (i.e. Seth) pulled out." This passage is quoted twice.

"...O N, I give you the 'Eye of Horus', which he has pulled out."

"...O N, I give you the 'Eye of Horus', which is on Seth's brow."

"...O N, I give you the 'Eye of Horus'; little is that which Seth has eaten of it."

"...O N, I give you the 'Eye of Horus' which he has snatched away from Seth."

"...O N, I give you the 'Eye of Horus' which he rescued from Seth."

"...O N, I give you the 'Eye of Horus' which smote Seth."

"...O N, I give you the 'Eye of Horus' which was torn from Seth."

"...O N, I give you the 'Eye of Horus' which he has guarded and saved from Seth." (Faulkner 2004: III, 70-75).

58. Text 942

A somewhat fragmentary text that includes the passages:

"Seth who turned the land upside down."

"Seth has been placed beneath her coils for her." (Faulkner 2004: III, 81).

59. Text 956

A text that includes the following two passages:

"My mother has installed me in the midst of herself, because what is disliked is that Seth should see me when I reappear."

"...the powers of Seth are sealed off." (Faulkner 2004: III, 88).

60. Text 957

A lengthy text that includes the following two passages:

"Nekhbet has installed me in the midst of herself, because what is disliked is that Seth should see me when I reappear."

"...the powers of Seth will be sealed off." (Faulkner 2004: III, 89).

61. Text 960

A text that begins with the sentence:

"Re who excludes the sun-folk, who all belong to me<...> who displays beauty and who kicks Seth." (Faulkner 2004: III, 91).

62. Text 993

A lengthy text that includes the following passage:

"She who bent Seth on account of her utterance." (Faulkner 2004: III, 101).

63. Text 1000

A text for entering into the sun-disk that includes this opening sentence:

"O you who are strong in your striking-power; who do not turn aside because of what he (i.e. Seth) would do, here am I." (Faulkner 2004: III, 106).

64. Text 1013

A lengthy text concerned with not eating faeces in the realm of the dead, it includes the following passage:

"O you who are at the head of the Chaos-gods, who guide them of the celestial expanses, do not let me pass into the tomb against Re <...> among the 'confederacy of Seth'.

O you who are over Shusety, *let me take possession of my body <...> Geb <...> for I have made Horus triumphant over Seth."* (Faulkner 2004: III, 113).

65. Text 1021

A spell to save one from slaughter that contains the phrase:

"...while Re stands on the bonds of Seth." (Faulkner 2004: III, 121).

66. Text 1028

A lengthy text that includes the phrase:

"...See, the throat of Seth is brought to me, and it is I who present <...>." (Faulkner 2004: III, 126).

67. Text 1076

A 'cannibal' text.

"His name is 'One who spits out the Nile', who gives himself. Nehebkau. *He who eats his fathers. He who eats his mothers. He who drives off Seth when he is angry. He who begot the 'Bull of On'. He who swallowed the flood. 'Falcon-face' who issued from* Edjo. *Four-faces who issued from the horizon."* (Faulkner 2004: III, 146).

68. Text 1079

"I am he who wrapped his standard, who issued from the wrrt-*crown; I have come that I may establish offerings in Abydos; I have opened up* Rostau *that I may ease the suffering of Osiris. It was I who created water, who assigned my standards, and who prepared my path in the Valley. O Great One, prepare a bright path for me, that I may be allowed to pass, and I will remove pain from the Self-created. As for those who squat, it is Geb who will establish them in* Rostau *in the realm of his son Osiris for fear of his brother Seth may he not harm him. As for anyone who knows the names of those who squat, he will be with Osiris forever and he will never perish.* (Faulkner 2004: III, 147).

69. Text 1119

"This is he who proclaims Osiris; water is about him and life is in his mouth. As for Osiris who was made in the field, his arms drive off Seth for him, and every limb of his is in the place which they reached. The limbs of his which he allots to his semblance are necessary.

Hail to you, Osiris, possessing your mansions, you who endure; the ill-disposed is inert, but your heart is stout, O you who do not fight, but drive off uproar. I speak of the content of the chest of red stuff of him who is spiteful. Assess me, Osiris, for I have assessed you; may my bones be hale and my limbs strong." (Faulkner 2004: III, 164).

70. Text 1120

"I stand up with Osiris when he stands up; O Osiris, your soul comes to you and your throat is opened. Come, Osiris – four times – that the sweet breezes may come to you, for his power (i.e. Seth's power) *is laid low, and they have forsaken the wrath which is on him forever."* (Faulkner 2004: III, 164).

71. Text 1122

"He does not know Seth because of Osiris. Stand, that I may raise you; open your ears, for I give you the 'Sacred Eye'." (Faulkner 2004: III, 165).

72. Text 1138

"Re-Atum is dead. Fire. Fire. I have come that I may be strong in your company. It is the Aggressor who joined the Scowler when Seth made the 'Eye of Darkness' passed by. I am a destroyer with the 'Lord of Robbery' following me, I am he who passes by and splits open the darkness, and fire has no power over me as over anyone else who belongs to the night. The t-*bird belongs to me, and I have split open the darkness."*
(Faulkner 2004: III, 174).

The positive texts that mention Seth number 27 which represents 2.0% of the total texts.

1. Text 16/17

A medium sized text that contains the following passage:

"...the powers of Seth served him over and above his own powers." (Faulkner 2004: I, 10).

The 'him' referred to in this passage is Horus and the passage appears to indicate that Seth was unable to avoid adding his strength to that of the young Horus, a strange state of affairs if one accepts only the adversary of Horus role for Seth but perfectly acceptable if one accepts the view of Seth as the strongest of the gods helping another god.

2. Text 112

This is a text for preventing a man's heart giving witness against him (presumably when it is weighed against the feather of truth). Here the heart is afraid of Seth as illustrated by the passage:

"the breaker of bones who wailed when he saw Seth." (Faulkner 2004: I, 106).

3. Text 119

Here, along with other gods, Seth is helping to protect the deceased from an assault from the rear by an unnamed being.

"Twice he has placed someone behind me, so that he cannot reach me. He has placed Horus son of Isis behind me, so that he cannot reach me. He has placed Seth behind me, so that he cannot reach me. Twice he has placed someone behind me, so that he cannot reach me. He has placed Geb behind me, even he who went forth from his 'Eye', so that he cannot reach me on the great path which the 'Sole One' inherited, the way to which is unknown to men and upon which the gods never go." (Faulkner 2004: I, 111).

4. Text 160

This text contains a passage concerned with Seth in his role as protector of the solar barque:

"I know the name of this serpent which is upon the mountain, its name is Whn.f. Now at eventide he will turn his eye against Re and a stoppage will occur in the crew and a great astonishment in the voyage, and Seth will bend him with his hand." (Faulkner 2004: I, 138).

5. Text 353

A spell for having power over water; whilst the text refers to Seth's power over the water in Osiris's eye, here it is meant in a beneficial way as it provides the narrator of the spell with power over water:

"The doors of the 'Great One' are opened for Osiris; the doors of the firmament are thrown open for Thoth. O Nile-god, the 'Great One of the sky in this your name of <...>', grant that I may have power over water just as Seth had power over the water in the eye of Osiris on that night of the great storm. May you permit me to despatch for myself the 'Great Ones who preside over the flood' just as their august god whose name they do not know sent them. I am their august god whose name they do not know, and they are despatched for me (Faulkner 2004: I, 284-85).

6. Text 407

A text concerned with knowing the seven knots of the celestial cattle which contains the following passage:

"O Seth, possessed of your power, great Longhorn dwelling in the northern sky; give to me air among the wtnw who give rest to the celestial cattle." (Faulkner 2004: II, 58).

7. Text 408

Very similar to the above text and again concerned with the seven knots of the celestial cattle it contains the following passage:

"O Seth, possessed of your power, Great Longhorn dwelling in the northern sky when the Longhorn is caused to ascend to the northern sky, see you have come under my feet; give to me air among the wtnw who give rest to the celestial cattle." (Faulkner 2004: II, 60).

8. Text 519

The deceased becomes a god with iron bones and golden flesh.

"Ho N! Raise yourself upon your iron bones and golden flesh, for this body of yours belongs to a god; it will not grow mouldy, it will not putrefy, it will not be destroyed. The warmth which is on your mouth is that which issued from the nostrils of Seth, and the winds of the sky will be destroyed if the warmth which is on your mouth is destroyed; the sky will be deprived of the stars if the warmth which is on your mouth is lacking. May your flesh be born to life, and may your life be more than the life of the stars in their season of life." (Faulkner 2004: II, 148-149).

9. Text 528

Both the deceased and his *ka* are purified.

"Ho N! Wake up, raise yourself, so that you may be pure and that your double may be pure! Your purification is the purification of Horus and Seth, your purification is the purification of Thoth and

Dwn-'nwy, *your purification is the purification of your double your purification also is among your brethren the gods."* (Faulkner 2004: II, 152).

10. Text 530

Similar to the previous text.

"Purity, purity for your double! You are pure for your double, your head is censed with sweet-smelling incense, you are made strong by means of incense, the fragrance of a god is on your flesh, the two Great Ones (here referring to Horus and Seth), *the 'Lords pre-eminent in Upper Egypt', cleanse you. The incense comes, the incense comes; the ear of corn comes, the ear of corn comes; there comes the spinal cord which issued from the backbone of Osiris, there comes the marrow, there comes the marrow, there comes the limbs which issued from Osiris, and Horus censed him because of his 'Eye'. O N, I cense you because of the 'Eye of Horus', I make a god of you because of the 'Eye of Horus', I equip you as a god, it equips you as a god, its perfume diffuses over you, and the perfume of the 'Eye of Horus' is on you."* (Faulkner 2004: II, 153).

11. Text 564

"This is Osiris, the West <...> if he knows his name, Osiris will know his name. Not <...> I will not be in it, for I am Seth who is among the gods and I will not perish." (Faulkner 2004: II, 169).

12. Text 571

A text concerned with building a mansion amongst the waters, it includes the following passage:

"...and he has found Seth in it with his staff in his hand subduing the patricians for me." (Faulkner 2004: II, 73).

13. Text 581

A text concerned with not eating faeces, it contains the following passage:

"I am bound for the northern sky and I will dwell in it with Seth." (Faulkner 2004: II, 184).

14. Text 630

A text concerned with giving air to the deceased, it concludes with the following passage:

"..I speak about the lone air which is in the 'Mansion of Seth'; its name is <...>. O N <...> is the 'Lord of the air'. I know the air by this its name is Seth." (Faulkner 2004: II, 213-214).

15. Text 633

A text concerned with air being in a man's nose in the realm of the dead.

The air is in N's nose like Seth. N has spoken to Seth, N has been informed." (Faulkner 2004: II, 215).

16. Text 647

A lengthy text concerned with obtaining protection through Ptah, it contains the following passage:

"I am the 'Lord of Life', ruling in the sky, while Seth is my protection because he knows the nature of what I do; I am the 'Lord of Life'." (Faulkner 2004: II, 223)

17. Text 649

A medium sized text that contains the following passage:

"O Lion-man of his, open a path for me, for I am Seth about to sail the bark." (Faulkner 2004: II, 224).

18. Text 665

A medium sized text that includes the following passage:

"Seth comes, one who provides shares whenever food is provided." (Faulkner 2004: II, 236).

19. Text 686

A text concerned with driving away snakes, it includes the following passage:

"...a path has been cleared for me by Seth." (Faulkner 2004: II, 251).

20. Text 694

A short text that contains the following passage that alludes to Seth's might amongst the gods:

"I have put the awe of you into the spirits like Seth among the gods." (Faulkner 2004: II, 259).

21. Text 725

A medium sized test that includes the following passage:

"May your heart be glad and may your feet dance; may your tomb be as well-founded as the tomb of Horus and the burial-place of Seth who is in Hnt.*"* (Faulkner 2004: II, 276).

22. Text 769

A text concerned with ascending to heaven that begins with the following passage:

"Stand up, O 'Ladder of Horus'! Stand up, O 'Ladder of Seth'! Stand up, O great and mighty ladder which was made for Osiris, so that he might ascend on it to the sky." (Faulkner 2004: II, 299).

23. Text 772

A text concerned with what the dead person will live upon that contains the following passage:

"I will live on seven portions which are being brought; their seven loaves are with Horus and with Seth." (Faulkner 2004: II, 302).

24. Text 857

The deceased has the soul of Horus and the strength of Seth.

"There is double satisfaction for the 3ms-*club of tamarisk which smites the disaffected, and he who controls the land is powerful. You have the soul of Horus, you have the strength of Seth, may you control this land, O N, as Horus may there be given to you the water which issued from the 'Eye of Horus', the name of which was made out as* 3ms-*club when it was turned about throughout the deserts under the fingers of Seth.*

Raise yourself! May you protect N from those who would do anything evil against her. There is double satisfaction for the 'White Eye of Horus' which smites the plebs and N is protected from those who would do anything evil against her. He will not live, namely him who you strike, his head will not be knit on." (Faulkner 2004: III, 37).

25. Text 945

A lengthy text that contains the phrase:

"My strength is Seth." (Faulkner 2004: III, 84).

26. Text 1017

A lengthy text concerned with living by magic and by means of protection in the 'Two Houses', it contains the following passage:

"My wrapping is the 'Great Commander'. I give incense and water to my dead father, because I have offered an im3-*tree, because I have uprooted an acacia, because it is I who see my pool, for I have dug it in company with Seth."* (Faulkner 2004: III, 118).

27. Text 1128

Some of the gods comprising the crew of the Night-bark are named.

"Circle of fire. Circle of fire. The fire of the Night-bark. The company which is in the bow is Isis, Seth and Horus. The company which is in the stern is Hu, Sia and Re." (Faulkner 2004: III, 166).

The neutral texts that mention are 32 in number which represents 3.0% of the total texts.

1. Text 162

A text designed to give power over the four winds which included the following passage:

"Re grasps my hand and sets me in this field of his in the midst of rushes, and I flourish in it like the condition of Apis and Seth." (Faulkner 2004: I, 140).

2. Text 181

The deceased will not perform detestations.

"O Hearer! O Unstopper! – and vice versa – hear me, unstop me, save me when I am heard, for I am the 'Bull of Kenzet', a possessor of bread in On; *four portions are in the sky and three portions are on earth. These things have been made for me as gifts in* On *which have been given to me, for I am the Bull with curly hair, having five portions in the 'House of Horus' and two portions in the 'House of Seth'; three portions are in the sky and three portions are on earth. It is the Night-bark and the Day-bark which are daily taken for me to the 'House of the God'. Faeces is my detestation, and I will not eat it, nor will I drink urine: I will not walk upside down, for it is Isis who rows me every day."*
(Faulkner 2004: I, 152).

3. Text 187

Another text concerned with the detestation of faeces that includes the following passage:

"I will live on those three portions which were made for Osiris; one is for Horus, another is for Seth, and another for me, and I am their third." (Faulkner 2004: I, 156).

4. Text 220

Another detestation of faeces text that includes this passage:

"Why will you not eat filth or drink urine because of the emptiness of Horus and Seth?" (Faulkner 2004: I, 175).

5. Text 268

A text for becoming Sobek, 'Lord of the Winding Waterway' that includes the following passage:

"N is the fnt-snake which issued from the shank and ate the 'Chaos-god', whom Seth exhaled for him from within the secrets of Geb." (Faulkner 2004: I, 203).

6. Text 280

A medium sized text that includes the following passage:

"O N, you are the 'Elder Horus', you have judged between the Rivals, namely the two who would destroy the sky; you have adzed Orion with the two adzes of Seth, you have given judgement in this sky for Re, light and dark are at your will." (Faulkner 2004: I, 211).

7. Text 318

A medium sized text that includes the following passage:

"...while the head of Horus remained with that of Seth – and vice versa." (Faulkner 2004: I, 246).

8. Text 354

A text used in 'purification' rituals.

"Spell for a wnwn-plant. Your purification is the purification of Horus, Seth, Thoth and dwn-ᶜwy. Your purification is on your mouth; may you cleanse all your bones, may you provide what appertains to you. Smyn, smyn, which splits open your mouth! Taste its taste in front of them of the God's booth. Your purification is natron from the cleansing of the 'Followers of Horus'." (Faulkner 2004: I, 285).

9. Text 373

A text concerned with breathing air amongst the waters. Seth (as the Outcast) is mentioned twice but overall in a neutral manner.

"Hidden are the ways for those who pass by; light is perished and darkness comes into being' – so says Nephthys.

'Why is it said?' - so says the 'Outcast'.

d.f-ȝw is upon the 'Outcast'<...> It means that the 'Outcast', the son of Nut, has fallen on his side and that his breath has been taken away' – so says d.f-ȝw, and the arm of Him who rests wearily is uplifted.

The doors of the hns-water are opened, and the winds pass out; its nt-crowns are parted, and the air goes in. I have gone down in order to present Ma'et with water, for breath is in my nose; I will go forth and open the Eye, Re upon earth, for breath is in my nose. It is the 'Outcast' who speaks to me and informs me that life is provided and that air is breathed among the waters." (Faulkner 2004: II, 9-10).

10. Text 396

A medium sized text which includes the following two passages:

"O Ferryman, bring Horus to me for his 'Eye' and the 'Outcast' to me for his testicles;"

"Bring me her mast-crutch, for the 'reeds' are the bands which are under the bright hair of Seth;" (Faulkner 2004: II, 22-23).

11. Text 400

A spell for joining the ferry-boat to the realm of the dead, it includes the following passage:

"I have extended my arm over the arm of Horus and the sandal of Seth."

Faulkner suggests that this was intended to imply that the deceased had exercised some sort of restraint over both of the gods. (Faulkner 2004: II, 43-45).

12. Text 479

A lengthy text concerned with escaping from fish-traps and containing the following passage:

"That vessel in which you cook is the contentious shooters of 'Seth of Ombos'."
(Faulkner 2004: II, 122).

13. Text 524

A spell concerned with protection against ones foes.

"O N, I am Horus who went forth as Horus and Seth, and my father said to me; Come, betake yourself to my father N and do not let him be subdued at the hands of his foes in your name of Horus. You have come that you may join him up, N do not be far from him. Place yourself and your father in his embrace, do not ever let go of him, and smite his foes from him."
(Faulkner 2004: II, 151).

14. Text 526

Isis and Nephthys place the heart in the body.

"I am Nephthys, and I have come that I may lay hold of you and that I may place your heart in your body for you: I bring you Horus and his 'Great-of-Magic', I bring you Seth and his 'Great-of-Magic'.

I am Isis, and I have come that I may lay hold of you and that I may place your heart in your body for you; I bring you Horus and his 'Great-of Magic', I bring you Seth and his 'Great-of-Magic'." (Faulkner 2004: II, 152).

15. Text 640

A spell to prevent the deceased from entering into the shambles, the place that is the realm of the dead.

"My word is spoken, the knot is tied behind me in the sky, the earth is guarded by Re every day. I have made the knot firm against the inert ones at my feet on that day of cutting off the tress.

The knot is tied behind me by Seth, in whose power the 'Ennead' were at first, before uproar had come into being, so that you might make me hale as this one who slew my father, for I am he who takes possession of the 'Two Lands'.

The knot is tied behind me by Nu who saw the 'First Occasion' before the gods were born <...> I am Pnty, *I am the heir of the great gods."* (Faulkner 2004: II, 218).

16. Text 660

A lengthy text that includes the following passage:

"I will cut off your heads, O you who oppose my path; I will lift up your heads on my hands, for my birth was the birth of a god on that day when the hdn-*plant was fashioned, before sky and earth had come into being, before water had come into being, before the Abyss had come into being, before Geb and Nut had come into being, before Osiris and Isis had come into being, before Seth and Nephthys had come into being."*
(Faulkner 2004: II, 230).

17. Text 772

A medium sized text that includes the following passage:

"I will live on seven portions which are being brought; their seven loaves are with Horus and with Seth." (Faulkner 2004: II, 302).

18. Text 803

"Words spoken by Nut who enfolds him and who puts her arms about N in life: N will not die.

O Nut, you have carried off Horus and his greatly magical; you have carried off Seth and his greatly magical; enfold N with life in your name of 'Great Protectress'."
(Faulkner 2002: III, 4).

19. Text 821

The deceased is likened to a number of gods and their *kas.*

"Provide for my father N <...> my father N <...>. Betake yourselves to him, grasp him by his legs <...> you shall live <...>. Someone has gone to his double, Horus has gone to his double, Seth has gone to his double, Thoth has gone to his double, Dwn-'mwy *has gone to his double, Osiris has gone to his double, the 'Eyeless One' has gone to his double. Ho N! You have departed living and you shall not depart dead; your mother has come to you, Nut has come to you so that she may cleanse you and provide for you as a god, for you are the greatest of her children. Geb is gracious to you, he loves you and he will protect you."*
(Faulkner 2004: III, 12).

20. Text 832

A medium sized text that contains the following passage:

"Sky and earth and the 'Mounds of Horus' have been given to you, you have travelled about the 'Mounds of Seth'." (Faulkner 2004: III, 210).

21. Text 841

A medium sized text that contains the following passage:

"Seth is released from bonds <...>Seth is released from the 'Eye of Horus', who is firmly established..." (Faulkner 2004: III, 29).

22. Text 843

A text concerned with the bread and beer offerings.

"<...> incantations which are given for N. This hwg-cake is upon Anubis. The 'confederacy of Horus and Seth' has no power over him, they being far removed from this which is given to you for this bread and this beer." (Faulkner 2004: III, 30).

23. Text 846

A medium sized text that includes the following passage:

"Disturber who is sent in storm, messenger of Seth living on what you steal: Oppose your face to the earth-god <...>." (Faulkner 2004: III, 31).

24. Text 858

A lengthy text which contains the two following passages:

"O N, take the finger of Seth which causes the white 'Eye of Horus' to see.

O N, Take the white 'Eye of Horus', which illumines the tip of the finger of Seth."

"I bring what expands the heart of Seth, I give what expands the heart of Seth, I give them to you, so seize them and join them to yourself." (Faulkner 2004: III, 37-38).

25. Text 859

A medium sized text that contains the two following passages:

"O N, take the white 'Eye of Horus' which illumines the tip of the finger of Seth."

"O N, I bring to you the two 'Eyes of Horus', I bring what expands the heart of Seth, I give what expands the heart of Seth, I give them to you." (Faulkner 2004: III, 38-39).

26. Text 882

A short text that terminates with the following passage:

"Horus secures the rope of Seth when he ferries him across, and see, my bark is placed on those who are yonder." (Faulkner 2004: III, 47).

27. Text 901

A text concerned with a spell for proceeding to the gates and with those who are in charge of the gates of the tomb, it concludes with the following sentence:

"The room of 'Her who is hidden, mistress of paths', who guides Horus and Seth when the bark passes by." (Faulkner 2004: III, 6).

28. Text 941

A medium sized text that contains a reference to *"the company of Seth..."* (Faulkner 2004: III, 80).

29. Text 996

"I have come here with a skin-bottle; the beer in it is stale, the cup in it is broken, the vessel in it is the <...> of Khnum in his mouth. He has moulded me <...> he has treated me ill for a year.

"What is it into which you have looked?" says Thoth <...> drinking water for that pregnant woman and beer for that pregnant woman – and vice versa <...> who permits Seth to breathe because he is dishevelled through them; Seth will come <...> As for my restraint of Nrt, that hoof which is in the coil of Re will be given to him who comes for it, and he will have power over <...>, the great ones shall become lesser ones, and it shall not come to pass that I speak but am not heard. Shall I who say this be opposed when Hnnsw speaks?" (Faulkner 2004: III, 104).

30. Text 1011

A lengthy text that contains the following passage:

"Three portions of mine are in the 'House of Horus', two portions of mine are in the 'House of Seth'." (Faulkner 2004: III, 111).

31. Text 1118

"The Mansion of Osiris. The land of spirits. Seth of the land of spirits." (Faulkner 2004: III, 163).

32. Text 1143

"Drive off the terrible ones from the earth-gods, protect the Great Lady, separate the two Combatants in 603 storms. There are 600 in the breadth of what is over this lake. O Shu, Nu, Atum, Re, Old One, I have passed by Shu, Nu Atum, Re, the Old One, the four Seths, Ptah, Sia who is in his Eye, the torch and the fire; his power is the terror of Nu who fashioned the body of Horus, more potent than his fellows; the Falcon, the Duck and the Plume on the 'Day of Scratching'; they are safe after the destruction, and what they pray for is eternity. Scatter toward them, O you whose face is hidden; make a plan for your arms according to your movements, Horus the Elder is in the middle of the upper stars and opposite the lower ones."

(Faulkner 2004: III, 177).

APPENDIX 3 THE BOOK OF THE DEAD

There are 26 spells that refer to Seth in a negative manner, these represent 1.4% of the total number of spells.

Spell 9 (Faulkner 1972: 37); a spell for going out into the day after opening the tomb, states:

'O you soul, greatly majestic, behold, I have come that I may see you; I open the Netherworld that I may see my father Osiris and drive away darkness, for I am beloved of him.

I have come that I may see my father Osiris and that I may cut out the heart of Seth who has harmed my father Osiris. I have opened up every path which is in the sky and on earth, for I am the well-beloved son of my father Osiris. I am noble, I am a spirit, I am equipped; O all your gods and all you spirits, prepare a path for me.'

Spell 17 (Faulkner 1972: 44-50; Allen 1974: 26-32); a spell for ascending and descending into the god's domain and becoming a blessed one in the beautiful west. This is a lengthy spell that includes the following passages:

'As for yesterday, that is Osiris. As for tomorrow, that is Re on that day in which the foes of the 'Lord of All' (i.e. the 'confederacy of Seth') were destroyed (Allen has: annihilated) and his son Horus was made to rule.'

'I restored the Sacred Eye after it had been injured on that day when the Rivals (i.e. Horus and Seth) fought.' Allen has: *'I filled out the eye after its impairment on that day when the Two Comrades fought.'*

'What does it mean? It means the day when Horus fought with Seth when he inflicted injury on Horus's face and when Horus took away Seth's testicles.'

'As for those gods the 'Lords of Justice', they are Seth and Isdes, 'Lord of the West'.'

Save me from that god who steals souls, who laps up corruption, who lives on what is putrid, who is in charge of darkness, who is immersed in gloom, of whom those who are among the languid ones are afraid. Who is he? He is Seth.'

'If Horus be respected, Seth will be divine, and vice versa.' This is a strange sentence contrasting with all the negative ones that concern Seth but may hark back to Horus and Seth being rulers of Lower and Upper Egypt.

'As for Wadjet, *'Lady of the Devouring Flame', she is the 'Eye of Re'. As for those few who approach her, it means that the confederacy of Seth are near her, because what is near her is burning.'*

Spell 18 (Allen 1974: 32-34); a medium length spell that contains the following phrase:

'The great Council that is at the great earth-fertilising in Busiris means when Seth's gang came having assumed their form of goats. Then (they) were slaughtered before these gods so that their blood dripped from them, and were given by assignment to the dwellers in Busiris.'

Spell 19 (Allen 1974: 34-35); a spell for wreaths of vindication begins with the following passage to be said by the deceased:

'Thy father Atum binds for thee this beautiful wreath of vindication on this thy brow. Live, beloved of the gods; mayest thou live forever. Osiris presiding over the Westerners has vindicated thee against thy enemies. Thy father Geb assigns to thee his whole inheritance. Come! Praise be to thee as one vindicated, O Horus, son of Isis and son of Osiris, on the throne of thy father Osiris, overthrowing thy enemies. He definitely assigns to thee the whole of the Two Lands. Atum has assigned and the Ennead has confirmed the two regions of beauty to the vindicated one, Horus the son of Isis and son of Osiris, forever and ever, even to Osiris N (the N here being the name of the deceased). Osiris presiding over the Westerners, the two sanctuaries of the gods together and every god and every goddess who is in the sky and in the earth are vindicating Horus, the son of Isis and son of Osiris, against his enemies before Osiris presiding over the Westerners and vindicating Osiris N. against his enemies before Osiris presiding over the Westerners, Unnofer the son of Nut, on this day of his vindication against Seth and his gang.'

Spell 20 (Faulkner 1972: 50; Allen 1974: 35-36) has the deceased appealing to Thoth to vindicate him before the tribunals of the gods and includes the following passage:

'In the presence of the great tribunal, which is in Heliopolis, on that night of battle, and of felling those who rebelled.' This refers to the battle between Horus and Seth and the defeat of the latter and his confederacy.

Spell 23 (Faulkner 1972: 51-52; Allen 1974: 36) is a spell for opening the mouth of the deceased and includes the following passage:

'Thoth comes indeed, filled and equipped with magic, and the bonds of Seth which restricted my mouth have been loosened. Atum has warded them off and has cast away the restrictions of Seth.'

Spell 28 (Allen 1974: 38-39) is a spell for not allowing the breast of the deceased to be taken away from him and includes the following passage:

'O crushers of Osiris, he has seen Seth. O turn back in pursuit of him who smote him, for he has caused destruction.'

Spell 60 (Allen 1974: 55) is a spell for having water available to the deceased, it states:

'I am N. Opened for me are the double doors of the sky, parted for me are the double doors of the celestial waters, by Thoth and by Hapi, that is, Hapi of the sky, vast at early morn.

May ye let me have water available as when Seth robbed his foe on this day when the 'Two Lands' raged.

The elders escort to me the oblation that is in the corner (i.e. of the sky). As they escort this great God, the equipped blessed one whose name is unknown, so the eldest escorts me to the oblation. I am N.'

Spell 65 (Faulkner 1972: 69; Allen 1974: 60-61) is a spell for going out into the day and having power over one's enemies and includes the following passage:

'Do not permit me to be carried off as booty to Osiris, for I have never been in the 'confederacy of Seth', O you who sit on your coils before Him whose soul is strong, let me sit on the throne of Re and take possession of my body before Geb; may you grant that Osiris may go forth vindicated against Seth; may the dreams of Seth be the dreams of a crocodile.'

Spell 78 (Faulkner 1972: 74-78; Allen 1974: 67-69) is a lengthy spell for being transformed into a divine falcon; it contains the following passages:

'I say: How mighty is Horus! I cause them to know that the terror of him is great, and that his horn is sharp against Seth.'

'I desire triumph over my enemies. May the mysteries be uncovered for me, may the secret caverns be opened to me, may I enter into the 'Lord of the Soul', greatly majestic, may I come forth to Busiris and go all over his mansion, may I tell him the affairs of his son whom he loves, while the heart of Seth is cut out.'

'Be high upon your seat, O Osiris: may your breast live and your buttocks be vigorous. Let your heart jubilate, for you triumph over Seth, and your son Horus has been placed upon your throne.'

Spell 80 (Faulkner 1972: 78-79; Allen 1974: 80) is a spell for making transformation into a god and giving light and darkness; it contains the following passage:

'I filled the eye when it was nothing before the 6th day feast had come. I judged Seth in the upper chambers in addition to the elders (who were) with him.'

Spell 83 (Faulkner 1972: 80-81; Allen 1974: 71-72) is a spell for being transformed into a phoenix; it contains the following passage:

'Horus who makes brightness with his person, that god who was against Seth.'

Spell 86 (Faulkner 1972: 83-84; Allen 1974: 73-74) is a spell for being transformed into a swallow, and contains the following passage:

'Horus is in command of the Sacred Bark, and the throne of his father Osiris has been given to him, while that Seth, the son of Nut, is in bonds because of what he has done.'

Spell 90 (Faulkner 1972: 85; Allen 1974: 75) is a spell for removing foolish speech from the mouth, and contains the following passage:

'Turn away at the sentence which Isis spoke when you came to put folly into the mouth of Osiris at the desire of his enemy Seth, saying to you: 'May your face be downcast at seeing this face of mine!''

Spell 99 (Faulkner 1972: 90-97; Allen 1974: 78-81) is a lengthy spell concerned with the provision of a boat for the deceased to cross the celestial river. It consists of three parts: in part one the celestial ferryman, Mahaf, is requested to arouse Aqen who has charge of the boat; in part two Aqen having been aroused raises objections and in part three the deceased has to declare the names of the various parts. It includes the following passages:

'O ferryman, bring me this which was brought to Horus on account of his eye and which was brought to Seth on account of his testicles; there leaps up the 'Eye of Horus' which fell in the eastern side of the sky so that it may protect itself from Seth.'

'...her end-pieces are the hair which is under the tail of Seth;'

'It is the cloth which came out of Sutyu when Horus and the Ombite kissed on New Year's Day.'

'"Tell me my name," say the oar-loops. (Allen has halyard-bags) *'You have been made with the hide of the Mnevis-bull and the tendons of Seth.'*

Spell 110 (Faulkner 1972: 103-108; Allen 1974: 87-90) is concerned with carrying out various activities in the Fields of Rushes and contains the following passage:

'He says: 'The Falcon has been taken by Seth, and I have seen the damage in the Field of Offerings; I have released the Falcon from Seth, I opened the paths of Re on this day when the sky moaned because of Seth and the water rose high because Seth was vexed at the wind for its bringing life to him who was in his egg and rescuing him who was in the womb (i.e. Horus) from the 'Silent Ones'.'

Spell 112 (Faulkner 1972: 108-109; Allen 1974: 91) is a spell for knowing the 'Souls of Pe' and contains the following passage which is virtually identical to Coffin Text 157:

'And Re said: "Look again at yonder black pig." And Horus looked at this black pig, and Horus cried out because of the condition of his injured eye, saying: "Behold, my eye is like that first wound which Seth inflicted on my eye," and Horus fainted before him. The Re said: "Put him on his bed until he is well." It so had happened that Seth had transformed himself into a black pig and had projected a wound into his eye, and Re said: "The pig is detestable to Horus."

Spell 134 (Faulkner 1972: 122-123; Allen 1974: 109-110) is a spell for making a spirit worthy; it contains the following passage:

'N. is Horus; his mother Isis bore him, Nephthys nursed him, just as they did for Horus, in order to drive away the 'confederacy of Seth'.'

Spell 137a (Faulkner 1972: 127-130; Allen 1974: 113-115) is a spell for four torches that are used in ceremonies for the dead spirit; it contains the following two passages:

1. *'The 'Eye of Horus' comes intact and shining like Re in the horizon; it covers up the powers of Seth who would possess it, for it is he who would fetch it for himself, and it is hot against him when he is at the feet of the intact 'Eye of Horus'.'*
2. *'...so spread your protection over N. as when you removed the impediment from Osiris, 'Foremost of the Westerners', so that he might live with the gods and drive Seth from him; as when at dawn Horus became strong that he himself might protect his father Osiris when wrong was done to your father when you drove Seth off.'*

Spell 137b (Faulkner 1972: 132; Allen 1974: 115) is a spell for kindling a torch for N. and states:

'The bright 'Eye of Horus' comes, the glorious 'Eye of Horus' comes; welcome, O you who shine like Re in the horizon. It drives off the powers of Seth from upon the feet of Him who brings it. It is Seth who would take possession of it, but its heat is against him; the torch comes. When will it arrive? It comes now, traversing the sky behind Re on the hands of your two sisters, O Re. Live, live, O 'Eye of Horus', for he is the 'Pillar-of-his-Mother' priest.'

Spell 145 (Allen 1974: 123-133) is a spell for entering the secret portal of Osiris in the 'Fields of Rushes'; it contains the following two passages:

1. *'I am pure with these waters wherewith* Unnefer *purified himself at his going to law with Seth; I caused that* Unnefer *triumphed.'*
2. *'I am pure with those waters wherewith* Isdez *purified himself when he entered to question Seth there within the secret chamber.'*

Spell 151 (Faulkner 1972: 145-148; Allen 1974: 147-150) is a spell for a secret head which contains the following passage:

'...lead him on fair roads that he may obstruct the 'confederacy of Seth' for you (Allen has: *'thou smitest for him 'Seth's Gang', thou overthrowest for him his enemies beneath him').'*

Spell 163 (Faulkner 1972: 158-160) is a spell for preventing a man's corpse from rotting; Allen does not refer to any mention of Seth but Faulkner has the following passage:

'His head shall not be cut off. He shall not be destroyed by the knife of Seth.'

Spell 173 (Faulkner 1972: 172-173; Allen 1974: 181-182) is a spell of praise for the deceased in the realm of the dead. It contains the following four passages:

1. *'Ho Osiris! I am your son Horus; I have come that I may slay for you him who mutilated you.'* Allen has *'I have come to slay for thee thy injurer.'*

2. 'Ho Osiris! I am your son Horus; I have come, having thrust my hand against those who rebelled against you.' Allen has 'I have put forth my hand against them that rebel against thee.'
3. 'Ho Osiris! I am your son Horus; I have come, having brought to you the 'confederacy of Seth' with their bonds on them.' Allen has 'I have brought to thee Seth's gang, their bonds upon them.'
4. 'Ho Osiris! I am your son Horus; I have come, having made for you a massacre of those who rebelled against you.' Allen has 'I have slain for thee.'

Spell 175 (Faulkner 1972: 175; Allen 1974: 183-185) is a spell for not dying again; it contains the following passage:

'N.: But the soul of Seth will travel further than all the gods.

ATUM: I have caused his soul which is in the bark to be restrained, so that the body of the god may be afraid.'

Allen has N. requesting of Atum: "And has Seth's soul, rather than those of all the other gods, been sent to the West?" To which Atum replies: "I have put under guard his soul that is in the bark, that he may not cause the god's body to fear."

Spell 189 (Faulkner 1972: 185-188; Allen 1974: 211-213) is a spell for preventing a man from going upside down and from eating faeces; the last two paragraphs state:

'Men will thresh for me as for the Apis-bull who presides over Sais. Men will reap for me as for Seth, 'Lord of the Northern Sky'.

O you who turn back the ished-tree on your own account, who uproot falsehood, whose faces are pure, shall I be with the confederates of Seth on the mountain of Bakhu? I will dwell with those potent noble dead in order to excavate the pool of Osiris and to rub his heart, and there shall be no accusation against me, N, by any living person.'

The positive spells that mention Seth are 13 in number, which represents 0.7% of the total texts.

Spell 8 (Allen 1974: 10) is a spell for penetrating the West and going forth by day

'This is Osiris the Westerner. Osiris knows his spell, that he may not be yonder. I shall not be yonder, for I am Seth who is among the gods. I have not perished. "Horus replaces thee; he counts thee among the gods in Heliopolis." I know what was done in Rosetau and in the 'Sacred Land'.

Spell 32 (Faulkner 1972: 56-58; Allen 1974: 42-44) is a spell for repelling a crocodile which comes to take away a spirit's magic from him in the realm of the dead; it contains the following passage:

'Get back, you 'crocodile of the West', who lives on the 'Unwearying Stars'! Detestation of you is in my belly, for I have absorbed the power of Osiris, and I am Seth.'

Spell 38A (Faulkner 1972: 58-60; Allen 1974: 45) is a spell for living by air in the realm of the dead; it contains the following passage:

'I have associated with Horus and Seth, the 'Two Lords'.' Allen has: 'Horus fraternizes with Seth, and the Elders intercede for me on my behalf.'

Spell 39 (Faulkner 1972: 60-61; Allen 1974: 46-47) is a spell for repelling a rerek-snake in the realm of the dead. It is in fact the spell that enables the snake, Apophis, to be defeated by Seth each night when he attempts to attack Re in his barque. It contains the following passage:

'O Re, your crew...may you rest there, for your possessions are there. Bring to the house, bring your 'Eye' to the house, bring what is good; may no evil opposition come forth from your mouth against me, for I am Seth, who can raise a tumult of storm in the horizon of the sky like one whose will is destruction.'

Spell 50 (Faulkner 1972: 65; Allen 1974: 51) is a spell for not entering the god's place of execution; it contains the following passage:

'The knot was tied about me by Seth, in whose power the 'Ennead' were at first, before uproar had come into being, when he caused me to be hale.'

Spell 54 (Faulkner 1972: 65; Allen 1974: 53) is a spell for giving breath to N. in the realm of the dead; it reads as follows:

'O Atum, give me the sweet breath which is in your nostril, for I am this Egg which is in the 'Great Cackler', I am the guardian of this great being who separates the earth from the sky. If I live, she will live; I grow young, I live, I breathe the air. I am he who splits iron, I go round about the Egg. Tomorrow is mine through the striking-power of Horus and the strength of Seth. O you who sweeten the state of the 'Two Lands', you with whom are *provisions, you with whom is lapis-lazuli, beware of Him who is in his nest; the Youth goes forth against you.'*

Spell 62 (Faulkner 1972: 68; Allen 1974: 55) is a spell for drinking water in the realm of the dead; it states:

'May the great water be opened for Osiris, may the cool water of Thoth and the water of Hapi be thrown open for the 'Lord of the Horizon' in this my name of Pedsu. May I be granted power over the waters like the limbs of Seth, (Allen has: *'Mayest thou let me have water available like the members of Seth') for I am he who crosses the sky, I am the 'Lion of Re', I am the 'Slayer' who eats the foreleg, the leg of beef is extended to me, limitless eternity is given to me, for I am he who inherited eternity, to whom everlasting was given.'*

Spell 108 (Faulkner 1972: 101-102; Allen 1974: 86-87) is a spell for knowing the souls of the Westerners. Concerned with defeating a serpent that is threatening to stop the Sacred Bark, it contains the following passage:

'Seth will project a lance of iron against him and will make him vomit up all that he has swallowed. Seth will place him before him and will say to him with magic power: "Get back at the sharp knife which is in my hand! I stand before you, navigating aright and seeing afar. Cover your face, for I ferry across; get back because of me, for I am the Male! Cover your head, cleanse the palm of your hand; I am hale and I remain hale, for I am the great magician, the son of Nut, and power against you has been granted to me. Who is that spirit who goes on his belly, his tail and his spine? See, I have gone against you, and your tail is in my hand, for I am one who exhibits strength. I have come that I may rescue the earth-gods for Re so that he may go to rest for me in the evening. I go round about the sky, but you are in the fetters which were decreed for you in the Presence, and Re will go to rest alive in his horizon."'

Allen has: *'Then Seth will hurl a spear of metal against him and cause him to disgorge all that he has swallowed. Then Seth will pit himself against him and say as a spell: "Fall back before the sharp metal that is in my hand. I stand against thee, that the course be true. O farseer pray close thy eye and veil thy head, so that I may cross. Fall back before me, for I am a male. Veil thy head and cool thy upper lip, for if I stay sound thou stayest sound. I am the 'Great of Magic', son of Nut; my magic power has been given me against thee. What is it? It is blessedness, O goer on his belly, whose strength is due to his backbone. Behold, I go indeed, and thy strength with me. It is I who have taken over strength. I have come that I may dispose of the earth-gods for Re, that he may be set for me in the evening. We have circled this sky, while thou art in bonds. This is what was commanded against thee aforetime." Then he, Re, sets in life at his horizon.'*

Spell 111 (Allen 1974: 90-91) is a spell for not dying again in the god's domain, and is similar to Spell 108 in that it involves Seth defeating the snake. It contains the following passage:

'Then Seth will pit himself against him. He says: "Let not the halting of Re's journey be for long. I see the way. Close thy eye, thou whom I have bound for I am a male. Veil thy head, that I may proceed. It is I who have taken over strength. I have come, I have disposed of the earth-god for Re, that he may set in the evening. This magic power has been given me against thee."'

Spell 140 (Faulkner 1972: 132; Allen 1974: 116-117) is a spell to be used on the second month of winter; it lists Seth along with many other gods and goddesses as being joyful when the Sacred Eye is full and Apophis has been defeated.

Spell 153A (Faulkner 1972: 149-152; Allen 1974: 151-152) is a spell for escaping from the net; the final sentence reads:

'I ascend on your ladder which my father Re made for me, and Horus and Seth grip my hands.'

Spell 171 (Faulkner 1972: 170; Allen 1974: 178) is a spell for donning a pure garment; Seth, along with a host of other gods and goddesses is requested to bless the garment.

Spell 180 (Faulkner 1972: 177-180; Allen 1974: 190-192) is a spell for going forth by day and praising Re in the West; it contains the sentence:

'I traverse the Netherworld after the manner of Re, I give judgement like Thoth, I walk and am glad, I run at my own pace in my dignity of one whose affairs are secret, my shape is that of the double god Horus-Seth.' Allen has: *'My forms are those of the 'Two Gods'.'*

There are 12 neutral spells that mention Seth representing 0.6% of the total texts.

Spell 42 (Faulkner 1972: 62; Allen 1974: 48-49) is a spell for warding off harm that is done in Heracleopolis. It contains a list of body parts that are all identified with various gods and contains the following phrase:

'My back is Seth'.

Spell 94 (Faulkner 1972: 88) is a spell for requesting a water-pot and a palette; its first sentence states:

'O you great one who sees your father, 'Keeper of the Book of Thoth', see, I have come spiritualised, besouled, mighty and equipped with the writings of Thoth. Bring me the messenger of the earth-god who is with Seth. Bring me the water-pot and palette from the writing-kit of Thoth and the mysteries which are in them.'

Spells 96 and 97 (Faulkner 1972: 88-89; Allen 1974: 77) are spells for being beside Thoth and a spirit in the realm of the dead. The first sentence states:

'I am he who dwell in his 'Eye', I have come that I may give Maat *to Re, I have propitiated Seth with the bodily fluids of* Aker *and the blood which is in the spinal cord of Geb.'*

Spell 113 (Faulkner 1972: 109-112; Allen 1974: 92) is a spell for knowing the 'Souls of Nekhen' and describes how the 'Souls of Nekhen' will be with Horus until Seth comes to know that they are with him and complains.

Spell 125A (Allen 1974: 101) is a spell to do with the judgement of the deceased before the tribunal of 42 gods where he declares that he has not committed a series of specified sins; this variant states:

'I have come hither to see thy beauty, my hands uplifted in praise of thy real name. I came hither before the pine came into being, before the acacia was born, or the ground brought forth tamarisks. If I enter the secret seat, I speak with Seth, I make glad him who is close to me.'

Spell 149 (Faulkner 1972: 137-145; Allen 1974: 142-146) is a set of spells for knowing the mounds of Osiris in the Fields of Rushes. The following statement is made in connection with the eleventh mound:

'O Idu-town, let me pass, for I am 'Great of Magic', with the knife which issued from Seth, and my legs are mine forever.' Allen has: *'I am the 'Great of Magic', the keen one who escaped from Seth.'*

Spell 168 (Allen 1974: 173) requests that the 'Souls of the West' give a funeral offering to the Osiris N. and it contains the following phrase:

'...and these my members have tired not for Seth.'

Spell 174 (Faulkner 1972: 173-175; Allen 1974: 182-183) is a spell for letting a spirit go out from the great gate in the sky. It contains the sentence:

'As for the 'Lord of the Storm', the slavering of Seth is forbidden to him.' Allen has: *'the 'Lord of the Storm' has inhibited Seth's drivel. May he (i.e. Seth) lift me; then I will lift Atum.'*

Spell 178 (Faulkner 1972: 176; Allen 1974: 186-189) is a spell for raising the corpse and ensuring that his eyes and ears have power, and that his head is firm. It contains the following sentence:

'What N. detests is faeces; he rejects urine, even as Seth rejected it.'

Spell 182 (Faulkner 1972: 181; Allen 1974: 196-200) is a spell for giving breath to Osiris and protecting him in the god's domain. It contains the following sentence:

'I am Thoth; I have pacified Horus, I have calmed the 'Rivals' (i.e. Horus and Seth) in their time of raging;' Allen has: *'I pacified Horus and quieted the 'Two Comrades' in their time of wrath.'*

Spell 183 (Faulkner 1972: 184; Allen 1974: 200-202) is a spell for adoring Osiris and giving praise; it contains the following phrase:

'He has pacified the 'Rival Gods' for you (i.e. Horus and Seth), he has stopped the raging and the tumult for you, he has made the Rivals well-disposed to you, and the 'Two Lands' are peacefully reconciled before you; he has driven anger from their hearts for you, and they fraternise with each other.'

REFERENCES

Allen T. G. (1974). *The Book of the Dead or Going Forth by Day*. Chicago: The University of Chicago Press.

Allen J. P. (2005). *The Ancient Egyptian Pyramid Texts*. Atlanta: Society of Biblical Literature.

Allon N. (2007). Seth is Baal – Evidence from the Egyptian Script. *Egypt and the Levant:* S15-S22.

Armour R. A.(2001). *Gods and Myths of Ancient Egypt*. Cairo:The American University in Cairo Press 1986; repr Cairo: the American University in Cairo Press 2001.

Asheri D.,Lloyd A.and Corcella A.(2007). *A commentary on Herodotus*. Oxford: Oxford University Press.

Assmann J. (1984). *Ägypten. Theologie und Frömmigkeit einer frühen Hochkultur*. Stuggart: Kohlhammer.

Assmann J. (1995). *Egyptian Solar Religion in the New Kingdom. Re, Amun and the crisis of Polytheism*. London: Kegan Paul International.

Assmann J. (1996). *The mind of Egypt*. Munich:Carl Hans Verlag; repr London: Harvard University Press 2006.

Assmann J. (2001). *The search for god in Ancient Egypt*. Ithaca:Cornell University Press.

Assmann J.(2008). *Of God and Gods. Egypt, Israel, and the Rise of Monotheism*. Madison:The University of Wisconsin Press.

Ayrton E. R. and Loat W. L. S. (1911). *Pre-Dynastic cemetery at El-Mahasna*. London: The Egypt Exploration Fund.

Baines J. (1987). Practical Religion and Piety. *Journal of Egyptian Archaeology* 73:79-98.

Baines J. (2000). Egyptian Deities in Context:Multiplicity,Unity,and the Problem of Change. In B. N. Porter (Ed.), *One God or many? Concepts of Divinity in the Ancient World*: 27-35. Chebeague: Casco Bay Assyriological Institute.

Baker D. D. (2008). *The encyclopaedia of the Pharaohs*. London:Stacey International.

Bakry H. S. K. (1962).The stela of Pa-ahaty, the Follower of Seth. *Annales du Service des Antiquités de l'Égypte* 57: 7-8.

Baumgartel E. J. (1955). *The cultures of Prehistoric Egypt*. London:Oxford University Press.

Bickerstaffe D. (2009). *Refugees for Eternity. The Royal Mummies of Thebes IV:Identifying the Royal Mummies*. London:Canopus Press.

Bierbrier. M. (1982). *The Tomb-builders of the Pharaohs*. London: British Museum Publications Ltd.

Bietak M. (1997). The Center of Hyksos rule:Avaris (Tell el Dab'a). In E.D. Oren (Ed.), *The Hyksos:New Historical and Archaeological Perspectives*:87-139. Philadelphia:The University Museum, University of Pennsylvania.

Blackman A. M. (1998). Sacramental ideas and usages in Ancient Egypt. In A. B. Lloyd (Ed.), *Gods, Priests and Men*: 183-196. London:Kegan Paul International.

Blackman A. M.and Fairman H. W. (1942). The Myth of Horus II. *Journal of Egyptian Archaeology* 28:32-38.

Blackman A. M. and Fairman H. W. (1943). The Myth of Horus II. *Journal of Egyptian Archaeology* 29: 2-36.

Blackman A. M. and Fairman H. W. (1944). The Myth of Horus II. *Journal of Egyptian Archaeology* 30: 5-22.

Bleeker C. J. (1973). *Hathor and Thoth. Two key figures of the Ancient Egyptian Religion.*Leiden: Brill.

Booth C. (2005). *The Hyksos period in Egypt*. Princes Risborough:Shire Publications.

Bourghouts J. F. (1973). The Evil Eye of Apopis. *Journal of Egyptian Archaeology* 59:114-150.

Bourriau J. (2000).The Second Intermediate Period. In I. Shaw (Ed), *The Oxford History of Ancient Egypt*:184-217. Oxford: Oxford University Press

Bowman A. K. (1986). *Egypt after the Pharaohs*. Berkeley and Los Angeles:University of California Press.

Brand P. J. (2000). *The Monuments of Set I; Epigraphic, Historical and Art Historical Analysis*. Leiden: Brill.

Breasted J. H. (1906). *Ancient Records of Egypt*, Vols 1-5. Chicago:University of Illinois Press; repr 2006 Chicago: Chicago University of Illinois Press.

Brown T. S. (1965). Herodotus speculates about Egypt. *The American Journal of Philology* 86, No 1:60-76.

Bryan B. M.(2000). The 18th Dynasty before the Amarna Period. In I. Shaw (Ed), *The Oxford History of Ancient Egypt*: 218-271. Oxford:Oxford University Press.

Burkard G., and Thissen H. J. (2003). *Einführung in die altägyptische Literaturgeschichte*. Berlin: LIT Verlag.

Callender G. (2000). The Middle Kingdom Renaissance. In I. Shaw (Ed), *The Oxford History of Ancient Egypt*:148-183. Oxford:Oxford University Press.

Calverley A. M. and Broome M. F. (1935). *The Temple of King Sethos I at Abydos*, Vol II. London:The Egypt Exploration Society.

Cauville S. (2012). *Offerings to the Gods in Egyptian Temples*. Leuven:Peeters.

Chicago Reliefs (1936). *Reliefs and inscriptions at Karnak*, Volume 1: Ramesses III's Temple with the great enclosure of Amon part 1. Chicago:University of Chicago Press.

Clayton P. (1994). *Chronicle of the Pharaohs*. London:Thames and Hudson Ltd.

Cruz-Uribe E. (2009). Seth, God of Power and Might. *Journal of the American Research Center in Egypt* 45:201-226.

Daressy M. G. (1900). *Les sépultures des prêtres d'Amon à Deir el-Bahari. Annales du Service des Antiquités de l'Égypte* 1:141-148.

Darnell J. C.(2002). *Theban Desert Road Survey in the Egyptian Western Desert*;Volume 1: Gebel Tjauti Rock Inscriptions 1-45 and Wadi El-Hol Rock Inscriptions 1-45. Chicago: Oriental Institute Publications.

David A. R. (1980). *Cult of the Sun. Myth and Magic in Ancient Egypt*. London:J. M. Dent and Sons Ltd.

David A. R. (1981). *A Guide to Religious Ritual at Abydos*. Warminster:Aris and Phillips.

David A. R. (1982). *The Ancient Egyptians: Religious Beliefs and Practices*. London:Routledge & Kegan Paul.

Davies V. and Friedmann R. (1998). *Egypt*.London:British Museum Press.

Derchain P. (1990). L'auteur du Papyrus Jumilhac. *Revue d'Égyptologie* 41:9-30.

Dodson A (2000). The Layer pyramid of Zawiyet el-Aryan:Its Layout and Context. *Journal of the American Research Center in Egypt* 37:81-90.

Dodson A. and Hilton D. (2004). *The complete Royal Families of Ancient Egypt*. London: Thames & Hudson.

Dreyer G.(1998). *Umm el-Qaab I:Das prädynastische Königsgrab U-j und seine frühen Schriftzeugnisse*. Archäologische Veröffentlichungen des Deutschen Archäologischen Instituts, Abteilung Kairo 86. Mainz: Philipp von Zabern.

Ellis S. P. (1992). *Graeco-Roman Egypt*. Princes Risborough: Shire Publications Ltd.

Emery W. B. (1961). *Archaic Egypt*. Harmondsworth:Penguin Books.

Eyre C. (2002). *The Cannibal Hymn*. Liverpool:Liverpool University Press.

Fairman H. W. (1935). The Myth of Horus at Edfu I. *The Journal of Egyptian Archaeology* 21:26-36.

Fairman H. W. (1974). *The Triumph of Horus*. London:B.T. Batsford Ltd.

Faulkner R. O. (1936). The Bremner-Rhind Papyrus: I, A. The Songs of Isis and Nephthys. *The Journal of Egyptian Archaeology* 22, No 2: 121-140.

Faulkner R. O. (1937).The Bremner-Rhind Papyrus: III. D. The Book of Overthrowing 'Apep. *The Journal of Egyptian Archaeology* 23, No 2:166-185.

Faulkner R. O. (1947). The Wars of Sethos I. *The Journal of Egyptian Archaeology* 33:34-39.

Faulkner R. O. (1972). *The Ancient Egyptian Book of the Dead*. New York:The Limited Editions Club; repr 1985, London:Book Club Associates.

Faulkner R. O. (2004). *The Ancient Egyptian Coffin Texts*. Warminster: Aris and Phillips (Vol 1) 1973, (Vol 2) 1977, (Vol 3) 1978; repr 2004, Warminster: Aris and Phillips.

Faulkner R. O. (2007). *The Ancient Egyptian Pyramid Texts*. Stilwell:Digireads.com Publishing.

Fletcher J. (2000). *Egypt's Sun King*. London:Duncan Baird Publishers Ltd.

Frankfort H. (1948). *Kingship and the Gods:A Study of Ancient Near Eastern Religion as the Integration of Society and Nature*. Chicago:The University of Chicago Press.

Frankfurter D. (1998). *Religion in Roman Egypt*. Princeton:Princeton University Press.

Friedman F. D. (1994). Aspects of Domestic Life and Religion. In L.H. Lesko (Ed), *Pharaoh's Workers*:95-117. Ithaca: Cornell University Press.

Gardiner A. H. (1931). *Chester Beatty Papyrus I.* Oxford:Oxford University Press.

Gardiner A. H. (1932). *Late-Egyptian Stories.* Bruxelles:Bibliotheca Aegyptiaca.

Gardiner A. H. (1933). The Dakhleh Stela. *Journal of Egyptian Archaeology* 19: 19-30.

Gardiner A. H. (1935). *Hieratic Texts in the British Museum:The Chester Beatty Papyrus.* London:British Museum Press.

Gardiner A. H. (1947). *Ancient Egyptian Onomastica.* Oxford:Oxford University Press.

Gardiner A. H. (1961). *Egypt of the Pharaohs.* Oxford:Oxford University Press.

Garstang, J. (1907). *The Burial Customs of Ancient Egypt as illustrated by the Tombs of the Middle Kingdom.* London: John Constable.

Gaudard F. P. (2005). *The Demotic Drama of Horus and Seth.* Chicago: The University of Chicago.

Gauthier H. (1928). *Dictionnaire des noms géographiques contenus dans les textes hiéroglyphiques.* Cairo:Société royale de géographie d'Égypte.

Georganteli E. (2010). Economy and Art in Egypt from Alexander the Great to the Arab Conquest. In E. Georganteli and M. Bommas (Eds.), *Sacred and Profane:*101-120. London:D. Giles Limited.

Ghazouli E. B. (1964). 'The Palace and Magazines attached to the Temple of Seti I at Abydos'. *Annales du Service des Antiquités de l'Égypte* 58:99-186.

Goedicke H. (1984). The Canaanite illness. *Studien zur Altägyptischen Kultur* 11: 91-105.

Gordon A. H., Gordon A. A. and Schwabe C. W. (1995). The Egyptian *was*-sceptre and its Modern Analogues: Uses as Symbols of Divine Power or Authority. *Journal of the American Research Center in Egypt* 32:185-196.

Gordon-Rastelli L. (2011). Egypt on the Upper Rhine in Basel, Switzerland. *Kmt:A Modern Journal of Ancient Egypt* 22, No1:28-42.

Griffiths F. Ll. (1898). *The Petrie papyri: Hieratic papyri from Kahun and Gurob.* London:Quaritch.

Griffiths J. G. and Barb A. A. (1959).Seth or Anubis? *Journal of the Warburg and Courtauld Institutes* 22, No 3/4: 367-371.

Griffiths J. G. (1960). *The Conflict of Horus and Seth.* Liverpool:Liverpool University Press.

Griffiths J. G. (1969). Review of Seth, God of Confusion. A Study of his Role in Egyptian Mythology and Religion by Herman Te Velde. *Journal of Egyptian Archaeology* 55:226-227.

Griffiths J. G. (1970). *Plutarch's De Iside et Osiride.* Swansea:University of Wales Press.

Grimal N. (1992). *A history of Ancient Egypt.* Oxford: Blackwell Publishing; repr 2007, Oxford:Blackwell Publishing.

Gros de Beler A. (2004). *Egyptian Mythology.* Rochester:Grange Books.

Gunn B. and Gardiner A. H. (1918). New Renderings of Egyptian Texts:II The Expulsion of the Hyksos. *Journal of Egyptian Archaeology* 5, No 1: 36-56.

Hart G. (1986). *A Dictionary of Egyptian Gods and Goddesses.* London:Routledge and Kegan Paul.

Hawass Z. (2003). *The treasures of the Pyramids.* Cairo:The American University in Cairo Press.

Hawass Z. and Janot F. (2004). *The Royal Mummies: Immortality in Ancient Egypt.* Vercelli: White Star S.p.A.

Hays H. M. (2010). Funerary Rituals (Pharonic Period).In Dielman J. and Wendrich W. (Eds.), *UCLA Encyclopedia of Egyptology.* Los Angeles: http://digital2.library.ucla.edu/viewItem.do?ark=21198/zz001nf65w.

Herodotus (1999). *The Histories.* Translated by A. D. Godley. Harvard:Harvard University Press.

Hill M.(2007). Shifting ground:The new Kingdom from the reign of Thutmose III. In M. Hill (Ed), *Gifts for the Gods: Images from Egyptian Temples*:23-38. New Haven: Yale University Press.

Hornung E. (1970). Review of Te Velde's:Seth, God of Confusion. *Orientalistische Literaturzeitung* 65:17-20.

Hornung E.(1971). *Conceptions of God in Ancient Egypt. The One and the Many.* Ithaca, New York:Cornell University Press.

Ikram S. (1995). *Choice Cuts:Meat Production in Ancient Egypt*. Leuven:Peeters Publishers.

James T. G. H. (1962). Review of Le Papyrus Jumilhac. *Journal of Egyptian Archaeology* 48: 176-178.

James T. G. H. (2002). *Ramesses II*. Vercelli:White Star S.r.l.

Janssen J. J. (1968). The Smaller Dakhla Stela. *Journal of Egyptian Archaeology* 54:165-172.

Jay J. E. (2007). Religious Literature of late Period and Greco-Roman Egypt. *Religion Compass* 1 (No 1):93-106.

Kaper O. E. (1962). *Temples and Gods in Roman Dakhleh*. Groningen: Rijksuniversiteit Groningen.

Kaper O. E. (1997). The statue of Penbast:On the cult of Seth in the Dakhleh Oasis. In J. Van Dijk (Ed), *Essays on Ancient Egypt in honour of Herman Te Velde*:231-241. Groningen:Styx Publications.

Kaper O. E. (2001). Two decorated blocks from the temple of Seth in Mut el-Kharab. *Bulletin of the Australian Centre for Egyptology* 12:71-78.

Kees H. (1924). Nbd als Damon der Pinsternis. *Zeitschrift für ägyptische sprache und altertumskunde* 59:69-70.

Kemboly Mpay S. J. (2010). *The Question of Evil in Ancient Egypt*. London: Golden House Publications.

Kemp B. (2007). *How to read the Egyptian Book of the Dead*. New York:W. W. Norton & Company.

Kemp B. (2008). The Amarna Project: religion for all? *Ancient Egypt* 9, No 2:41-46.

Kenyon K. (1960). *Excavations at Jericho*. London:British School of Archaeology in Jerusalem.

Kessler D. (2001). The Political History of the Third to Eighth Dynasties in Egypt. In R. Schultz and M. Seidel (Eds), *The world of the Pharaohs*:40-45. Cairo:The American University in Cairo Press.

Kitchen K. A. (1973). *The Third Intermediate Period in Egypt (1100-650 B.C.)*. Warminster:Aris and Phillips.

Kitchen K. A. (1982). *Pharaoh Triumphant:The Life and Times of Ramesses II*. Warminster:Aris and Phillips.

Kurth D. (2004). *The Temple of Edfu: A Guide by an Ancient Egyptian Priest*. Cairo:The American University in Cairo Press.

Labib P.(1936). *Die Herrschaft der Hyksos in Ägypten und ihr Sturz*.Glückstadt–Hamburg and New York:J. J. Augustin.

Langdon S. and Gardiner A. H. (1920). The Treaty of Alliance between Hattusili, King of the Hittites, and the Pharaoh Ramesses II of Egypt. *Journal of Egyptian Archaeology* 6:179-205.

Leclant J. and Yoyotte J. (1957). Les Obelisques de Tanis. *Kemi* 14:43-80.

Lepsius R.(1849). *Denkmaeler aus Aegypten und Aethiopien nach den zeichnungen der von Seiner Majestaet dem koenige von Preussen Friedrich Wilhelm IV*. Berlin:Nicholas Buchhandlung.

Lesko B. S. (1994). Rank, Roles and Rights. In L.H. Lesko (Ed), *Pharaoh's Workers*:15-39. Ithaca:Cornell University Press.

Lewis N. (1986). *Greeks in Ptolemaic Egypt*. Oxford: Oxford University Press.

Lichtheim M.(1973). *Ancient Egyptian Literature: The Old and Middle Kingdoms*. Berkeley:University of California Press.

Lichtheim M. (1976). *Ancient Egyptian Literature: The New Kingdom*. Berkeley:University of California Press.

Lloyd A. B. (1982). The inscription of Udjahorresnet:a collaborator's testament. *Journal of Egyptian Archaeology* 68: 166-180.

Lloyd A. B. (1998). *Gods, Priests and Men. Studies in the Religion of Pharonic Egypt by Aylward M. Blackman*. London:Kegan Paul International.

Lloyd A. B.(2000a). The Late Period. In I. Shaw (Ed), *The Oxford History of Ancient Egypt*:369-394. Oxford:Oxford University Press.

Lloyd A. B. (2000b). The Ptolemaic Period.In I. Shaw (Ed), *The Oxford History of Ancient Egypt*:395-421. Oxford: Oxford University Press.

Luiselli M. M. (2010). The Personal Approach to the Divine in Ancient Egypt. In E. Georganteli and M. Bommas (Eds), *Sacred and Profane*: 63-86. London:D Giles Limited.

Manassa C. (2003). *The Great Karnak Inscription of Merneptah:Grand Strategy in the 13th Century BC*. New Haven: Yale Egyptological Studies Press.

Manetho (2004). Translated by Waddell W. G. Harvard:Harvard University Press.

Manlius N. (2002). Aardvarks to otters:ancient Egypt's unusual fauna. *Ancient Egypt* 3, No 1:24-31.

Manniche L. (1987). *Sexual Life in Ancient Egypt*. London: Routledge and Kegan Paul.

Meeks D. and Favard-Meeks C. (1999). *Daily Life of the Egyptian Gods*. London:Pimlico.

Mertz B. (1964). *Temples, Tombs and Hieroglyphs*. New York:Peter Bedrick Books.

Midant-Reynes B. (1992). *The Prehistory of Egypt*. Armand Colin:Paris; repr 2006, Oxford:Blackwell Publishing.

Montet P. (1933). La stele de l'an 400 retrouvee. *Kemi* 4:191-215.

Moorey P. R. S. (1988). *Ancient Egypt*. Oxford:Ashmolean Museum.

Moret A. (1931). La légende d'Osiris à l'époque thébaine d'après l'hymne à Osiris du Louvre. *Bulletin de l'Institut Français d'Archéologie Orientale* 30:725-750.

Morgan M. (2005). *The Bull of Ombos:Seth & Egyptian Magick*. Oxford:Mandrake and Mogg Morgan.

Morkot R. G. (2000). *The Black Pharaohs, Egypt's Nubian Rulers*. London:The Rubicon Press.

Munro I. (2010). The Evolution of the Book of the Dead. In J. H. Taylor (Ed), *Journey through the afterlife Ancient Egyptian Book of the Dead*: 4-79. London:The British Museum Press.

Naville M., Newberry P. E. and Fraser G. W. (1891). *The season's work at Ahnas and Beni Hasan 1890-91*. London: Gilbert and Rivington.

Naville E. (1896). *The Temple of Deir-el-Bahari, Part II*. London:Egypt Exploration Fund.

Newby P. H. (1980). *Warrior Pharaohs*. London:Book Club Associates.

O'Connor D. (2009). *Abydos; Egypt's First Pharaohs and the cult of Osiris*. London:Thames and Hudson.

O'Connor D. (2011). The Narmer Palette:a new interpretation. In E. Teeter (Ed), *Before the Pyramids*:149-160. Chicago:The University of Chicago Press.

Oakes L. and Gahlin L. (2002). *Ancient Egypt*. London:Hermes House.

Oden R. A. Jr. (1979). The Contendings of Horus and Seth (Chester Beatty Papyrus No. 1):A structural interpretation. *History of Religions* 18, No 4:352-369.

Oldfather C. H. (1933). *The Library of History of Diodorus Siculus*, volume 1. Harvard:Harvard University Press 1933.

Oren E. D. (1997). The Hyksos Enigma:Introductory Overview. In E.D. Oren (Ed), *The Hyksos:New Historical and Archaeological Perspectives*:xix-xi. Philadelphia: The University Museum, University of Pennsylvania.

Panagiotakopulu E (2004). Pharaonic Egypt and the origins of plague. *Journal of Biogeography* 31:269-275.

Parkinson R. B. (1991). *Voices from Ancient Egypt:An anthology of Middle Kingdom writings*. London:British Museum Press.

Parkinson R. B. (1995).'Homosexual' Desire and Middle Kingdom Literature. *Journal of Egyptian Archaeology* 81:57-76.

Peacock D. (2000). The Roman Period. In I. Shaw (Ed), *The Oxford History of Ancient Egypt*:422-445. Oxford: Oxford University Press.

Pellegrini A. (1898). Glanures. *Recueil de travaux relatifs à la philologie et à l'archéologie égyptiennes et assyriennes* xx:96.

Petrie W. M. F. (1885). *Tanis I*. London:Gilbert and Rivington.

Petrie W. M. F. (1901). *The Royal Tombs of the Earliest Dynasties*. London:The Egypt Exploration Fund.

Petrie W. M. F. and Quibell J. E. (1896). *Naqada and Ballas*. London:Bernard Quaritch.

Pinch G. (2002). *Egyptian Mythology*. Oxford:Oxford University Press.

Plutarch (2003). *Moralia*. Edited and translated by F. C. Babbit.Harvard:Harvard University Press.

Porter B. and Moss R. L. B. (1964). *Topographical Bibliography of Ancient Egyptian Hieroglyphic Texts, Reliefs and Paintings,* Volume I:Theban Necropolis, part II:Royal tombs and smaller cemeteries. Oxford:Clarendon Press.

Porter B. and Moss R. L. B. (1972). *Topographical Bibliography of Ancient Egyptian Hieroglyphic Texts, Reliefs and Paintings,* Volume II:Theban Temples. Oxford:Clarendon Press.

Porter B. and Moss R. L. B. (1974). *Topographical Bibliography of Ancient Egyptian Hieroglyphic Texts, Reliefs and Paintings,* Volume III:Memphis, part 1 Abu Rawash to Abusir. Oxford:Clarendon Press.

Porter B. And Moss R. L. B. (1975). *Topographical Bibliography of Ancient Egyptian Hieroglyphic Texts, Reliefs and Paintings,* Volume VII:Nubia, the Deserts, and outside Egypt. Oxford:Clarendon Press.

Power D. (2010). Plutarch's account of the Osiris Myth. *Journal of Near and Middle Eastern Studies* 1:87-98.

Reeves N. (2001). *Akhenaten:Egypt's False Prophet.* London:Thames & Hudson.

Reiblein A. (2011). Colour in Ancient Egypt. *Ancient Egypt* 11, No 5:32-39.

Reisner G. (1927). Hetep-Heres, mother of Cheops. *Bulletin of the Museum of Fine Arts.* Supplement to Vol XXV:2-36.

Roberts A. (1995). *Hathor Rising. The Serpent Power of Ancient Egypt.* Rottingdean:Northgate Publishers.

Robins G. (1997). *The Art of Ancient Egypt.* London:British Museum Press.

Rochemonteix M, Chassinat E, Cauville S and Devauchelle D. (1934-1985). *Le temple d'Edfou* I-XV. Cairo:Institut Français d'Archéologie Orientale.

Rohl D. (2007). *The Lords of Avaris.* London:Century.

Rossel S., Marshall F., Peters J., Pilgram T., Adams M. D. and O'Connor D. (2008). Domestication of the donkey: timing, process and indicators. *Proceedings of the National Academy of Sciences* 105, No 10: 3715-3720.

Ryholt K. S. B. (1997). *The Political Situation in Egypt during the Second Intermediate Period.* Copenhagen:The Carsten Niebuhr Institute of Near Eastern Studies, University of Copenhagen.

Saad Z. Y. (1957). Ceiling Stelae in Second Dynasty Tombs from the excavations at Helwan. Cairo:*Supplément aux Annales du Service des antiquités de l'Égypte.*

Sabbahy L. K. (1993). Evidence for the Titulary of the Queen from Dynasty One. *Göttinger Miszellen* 135:81-87.

Scharff A. (1926). Vorgeschichtliches zur Libyerfrage. *Zeitschrift für ägyptische sprache und altertumskunde* 61:16-30

Schibly H. S. (1990). *Pherekydes of Syros.* Oxford:Clarendon Press.

Schoer B. (2004). Seth from ancestral god to despicable demon. *Ancient Egypt* 4, No 6:36-41.

Schorsch D. And Wypyski M. T. (2009). Seth, "Figure of Mystery". *Journal of the American Research Centre in Egypt* 45:177-200.

Schott S. (1930). *Urkunden mythologischen Inhalts VI.* Leipzig: G. Steindorff.

Schott S.(1950).*Bemerkungen zum ägyptischen Pyramidenkult.* Cairo:Institut für Ägyptische Bauforschung und Altertumskunde.

Schweizer A. (2010). *The Sun God's Journey through the Netherworld. Reading the Ancient Egyptian Amduat.* Ithaca: Cornell University Press.

Seidlmayer S. (2000).The First Intermediate Period. In I. Shaw (Ed), *The Oxford History of Ancient Egypt*:118-147. Oxford:Oxford University Press.

Sellers J. B. (1992). *The Death of Gods in Ancient Egypt.* Marston Gate:Amazon.

Sethe K. and Helck W. (1906).*Urkunden des ägyptischen Altertums* IV. Berlin:G. Steindorff.

Shaw I. and Nicholson P. (1995). *British Museum Dictionary of Ancient Egypt.* London:British Museum Press.

Shorter A. W. (1925). A possible late representation of the god Ash. *Journal of Egyptian Archaeology* 11:78-79.

Simpson W. K. (Ed). (1973). *The Literature of Ancient Egypt.* New Haven:Yale University Press.

Simpson W. K. (1976). 'A Statuette of a devotee of Seth.' *The Journal of Egyptian Archaeology* 62:41-44.

Smith M. (2008).Osiris and the Deceased. In Dieleman J. and Wendrich W. (Eds.), *UCLA Encyclopedia of Egyptology.* Los Angeles:http://digital2.library.ucla.edu/viewItem.do?ark=21198/zz001nf6bg.

Smith R.W. and Redford D. B. (1976). *The Akhenaten Temple Project*. Warminster:Aris and Phillips.

Stevens A. (2009).Domestic Religious Practices.In Willeke W. and Dieleman J. (Eds.),*UCLA Encyclopedia of Egyptology*. Los Angeles:http://digital2.library.uca.edu/viewItem.do?ark= 21198/zz001nf63v.

Strabo (1932). *The Geography*. Translated by Jones H. L. Cambridge: Harvard University Press

Strudwick N. C. (2005). *Texts from the Pyramid Age*. Atlanta:Society of Biblical Literature.

Strudwick H. (2006). *The Encyclopaedia of Ancient Egypt*. London:Amber Books Ltd.

Sweeney D. (2002). 'Gender and Conversational Tactics in "The Contendings of Horus and Seth".' *The Journal of Egyptian Archaeology* 88:141-162.

Szpakowska K. (2003). *Behind Closed Eyes. Dreams and Nightmares in Ancient Egypt*. Swansea:The Classical Press of Wales.

Taylor J. (2000).The Third Intermediate Period. In I. Shaw (Ed), *The Oxford History of Ancient Egypt*:330-368. Oxford:Oxford University Press.

Taylor J. H. (2010a). Preparing for the Afterlife. In J. H. Taylor (Ed), *Journey through the afterlife. Ancient Egyptian Book of the Dead*:28-53. London:The British Museum Press.

Taylor J. H. (2010b). The Day of Burial. In J. H. Taylor (Ed), *Journey through the afterlife Ancient Egyptian Book of the Dead*:82-103. London:The British Museum Press.

Teeter E. and Johnson J. H. (2009). *The Life of Meresamun:A temple singer in Ancient Egypt*. Chicago:The University of Chicago.

Te Velde H. (1967). *Seth, God of Confusion:A study of his role in Egyptian mythology and religion*. Leiden:E.J. Brill.

Te Velde H. (1968).The Egyptian God Seth as a Trickster. *Journal of the American Research Center in Egypt* 7:37-40.

Te Velde H. (1977). *Seth, God of Confusion: A study of his role in Egyptian mythology and religion*. Second edition; Leiden:E. J. Brill.

Thomas A. P. (1986). *Egyptian Gods and Myths*. Princes Risborough:Shire Publications Ltd.

Thomas A. P. (2004). The Pre-Dynastic Cemetery at El Mahasna.In S. Hendrickx, R. F. Friedman, K.M. Cialowicz and M. Chlodnicki (Eds), *Egypt at its Origins 1: Studies in memory of Barbara Adams*:1041-1054. Leuven: Peeters

Tyldesley J. (1996). *Hatchepsut, the Female Pharaoh*. London:Viking Group.

Vandier J. (1961). *Le Papyrus Jumilhac*. Paris:Musée du Louvre.

Van Dijk J. (2000).The Amarna Period and the Later New Kingdom. In I. Shaw (Ed), *The Oxford History of Ancient Egypt*:272-313. Oxford:Oxford University Press.

Van Seters J. (1966). *The Hyksos:A new investigation*. New Haven and London:Yale University Press.

Von Bomhard A. S. (1999). *The Egyptian Calendar. A work for eternity*. London:Periplus.

Waddell W. G. (2004). *Manetho*. Harvard: Harvard University Press 1940; repr 2004 Harvard: Loeb Classical Library.

Wainwright G. A. (1932). Letopolis. *Journal of Egyptian Archaeology* 18:159-172.

Ward W. A. (1978). Seth as *Hiw* , "Braying Ass," in the Middle Kingdom. *Journal of Near Eastern Studies* 37, No 1: 23-34.

Ward W. A. (1994). Foreigners Living in the Village. In L.H. Lesko (Ed), *Pharaoh's Workers*:61-85. Ithaca:Cornell University Press.

Watterson B. (1984). *The Gods of Ancient Egypt*. London: B. T. Batsford Ltd.

Watterson B. (1998). *The House of Horus and Edfu: Ritual in an Ancient Egyptian Temple*. Stroud:Tempus.

Wenke R. J. (2009). *The Ancient Egyptian State: The Origins of Egyptian Culture (c. 8000-2000 B. C.)*. Cambridge: Cambridge University Press.

Wente E. (1979). Response to Robert A. Oden's "The Contendings of Horus and Seth (Chester Beatty Papyrus No. 1): A structural interpretation. *History of Religions* 18, No 4:370-372.

Wente E. (1990). *Letters from Ancient Egypt*. Atlanta:Scholars Press.

West M. L. (1999). *The East Face of Helicon*. Oxford:Clarendon Paperbacks.

Whitehouse H. (2002). Putting the Question to Seth, Lord of the Oasis. *The Ashmolean* 43 (Summer):2-5.

Whitehouse H. (2009). *Ancient Egypt and Nubia*. Oxford:Ashmolean Museum, University of Oxford.

Wilkinson R. H. (1992). *Reading Egyptian Art*. London:Thames and Hudson.

Wilkinson R. H. (1994). *Symbol and magic in Egyptian Art*. London:Thames and Hudson Ltd.

Wilkinson T. A. H. (1999). *Early Dynastic Egypt*. London:Routledge.

Wilkinson T. (2005). *The Thames and Hudson Dictionary of Ancient Egypt*. London:Thames & Hudson.

Willeitner J. (2001). Royal and Divine Festivals. In R. Schulz and M. Seidel (Eds), *Egypt:The World of the Pharaohs*: 450-457. Cairo:The American University in Cairo Press.

Wilson J. A. (1955). Buto and Hierakonpolis in the Geography of Egypt. *Journal of Near Eastern Studies* 14, No 4: 209-236.

Witt R. E. (1971). *Isis in the Ancient World*. Ithaca:Cornell University Press.

Youtie H. C. (1951). The Heidelberg Festival Papyrus:A reinterpretation. In P. R. Coleman-Norton (Ed), *'Studies in Roman Economic and Social History in Honor of Allen Chester Johnson'*. Princeton: University of Princeton Press.

Zandee J. (1963). Seth als Sturmgott. *Zeitschrift für ägyptische sprache und altertumskunde* 90:144-156.

Zandee J. (1968). Review of H. Te Velde's 'Seth, God of Confusion:a study of his role in Egyptian mythology and religion'. *Bibliotheca Orientalis* 25:184-189.

Zivie A. (1997). Seth, échanson royal, et sa tombe de Saqqara. In J. Van Dijk (Ed), *Essays on Ancient Egypt in Honour of Herman te Velde*:371-380. Groningen: Styx Publications.

Zivie-Coche C. (2011). Foreign Deities in Egypt. In J. Dielman and W. Wendrich (Eds), *UCLA Encyclopaedia of Egyptology*:1-10. Available at

www.ingramcontent.com/pod-product-compliance
Lightning Source LLC
Chambersburg PA
CBHW061543010526
44113CB00023B/2783